Phillip K. Trocki

Modern Curriculum Press
Cleveland/Toronto

EXECUTIVE EDITOR   Wendy Whitnah

PROJECT EDITOR   Diane Dzamtovski

EDITORIAL DEVELOPMENT
DESIGN AND PRODUCTION   The Hampton-Brown Company

ILLUSTRATORS   Anthony Accardo, Joe Boddy, Harry Briggs, Roberta Collier-Morales, Mark Farina, Sandra Forrest, Carlos Freire, Ron Grauer, Meryl Henderson, Masami Miyamoto, Rik Olson, Doug Roy, John Sandford, Rosalind Solomon.

PHOTO CREDITS   5, Michael S. Yamashita/Westlight; 9, Catherine Ursillo/Photo Researchers; 13, Lawrence Migdale; 17, Henry Georgi/Comstock; 21, Janeart Ltd/Image Bank; 29, Steinhart Aquarium/Photo Researchers; 30, H.L. Parent/Photo Researchers; 31, E.R. Degginger/Earth Scenes; 33, Craig Aurness/Westlight; 35, Spencer Grant/Photo Researchers; 37, Michael Fredericks, Jr./Earth Scenes; 41, Mary Evans Picture Library/Photo Researchers; 44, Robert Landau/Westlight; 45, Masud Quraishy/Photo Researchers; 46, Leonard Lee Rue III/Photo Researchers; 53, Don Klumpp/Image Bank; 57, Don King/Image Bank; 61, Garry Gay/Image Bank; 69, Uniphoto/Pictor; 70, G. and V. Chapman/Image Bank; 72, Joel Glenn/ Image Bank; 77, Keith Gunnar/Photo Researchers; 78, Frans Lanting/Photo Researchers; 81, Spencer Grant/Photo Researchers; 85, Harry Angels N.A.S./Photo Researchers; 87, George R. Cassidy/Animals Animals; 93, Wilf Schurig/Animals Animals; 101, Lawrence Migdale; 105, Bob Daemmrich/Uniphoto; 106, Carson Baldwin, Jr./Earth Scenes; 109, Bob Daemmrich/Uniphoto; 113, Henry Georgi/Comstock; 116, Tom and Pat Lesson/Photo Researchers; 117, Lawrence Migdale; 133, Ron Blakeley/Uniphoto; 141, Jen and Des Bartlett/Photo Researchers; 143, Charles Mahaux/Image Bank.

COVER DESIGN   The Hampton-Brown Company
COVER PHOTO   G & J Images/Image Bank

Typefaces for the cursive type in this book were provided by Zaner-Bloser, Inc., Columbus, Ohio, copyright, 1993.

ISBN 0-8136-2818-0

8 9 10   97

TABLE OF CONTENTS

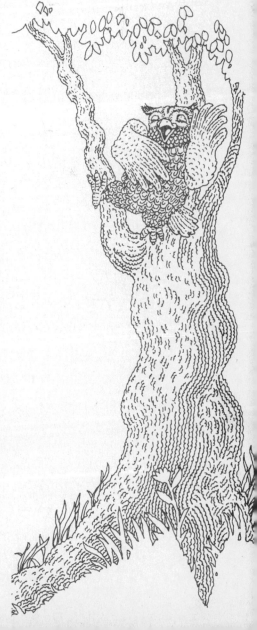

Learning to Spell a Word

1. Say the word.
   Look at the word and say the letters.

2. Print the word with your finger.

3. Close your eyes and think of the word.

4. Cover the word and print it on paper.

5. Check your spelling.

Making a Spelling Notebook

A Spelling Notebook will help you when you write. Write the words you're having trouble with on a sheet of paper. Add the paper to a notebook or folder. Whenever you need help to spell a word, look in your Spelling Notebook.

Name _____

Consonant Sounds

Warm Up

What stunt was performed by a woman nearly a century ago?

Free Fall

Every year, thousands of people travel to Niagara Falls. This 160-foot waterfall is between New York and Canada. Most people just watch the falls. On October 24, 1901, one person did more than just look. She was the first person to go over the falls in a wooden **barrel!**

Her name was Anna Taylor. This, her first real adventure, could have been her last. She was sure that if she survived the fall she would find **fame** and fortune.

Hundreds of people stood along the banks of the Niagara River. They cheered as the barrel was dropped into the river. The barrel floated with the **swift** current toward the falls. Then it tumbled down the **twelve**-story high falls. For a while, there was no sign of Anna Taylor. The crowd was **silent.** Finally the oak barrel bobbed up.

The barrel was brought ashore. As Anna stepped out, the crowd cheered wildly. It wasn't **until later** that people found out that she couldn't swim!

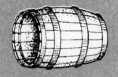
Look back at the boldfaced words. Say each word. What consonant sounds do you hear in each word?

On Your Mark

Take your Warm Up Test. Then check your spelling with the List Words on the next page.

5

Pep Talk

The vowels are **a, e, i, o, u,** and sometimes **y** and **w.** All the rest of the letters are **consonants.** In most words, you can hear the sounds of several consonants. Listen for the **w, l,** and **d** sounds in wild. Sometimes a consonant in a word is doubled, but you hear it only once. Listen for the one sound the double consonants stand for in banner and dollar.

LIST WORDS

1. banner
2. hundred
3. fame
4. later
5. seven
6. hammer
7. twelve
8. barrel
9. dollar
10. letters
11. silent
12. wild
13. until
14. swift
15. bottles
16. pineapple
17. film
18. gallon
19. traffic
20. eleven

Game Plan

Spelling Lineup

Write consonants to complete each List Word. Then circle any words with double consonants.

1. fa _m_ e
2. twe _l v_ e
3. bo _t t_ les
4. wi _l d_
5. le _t t_ ers
6. e _l_ e _v_ en
7. swi _f t_
8. la _t_ er
9. ga _l l_ on
10. tra _f f_ ic

11. se _v_ en
12. hun _d_ _m_ ed
13. fi _l m_
14. _S_ i _l_ ent
15. do _l l_ ar
16. un _t_ i _l_
17. ba _n_ _n_ er
18. ha _m_ _m_ er
19. ba _r_ _r_ el

20. pi _n_ ea _p_ _p_ _l_ e

Definitions

Read each definition clue. Write List Words in the spaces.
Then use the numbered letters to solve the riddle.

1. cars T r a f f i c
   11   4

2. 12 − 1 = T w e l v e
              9

3. a flag b a n n e r
                  7

4. quiet S i l e n T
         2   10 6

5. not tame W i l d
              8

6. fast S w i f T
       3   5

7. popularity f a m e
               1

Riddle: What runs and falls but never walks?

Answer: a S w i f T r i l e r
           1 2 3 4 5 6 7 8 9 10 11

Vocabulary

Write List Words under the correct headings. The first one
has been done for you.

numbers
1. __hundred__
2. Seven
3. Twelve
4. _____

fruit
5. _____

money
6. dollars

tool
7. _____

measurement
8. _____

containers
9. _____
10. _____

time words
11. _____
12. _____

Flex Your Spelling Muscles

Writing

Imagine that you were among the crowd who watched Anna Taylor float down Niagara River and go over Niagara Falls. Write a brief news report telling what you saw, heard, and felt. Don't forget to include what happened when it was all over. Use as many List Words as you can.

Proofreading

This travel article has ten mistakes. Use the proofreading marks to fix each mistake. Write the misspelled List Words correctly on the lines.

Proofreading Marks
⬭ spelling mistake
≡ capital letter

Niagara Falls Is Worth the Trip

When traveling to niagara Falls during the summer, be ready for some delays. The traffik can be heavy. When you finally get to the falls, spend some time watching the wyild, swiff water. Don't worry. it's unlikely that a barral will come crashing down. Latar, after you leave, your ears will still hear the roar of the water. take plenty of filmm and send leterz and postcards home to friends. There are many scenic places you'll want to share.

1. _____
2. _____
3. _____
4. _____
5. _____
6. _____
7. _____

Now proofread your news report. Fix any mistakes.

Go for the Goal

Take your Final Test. Then fill in your Scoreboard. Send your mistakes to the Word Locker.

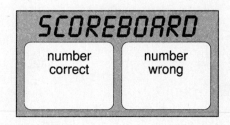

SCOREBOARD

| number correct | number wrong |

★ ★ ★ ★ ★ ★ ★ ★ ★ **All-Star Words** ★ ★ ★ ★ ★ ★ ★ ★ ★

vessel   slipper   splendid   enemy   instant

Work with a partner to write one paragraph using all the All-Star Words. Trade papers with other students to see how they used the words. How are the paragraphs alike or different?

Short-Vowel Sounds

Warm Up

What type of sculpture disappears with the tide?

Dig It

It all starts when the tide goes out. The artists come to the beach with their pails and shovels. They lift and sift and make **bumps** in the sand, but they aren't making just sand castles. This is the annual sand castle **contest** in Carmel, California which happens every October. In this contest, artists make not only castles, but also animals, fish, and anything else they can think of.

Artists mold and carve the wet sand for hours. They use pails, shovels, **sticks,** and other small tools, but mostly their **hands.** They build as far as the water's edge. The results are sometimes wacky, but always creative and fun to look at. The **judges** must have a hard time choosing a winner.

When the contest is over, the sculptors don't have to put the sand back. Before long the tide will come in and take care of things.

Look back at the boldfaced words. Say each word. Listen for the vowel sounds. What vowel sound do you hear in each word?

On Your Mark

Take your Warm Up Test. Then check your spelling with the List Words on the next page.

Pep Talk

The letters **a, e, i, o,** and **u** are vowels. You hear short-vowel sounds in these words:

/a/ in <u>stand</u>
/i/ in <u>sticks</u>
/e/ in <u>spent</u>
/ä/ in <u>locked</u>
/u/ in <u>judge</u>

Listen for the short-vowel sounds in each List Word.

LIST WORDS

1. hands
2. dentist
3. lifted
4. crack
5. bumps
6. practice
7. solid
8. clasp
9. sticks
10. spent
11. locked
12. adopt
13. judge
14. contest
15. stand
16. shrimp
17. stamp
18. trust
19. fender
20. pencil

Game Plan

Spelling Lineup

Write each List Word under the correct short-vowel sound. If a word has two short-vowel sounds, use the stressed one.

/a/

1. hands
2. stand
3. crack
4. clasp
5. stamp
6. stand

/i/

7. _____
8. _____
9. _____

/u/

10. bumps
11. judge
12. trust

/e/

13. _____
14. _____
15. _____
16. _____

/ä/

17. fender
18. _____
19. _____
20. _____

Alphabetical Order

Write this group of List Words in alphabetical order.
Remember, if two words begin with the same letter,
look at the next letter to help you decide the next word.

lifted
clasp
locked
adopt
judge
bumps
spent
stamp
contest
pencil

1. _____   7. _____

2. _____   8. _____

3. _____   9. _____

4. _____   10. _____

5. _____

6. _____

Hidden Words

Each word given is hidden in a List Word. Write the
List Word on the line. Circle the letters that spell the
hidden word.

1. rust _____   7. pen _____

2. lid _____   8. end _____

3. hand _____   9. tan _____

4. rim _____   10. rack _____

5. den _____   11. act _____

6. tick _____   12. test _____

Flex Your Spelling Muscles

Writing

Use the List Words to create a poster to advertise a sand sculpture contest or another contest you know about. Don't forget to include important information, such as when and where it will take place.

Proofreading

The following how-to article has nine mistakes. Use the proofreading marks to fix each mistake. Write the misspelled List Words on the lines.

Proofreading Marks
⬭ spelling mistake
⊙ add period

You can create a solud sand sculpture that won't disappear with the tide All you need is two cups of sand, one cup of cornstarch, and one cup of water. Heat the mixture over low heat until thick. Set aside and let it cool Then, use your handz to mold your sculpture and smooth out the bomps. Use the tip of a pensil to create designs. Let your sculpture dry and harden Invite your friends to create sculptures, too. Hold a contess and ask a parent or teacher to be the judj.

1. _____

2. _____

3. _____

4. _____

5. _____

6. _____

Now proofread your poster. Fix any mistakes.

Go for the Goal

Take your Final Test. Then fill in your Scoreboard. Send your mistakes to the Word Locker.

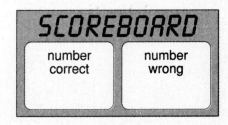

SCOREBOARD

number correct	number wrong

★ ★ ★ ★ ★ ★ ★ ★ ★ **All-Star Words** ★ ★ ★ ★ ★ ★ ★ ★ ★

timid   mascot   extend   public   fond

Make a list of the All-Star Words. Then, write a word or phrase that means the same or almost the same as each word. Check your definitions against your dictionary. Read each meaning aloud to a partner. Ask your partner to name the All-Star Word it goes with.

Long-Vowel Sounds

Warm Up

What playground rules should you follow?

Playground Rules

A playground is a place to have fun. Getting hurt could spoil your fun, so here are some simple **rules** for playing **safely**:

* Ride the slide one person at a time. A pile-up could be dangerous. Always slide feet first and your head will thank you.
* Ride the seesaw with a person of **equal** weight. Never get off without first alerting your partner.
* Keep a **tight** grip when you ride the swings. Use both hands and always remain seated.
* Play games with others. Never be the only one on a playground. Wait for your friends.

If you follow **these** rules, you'll have a good time and stay safe.

Say each boldfaced word. What do you notice about the vowel sounds?

On Your Mark

Take your Warm Up Test. Then check your spelling with the List Words on the next page.

Long vowels sound like their names.

/ā/ as in <u>scale</u>

/ē/ as in <u>these</u>

/ī/ as in <u>arrive</u>

/ō/ as in <u>stove</u>

/yo͞o/ as in <u>cubes</u>

/o͞o/ as in <u>rules</u>

The long vowel sound of u is /yo͞o/ or /o͞o/. Listen for the long-vowel sounds in each List Word.

LIST WORDS

1. these
2. deny
3. rules
4. safely
5. locate
6. crime
7. stove
8. scale
9. costume
10. arrive
11. opened
12. musical
13. equal
14. idea
15. tight
16. clover
17. rodent
18. tuba
19. cubes
20. pride

Game Plan

Spelling Lineup

Write each List Word. Circle the letters that spell long-vowel sounds. Words of two or more syllables may contain more than one long-vowel sound.

1. these
2. rules
3. locate
4. scale
5. costume
6. arrive
7. crime
8. stove
9. rules
10. cubes
11. tight
12. clover
13. pride
14. opened
15. medical
16. equal
17. safely
18. opened
19. sale
20. _____

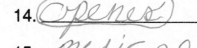

Classification

Write the List Word that belongs in each group.

1. sink, refrigerator, _____

2. piano, flute, _____

3. find, place, _____

4. this, those, _____

5. play, show, _____

6. mask, makeup, _____

7. laws, orders, _____

8. squares, boxes, _____

9. thought, plan, _____

10. rat, mouse, _____

Word Building

Add and subtract letters to form List Words.

1. right – r + t = _____

2. rival – riv + equ = _____

3. arrow – ow + ive = _____

4. rover – r + cl = _____

5. pale – p + sc = _____

6. any – a + de = _____

7. timely – tim + saf = _____

8. price – ce + de = _____

9. loaned – loa + ope = _____

10. time – t + cr = _____

Flex Your Spelling Muscles

Writing

Most sports and games have rules so that everyone can play safely. Choose a sport or game you know about. Then use the List Words to write some rules that go with it.

Proofreading

The following story has nine mistakes. Use the proofreading marks to fix each mistake. Then write the misspelled List Words on the lines.

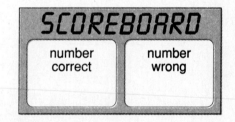

Proofreading Marks

◯ spelling mistake

∧ add something

The strangest thing happened yesterday. When Bo and I arrived at the school playground together the gate was shut tyght.

"Do you know why the gate is closed " I asked Bo.

"No, it never has been before. Do you think someone didn't know the rooles " he asked.

"Maybe. Let's try to get in," I said.

When we got the gate upened, we couldn't believe what we saw. By the swings sat a big cardboard stoove. On the slide was a tubah.

"What is all this " I asked.

"I don't know!" said Bo.

Just then a clown wearing a silly catsume came walking through the gate. Bo and I had forgotten! It was the day of our school carnival!

1. _____   3. _____   5. _____

2. _____   4. _____   6. _____

Now proofread your game rules. Fix any mistakes.

Go for the Goal

Take your Final Test. Then fill in your Scoreboard. Send your mistakes to the Word Locker.

SCOREBOARD

number correct	number wrong

★ ★ ★ ★ ★ ★ ★ ★ ★ ★ **All-Star Words** ★ ★ ★ ★ ★ ★ ★ ★ ★ ★

remove   spice   rude   cone   tomato

With your partner, write a silly recipe using the All-Star Words.
Swap recipes with other students to see how they used the words.

Hard and Soft c and g

LESSON 4

Warm Up

What kind of sculpture never gets into a museum?

Cool as Ice

If you saw someone wearing ski pants, heavy kneepads, a warm jacket, a baseball cap, rubber boots, and warm gloves, who would you think the person was? A skier? A baseball player in the Arctic? Possibly, but that person could also be an ice sculptor. An ice sculptor carves works of art out of giant ice cubes. Not a very **common** job, is it?

Simple blocks of ice can become any creation. An animal, a mermaid, or maybe a horse-drawn chariot. A frozen cart could carry two icy riders. It can take a sculptor hours and hours of cutting, chipping, and smoothing to complete one carving.

Unlike most works of art, ice sculptures are not meant to last. Once they're displayed, they melt. The sculptures are often used as party decorations. These **graceful** figures are usually placed in the **center** of the food table, in a **corner**, or on a **stage** by themselves. Talking about the sculptures puts guests at ease. They can easily "break the ice" by talking about the frozen art.

 Say each boldfaced word. Listen for the sounds that **c** and **g** make. What do you notice about the sounds for **c** and **g**?

On Your Mark

Take your Warm Up Test. Then check your spelling with the List Words on the next page.

The letter **c** can make a hard sound as in common and cactus and a soft sound as in force and celery. Listen for the hard and soft sound of **c** in circle.

The letter **g** can make a hard sound as in gifts and graceful and a soft sound as in edge and stage. Listen for the hard and soft sound of **g** in baggage.

Game Plan

Spelling Lineup

Write each List Word under the correct heading. Four words will be written more than once.

LIST WORDS

1. edge
2. common
3. circle
4. cactus
5. gifts
6. gentle
7. stage
8. strange
9. corner
10. graceful
11. center
12. baggage
13. category
14. gerbil
15. cement
16. prices
17. force
18. celery
19. decide
20. energy

hard **c** as in carton

1. _____
2. _____
3. _____
4. _____
5. _____

soft **c** as in cent

6. _____
7. _____
8. _____
9. _____
10. _____
11. _____
12. _____
13. _____

hard **g** as in grade

14. _____
15. _____
16. _____
17. _____

soft **g** as in germ

18. _____
19. _____
20. _____
21. _____
22. _____
23. _____
24. _____

Classification

Write the List Word that belongs in each group.

1. ordinary, usual, _____

2. square, triangle, _____

3. lettuce, cucumber, _____

4. middle, core, _____

5. luggage, suitcases, _____

6. group, set, _____

7. actors, play, _____

8. tame, kind, _____

9. desert, sand, _____

10. mouse, hamster, _____

11. birthday, party, _____

12. electrical, solar, _____

13. sidewalk, concrete, _____

14. cost, money, _____

Dictionary

Write the List Word that comes between each pair of guide words in the dictionary.

1. deal/ear

_____

2. effort/fact

_____

3. stone/stump

_____

4. coral/crayon

_____

5. early/egg

_____

6. grab/great

_____

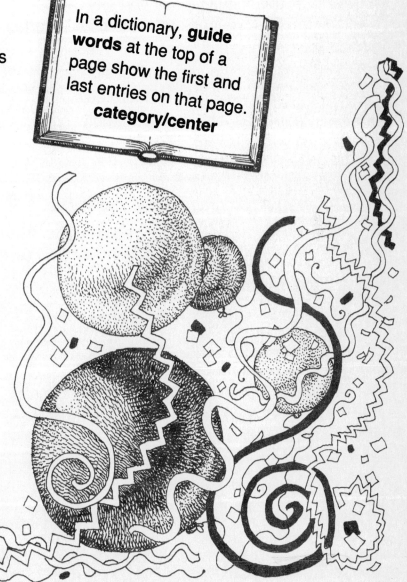

In a dictionary, **guide words** at the top of a page show the first and last entries on that page. **category/center**

Flex Your Spelling Muscles

Writing

Ice is only one material that sculptors use. Think of a sculpture you have seen in a picture, a store, or a museum. Write a paragraph telling what you liked or did not like about it. Use as many List Words as you can.

Proofreading

Mary's art review has ten mistakes. Use the proofreading marks to fix the mistakes. Write the misspelled List Words correctly on the lines.

Proofreading Marks
- ⬭ spelling mistake
- ∧ add something

Sculpture Display Wows Crowds!

Ana Cardona's powerful new sculpture is generating a great amount of energee at the art museum! The 10-foot sement kactus rises from thefloor in graseful lines taking senter staje. The public, of course, will deside for themselves. However, this reporter feels Ana Cardona's work has opened upa whole new categorry of sculpture art.

1. _____
2. _____
3. _____
4. _____
5. _____
6. _____
7. _____

Now proofread your paragraph. Fix any mistakes.

8. _____

Go for the Goal

Take your Final Test. Then fill in your Scoreboard. Send your mistakes to the Word Locker.

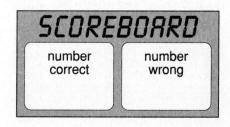

SCOREBOARD

number correct	number wrong

★ ★ ★ ★ ★ ★ ★ ★ ★ **All-Star Words** ★ ★ ★ ★ ★ ★ ★ ★ ★

gobble   college   damage   gasp   prince

Write a sentence for each All-Star Word. Then, read each sentence aloud to a partner, saying *blank* in place of the All-Star Word. See if your partner can complete each sentence with the correct missing word.

Beginning Consonant Blends

Warm Up

What sport was once called "baggataway"?

Lacrosse

North American Indians originally called this sport "baggataway." Today it's called *lacrosse*. Lacrosse is played by two teams on a grassy area a little larger than a football field. Each team has ten players. They wear heavy **gloves,** helmets, and shoulder pads to **protect** themselves. Each player carries a stick called a *crosse*. It is usually made of wood with a small pocket at the end. The pocket has a **screen** made of loose net so that the players can catch and throw the ball into it. Only the goalkeepers can touch the ball with their hands. The object of the game is to score goals. The team scoring the most goals wins. It is a game that requires both **speed** and **skill.**

The game was first used by Canadian Indians to train warriors. There were very few rules. Later, the French settlers gave it the name *lacrosse*. They added a few rules to make it safer to play. In 1867, it was adopted as the national game of Canada. Today it is popular in places as far away as Australia.

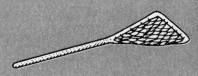

Say each of the boldfaced words. How many consonant sounds do you hear at the beginning of each word?

On Your Mark

Take your Warm Up Test. Then check your spelling with the List Words on the next page.

Pep Talk

A **consonant blend** is two or more consonants that come together in a word. Their sounds blend together, but each sound is heard. Listen to the sounds of these consonant blends:

gloves
straight
screens
craft
protect

Listen for the consonant blend in each List Word.

1. gloves
2. speed
3. skill
4. screens
5. protect
6. front
7. craft
8. brains
9. scared
10. proper
11. trace
12. dream
13. straight
14. splinter
15. screech
16. spaces
17. stuff
18. greedy
19. sprinkle
20. strict

Game Plan

Spelling Lineup

Add a consonant blend to each group of letters to form a List Word.

1. s t r ict
2. _____ ains
3. _____ uff
4. _____ eens
5. _____ inkle
6. _____ ill
7. _____ ared
8. _____ eedy
9. _____ inter
10. _____ eech
11. _____ ace
12. _____ aft
13. _____ ont
14. _____ oves

15. _____ otect
16. _____ eed
17. _____ aight
18. _____ aces
19. _____ oper
20. _____ eam

Rhyming

Use the clues to write List Words. Each List Word must rhyme with the underlined word.

1. As I chopped wood last <u>winter</u>, I got a _____ .

2. My sister <u>loves</u> to wear red _____ .

3. A <u>raft</u> is a water _____ .

4. Studying <u>trains</u> takes _____ .

5. Sandpaper is <u>rough</u> _____ .

6. I heard a _____ at the <u>beach</u>.

7. _____ the <u>wrinkle</u> to make it smooth.

8. To win the race, you will <u>need</u> _____ .

9. A fence that isn't crooked has a _____ <u>gate</u>.

10. Hiking up mountains takes a lot of <u>hill</u> _____ .

Puzzle

Fill in the crossword puzzle by writing a List Word to answer each clue.

ACROSS
2. wire window coverings
3. to watch over or keep safe
5. afraid
7. not willing to share
8. harsh or stiff

DOWN
1. to copy a picture
2. not crooked or bent
3. correct or suitable
4. the part that faces forward
6. a sleeping person's mind picture

Flex Your Spelling Muscles

Writing

What is your most favorite sport? What is your least favorite sport? Write a paragraph that explains why you prefer one sport over the other. Use as many List Words as you can.

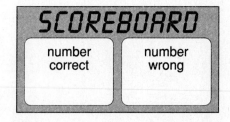

Proofreading

The article below has ten mistakes. Use the proofreading marks to fix each mistake. Write the misspelled words correctly on the lines.

Proofreading Marks
⬭ spelling mistake
≡ capital letter

Native American Kickball

Kickball races were once popular among Native americans in the Southwest and are still held by many groups in mexico. The players kicked a ball made of bone, wood, woven grass, or stone for many miles. some even raced barefoot with nothing to protekt their feet. They moved the ball in frunt of them with great skile and spead. they had to keep the ball going as strayht as possible in order to win. Sometimes they could kick the ball across flat spases to gain more ground and move ahead.

1. _____   4. _____

2. _____   5. _____

3. _____   6. _____

Now proofread what you wrote about your favorite sport. Fix any mistakes.

Go for the Goal

Take your Final Test. Then fill in your Scoreboard. Send your mistakes to the Word Locker.

SCOREBOARD

number correct	number wrong

★ ★ ★ ★ ★ ★ ★ ★ ★ **All-Star Words** ★ ★ ★ ★ ★ ★ ★ ★ ★

glow   crazy   program   scramble   strength

Write each All-Star Word. Then write a clue to go with it. Read each clue aloud to a partner. Ask your partner for the All-Star Word that goes with the clue.

Name _____

Instant Replay • Lessons 1–5

Time Out

Take another look at consonant sounds, short- and long-vowel sounds, the hard and soft sounds of **c** and **g,** and beginning consonant blends.

Check Your Word Locker

Look at the words in your Word Locker. Which words for Lessons 1 through 5 did you have the most trouble with? Write them here.

_____

_____

Practice writing your troublesome words with a partner. Try writing the letters of each word in the air. Your partner can spell the word aloud as you write.

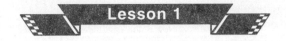

Lesson 1

In most words you can hear the sound of each consonant, as in <u>later</u>. Some words have double consonants that stand for one sound, as in <u>letters</u>.

List Words
banner
hammer
twelve
dollar
silent
wild
swift
bottles
pineapple
film

Write the List Word that belongs in each group.

1. nickel, quarter, _____

2. quiet, hushed, _____

3. wrench, pliers, _____

4. apple, peach, _____

5. quick, fast, _____

6. jars, packages, _____

7. free, untamed, _____

8. camera, movie, _____

9. four, eight, _____

10. flag, shield, _____

Lesson 2

Vowels can stand for short sounds, as in <u>contest</u> and <u>judge</u>.

List Words

dentist
lifted
practice
solid
clasp
adopt
judge
shrimp
trust
pencil

Write two List Words next to each short-vowel sound. If a word has two short vowel sounds, use the stressed one.

/a/ as in <u>hat</u>   1. _____ _____

/e/ as in <u>egg</u>   2. _____ _____

/ä/ as in <u>hop</u>   3. _____ _____

/i/ as in <u>hit</u>   4. _____ _____

/u/ as in <u>up</u>   5. _____ _____

Lesson 3

Vowels can also stand for long sounds, as in <u>these</u> and <u>stove</u>.

List Words

deny
safely
locate
costume
equal
idea
clover
rodent
tuba
pride

Write a List Word to complete each sentence.

1. A _____ is a musical instrument.

2. Ramon was filled with _____ when he won.

3. Anna wore a chicken _____ to the party.

4. Please help me _____ my lost book.

5. I can't _____ I'm happy it's summer.

6. We split the melon into _____ halves.

7. People say a four-leaf _____ is lucky.

8. Juan has a clever _____ for a story.

9. A field mouse is a _____ .

10. Drive _____ to avoid accidents.

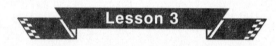

Lesson 4

Listen for the hard or soft sounds of **c** and **g** in <u>common</u>, <u>center</u>, <u>gifts</u>, and <u>stage</u>.

List Words

edge
circle
cactus
gentle
graceful
baggage
category
celery
decide
energy

Each sentence has two List Words, but one is misspelled. Circle the misspelled List Word and write it on the line.

1. Stand on the edge of the sircle for this dance. _____

2. Decide which bagadge is yours. _____

3. A deer is a gentle, gracfull animal. _____

4. I live on Palm Circle at the egge of town. _____

5. It took enargy to load the baggage. _____

6. Did you deside to buy the celery? _____

7. Be gentel and graceful with the baby. _____

8. Celary is a category of vegetable. _____

9. Solar energy is in a catagory of its own. _____

10. The caktus has a sharp edge. _____

Lesson 5

In a consonant blend, you can hear the sound of each consonant in a word, as in <u>sprinkle</u> and <u>protect</u>.

Write each group of List Words in alphabetical order.

List Words

gloves
protect
scared
proper
trace
straight
splinter
screech
greedy
strict

greedy scared straight proper gloves	trace screech strict protect splinter
1. _____	6. _____
2. _____	7. _____
3. _____	8. _____
4. _____	9. _____
5. _____	10. _____

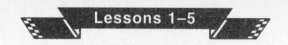

List Words

hammer
dollar
dentist
shrimp
pencil
deny
costume
celery
scared
straight

Write the List Word that matches each clue. Then read down the shaded boxes to solve the riddle.

1. a green vegetable

2. a unit of money

3. to declare untrue

4. a shellfish

5. a set of clothes

6. a doctor for the teeth

7. a pounding tool

8. a writing tool

9. not crooked or bent

10. frightened

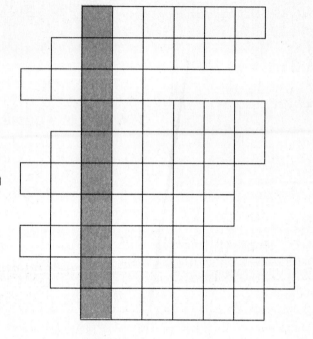

Riddle: Why did the chef put alphabet soup in the blender?

Answer: He wanted to see the _____ blend!

Go for the Goal

Take your Final Replay Test. Then fill in your Scoreboard. Send any misspelled words to your Word Locker.

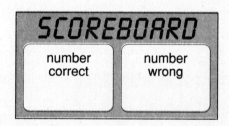

SCOREBOARD

| number correct | number wrong |

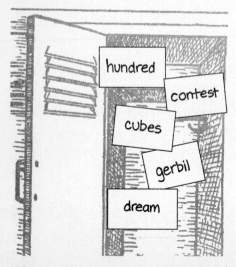

Clean Out Your Word Locker

Look in your Word Locker. Cross out each word you spelled correctly on your Final Replay Test. Circle the words you're still having trouble with. Add the words you circled to your Spelling Notebook. What do you notice about the words? Watch for those words as you write.

Consonant Blends

Warm Up

What problems might a two-headed snake have?

Double Header

You may have heard the saying that "two heads are better than one." This is definitely not true when it comes to a two-headed snake. **Different** kinds of animals have been born with two heads. For an unknown reason, a large number of these two-headed animals have been snakes.

It might seem that there would be some advantages in being a two-headed snake. You might think that a snake with two heads would have better hearing. However, a snake does not hear **sounds** as we do, since it has no ears. A snake cannot hear the **crunch** of a footstep. It feels the vibrations. Two heads would not help the snake's speech, either. A snake has no vocal chords and can only make hissing noises.

Two heads can only bring problems. Each head would want to be **independent.** Think about what would happen if one head wanted to go, and the other head wanted to stay where it was. Everything would come to a **halt.** The heads would spend all their time **protesting,** and the snake wouldn't get anywhere.

Say each boldfaced word in the selection. Listen for the consonant blends. What do you notice about where the blends are in the words?

On Your Mark

Take your Warm Up Test. Then check your spelling with the List Words on the next page.

Pep Talk

Remember, when two or more consonants come together in a word, their sounds may blend together. In a **consonant blend,** you hear each letter. A blend may be found anywhere in a word. Listen for the consonant blends in the List Words.

<u>cr</u>ept
<u>c</u>o<u>ld</u>er
ri<u>sk</u>
<u>sk</u>un<u>k</u>

LIST WORDS

1. crept
2. crunch
3. sounds
4. dusk
5. refund
6. colder
7. skunk
8. unfold
9. risk
10. milk
11. halt
12. different
13. protesting
14. twister
15. independent
16. absent
17. stretch
18. printing
19. blended
20. product

Game Plan

Spelling Lineup

Add one or two consonant blends to each group of letters to form a List Word.

1. differe ___ ___

2. ___ ___ ___ etch

3. refu ___ ___

4. twi ___ ___ er

5. du ___ ___

6. prote ___ ___ ing

7. unfo ___ ___

8. ___ ___ oduct

9. sou ___ ___ ___

10. indepe ___ ___ ent

11. ___ ___ unk

12. abse ___ ___

13. ___ ___ unch

14. ha ___ ___

15. ble ___ ___ ed

16. mi ___ ___

17. ___ ___ inting

18. co ___ ___ er

19. ___ ___ ept

20. ri ___ ___

Vocabulary

Write the List Word that matches each clue.

1. noises

   _____

2. a part of the day just before dark

   _____

3. to chew with lots of noise

   _____

4. not present

   _____

5. black and white animal

   _____

6. something to drink that's white

   _____

7. any item bought at a store

   _____

8. not ruled or controlled by others

   _____

Synonyms

Write the List Word that means the same or almost the same as each word given.

1. danger   _____

2. extend   _____

3. crawled   _____

4. repay   _____

5. evening   _____

6. complaining _____

7. cooler   _____

8. missing   _____

9. unusual   _____

10. mixed   _____

11. open   _____

12. tornado   _____

13. stop   _____

14. writing   _____

Flex Your Spelling Muscles

Writing

In what situations might a two-headed snake have difficulty making decisions? Write a conversation that the two heads might have about deciding what to eat or where to go. Use as many List Words as you can.

Proofreading

The following paragraph has ten mistakes. Use the proofreading marks to fix the mistakes. Then write the misspelled List Words correctly on the lines.

Proofreading Marks	
⬭	spelling mistake
⊙	add period
⌄	add apostrophe

When dusc falls, the spotted scunk looks for food. Its an indepedant animal that might take over another animal's home If a dog krept up on a spotted skunk it would be taking a risc. Youd hear some prootesing howls when the skunk sprayed the dog with a terrible smelling liquid

1. _____   4. _____

2. _____   5. _____

3. _____   6. _____

Now proofread your snake's conversation. Fix any mistakes.

Go for the Goal

Take your Final Test. Then fill in your Scoreboard. Send your mistakes to the Word Locker.

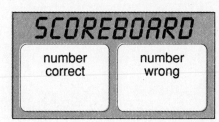

SCOREBOARD

number correct	number wrong

★ ★ ★ ★ ★ ★ ★ ★ **All-Star Words** ★ ★ ★ ★ ★ ★ ★ ★ ★

harvest   slender   stumble   branch   bask

Say each All-Star Word to your partner. Have your partner write the words and circle the consonant blends. Then switch roles and repeat the activity.

Vowels with r

Warm Up

How can you turn garbage into art?

Recycling for Art

Before you toss out that milk **carton** or that pair of **dirty** old shoes, think about keeping them. What for? Art, of course!

Believe it or not, **garbage** could transform you into an **artist.** With a little imagination and careful hunting, you can make found objects or discarded materials into artistic treasures. The best part is that you are also recycling!

Recycling for art is not a new idea. Artists have been working with used materials for hundreds of years. Sculptors have used everything from broken tea cups to **spare** tires. And painters have created masterpieces, on everything from old **boards** to discarded clothing. Scientists have even discovered that underneath some very famous paintings, completely different pictures have been painted! Very often artists could not afford the price of new canvas, so they simply painted over old ones.

The challenge for you is to find objects no one wants, and make them into something someone would want. And if the idea of turning junk into art bothers you, don't think of it as art. Think of it as just another way to clean up!

 Look back at the boldfaced words. Say each word. What do you notice about the way the vowels sound in each word?

On Your Mark

Take your Warm Up Test. Then check your spelling with the List Words on the next page.

Pep Talk

When the letter **r** comes after a vowel or vowels, it sometimes changes the vowel sound. Say each pair of words. Notice how the **r** changes the sound that the vowel or vowels make.

heat—heart
spot—sports
cub—curb

Game Plan

Spelling Lineup

Say each word below. Then write each List Word under the word with the same vowel sound. If a List Word has two syllables, use the vowel sound in the stressed syllable. Remember that some words use different letters to spell the same sound.

LIST WORDS

1. carton
2. heart
3. sports
4. artist
5. spare
6. dirty
7. shore
8. curb
9. fair
10. sherbet
11. boards
12. fearless
13. journal
14. cheerfully
15. garbage
16. organ
17. error
18. sparks
19. harbor
20. perfume

<u>part</u>

1. _____
2. _____
3. _____
4. _____
5. _____
6. _____

<u>fur</u>

7. _____
8. _____
9. _____
10. _____
11. _____

<u>short</u>

12. _____
13. _____
14. _____
15. _____

<u>care</u>

16. _____
17. _____
18. _____

<u>year</u>

19. _____
20. _____

Hidden Words

Each word below is hidden in a List Word. Write the List Word on the line. Circle the letters that spell the hidden word.

1. ports _____

2. cart _____

3. fume _____

4. park _____

5. air _____

6. full _____

7. hear _____

8. oar _____

9. less _____

10. arbor _____

Vocabulary

Write the List Word that matches each definition.

1. something extra

_____

2. festival

_____

3. trash

_____

4. a musical instrument

_____

5. not clean

_____

6. a person who draws or paints

7. edge of the street

_____

8. not afraid

_____

9. a dessert like ice cream

_____

10. mistake

_____

11. land at the edge of the sea

_____

12. diary

Flex Your Spelling Muscles

Writing

Imagine you are exhibiting your own works of "garbage art." Write an advertisement to tell about your show. Make it sound like something everyone would want to see. Use as many List Words as you can.

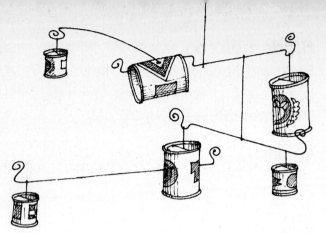

Proofreading

The editorial below has nine mistakes. Use the proofreading marks to fix the mistakes. Then write the misspelled List Words on the lines.

Proofreading Marks
⬭ spelling mistake
∧ add something

What is the problem with garbaje There is just too much of it. Who likes to look at dirtee beaches, or smell a polluted harber Who wants to see a milk cartone lying on the cerb It is time for people to stop this mess and be fare to our planet.

1. _____

2. _____

3. _____

4. _____

5. _____

6. _____

Now proofread your advertisement. Fix any mistakes.

Go for the Goal

Take your Final Test. Then fill in your Scoreboard. Send your mistakes to the Word Locker.

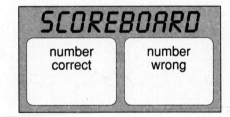

SCOREBOARD

number correct	number wrong

★ ★ ★ ★ ★ ★ ★ ★ ★ **All-Star Words** ★ ★ ★ ★ ★ ★ ★ ★ ★

starve   nurse   nervous   forth   hearth

With a partner, write a story using words or phrases that mean the same or almost the same as the All-Star Words. Trade stories with other students. Replace the words and phrases with the All-Star Words. Which way does the story sound the best?

Consonant Digraphs

Warm Up

What should you do if lightning strikes?

Flash!

Flash! Crackle! Boom! The lightning **reaches** across the sky. The softball game has come to a stop. Then the **thunder** sounds **sharply** in your ears. Everyone runs for cover.

Air is always full of electricity. When a storm develops, the electricity changes into positive and negative charges. Because opposites attract, the positive and negative meet. The path of electricity between them is lightning. It can move across the sky or go straight to the ground.

What should you do if you're outside when a storm with lightning strikes? Scientists say to look for shelter, but choose carefully. Don't **bother** to **gather** your belongings. Don't be **foolish** and stand under a tree. Lightning usually strikes the highest point around, such as a tree or **chimney.** Stay close to the ground if you can't find a building. Get down on your hands and knees if you have to. One of the safest places is in a car.

After **awhile** the lightning stops, but now it's pouring rain. No one wants to play "water" sports, so the game is called off until **Thursday.**

Look back at the boldfaced words. Say each word. Can you find two consonants together in each word that make only one sound?

On Your Mark

Take your Warm Up Test. Then check your spelling with the List Words on the next page.

Pep Talk

Consonant digraphs are two consonants together that make a completely new sound. A consonant digraph may be found anywhere in a word. Listen for the sounds of these consonant digraphs.

/sh/ as in <u>sharply</u>, <u>foolish</u>

/hw/ as in <u>whiskers</u>, <u>wheat</u>

/ch/ as in <u>chicken</u>, <u>reaches</u>

The consonant digraph **th** has two different sounds.

/th/ as in <u>thunder</u>

/*th*/ as in <u>bother</u>

LIST WORDS

1. thunder
2. farther
3. reaches
4. chicken
5. wheat
6. Thursday
7. foolish
8. gather
9. brother
10. awhile
11. chimney
12. sharply
13. leash
14. bother
15. shipment
16. feathers
17. charge
18. shovel
19. whiskers
20. crush

Game Plan

Spelling Lineup

Write each List Word under the correct heading.

/hw/ as in <u>whale</u>

1. _____

2. _____

3. _____

/th/ as in <u>thimble</u>

4. _____

5. _____

/sh/ as in <u>dish</u>

6. _____

7. _____

8. _____

9. _____

10. _____

11. _____

/ch/ as in <u>peach</u>

12. _____

13. _____

14. _____

15. _____

/*th*/ as in <u>mother</u>

16. _____

17. _____

18. _____

19. _____

20. _____

Sentence Completion

Write a List Word to complete each sentence.

1. The driver turned the corner _____ to avoid the dog.

2. Smoke goes up the _____ of our fireplace.

3. The _____ stays in her nest to guard her eggs.

4. Jason felt a little _____ wearing such a silly costume.

5. The spelling books will arrive in next month's _____ .

6. Hand Gretta a _____ so she can dig, too.

7. The oil on a duck's _____ helps it keep dry.

8. My cat has long, white _____ .

9. Kim's house is _____ from town than mine is.

10. Keep your dog on a _____ at all times.

Rhyming

Write the List Word that rhymes with each word given.

1. beaches _____

2. rather _____

3. father _____

4. large _____

5. sheet _____

6. hush _____

7. another _____

8. under _____

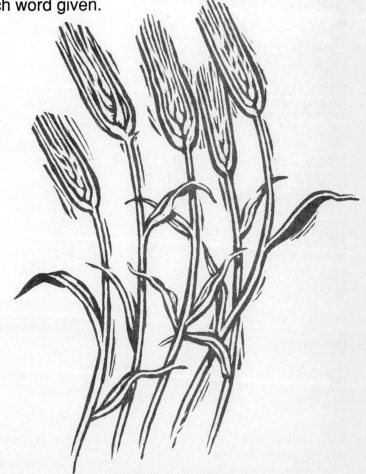

Flex Your Spelling Muscles

Writing

A thunder and lightning storm can be exciting and a little scary. Write a description of any kind of storm you have experienced. Include lots of vivid details. Use as many List Words as you can.

Proofreading

The newspaper report below has ten mistakes. Use the proofreading marks to fix the mistakes. Then write the misspelled List Words on the lines.

<table>
<tr><td>Proofreading Marks</td></tr>
<tr><td>◯ spelling mistake</td></tr>
<tr><td>≡ capital letter</td></tr>
<tr><td>⤸ take out something</td></tr>
</table>

Strange weather hit our our area last Thurzday. The day was warm until about noon when dark clouds began to gathur. heavy rain fell for awile until there was a loud crash of thundur. Suddenly, the rain turned to hail! this was the first hail storm our area has seen since 1963. The the hail came down so hard that one woman said it knocked the fithers off her prize chikin!

1. _____   4. _____

2. _____   5. _____

3. _____   6. _____

Now proofread your description. Fix any mistakes.

Go for the Goal

Take your Final Test. Then fill in your Scoreboard. Send your mistakes to the Word Locker.

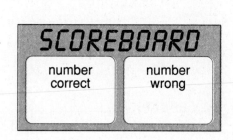

SCOREBOARD

number correct	number wrong

★ ★ ★ ★ ★ ★ ★ ★ ★ **All-Star Words** ★ ★ ★ ★ ★ ★ ★ ★ ★

whether   arithmetic   thankful   champion   shelter

Write a sentence for each All-Star Word. Leave a blank where the word would be written. Trade papers with your partner. See if you can complete each other's sentences.

Silent Letters

Warm Up

What is the "ghost galleon"?

Ghost Ship

Savage winds ripped her sails. Fierce waves spilled over her decks. A thundering crack was heard. Suddenly the towering mainmast broke and collapsed into the sea. The Santa Margarita was helpless, at the mercy of the wind and sea. In a short while, the mighty ship was gone, and over 120 people had drowned. In one of the most mysterious **wrecks** of all time, the Santa Margarita disappeared in 1622. Since then she has been **known** as the "**ghost** galleon."

It wasn't until 358 years later, in 1980, that the Santa Margarita was found. Pieces of the ship's cargo were found under the sand and water near an **island** in the Florida Keys. When the treasure-hunting divers saw the ship's cargo,

they quickly changed her nickname to the "gold-chain wreck." The name referred to the great amount of gold scattered on the ocean floor when the ship sank. Divers found a tangled mass of gold chains. When they untangled it, 43 glittering chains reached a total length of 180 feet! Each link was as thick as the **knuckle** of your **thumb.** In the 1600's, people often carried gold in the form of chains. Links could be unhooked and used like coins.

Say each of the boldfaced words in the selection. Which letters do not make a sound?

On Your Mark

Take your Warm Up Test. Then check your spelling with the List Words on the next page.

Pep Talk

Some words contain **silent letters.** We don't hear the sounds of those letters when we say the words. Study the silent letters in these words.

known	**w**rist	fol**k**s
honest	hal**f**way	fli**gh**t
	of**t**en	

Be extra careful when you spell such words. Now study the silent letters in the remaining List Words.

Game Plan

Spelling Lineup

Write each List Word under the correct heading.

LIST WORDS

1. ghost
2. thumb
3. known
4. often
5. folks
6. wrist
7. halfway
8. listen
9. knuckle
10. comb
11. wrecks
12. flight
13. honest
14. island
15. Wednesday
16. numb
17. wrench
18. crumb
19. soften
20. answer

silent **b**

1. _____
2. _____
3. _____
4. _____

silent **h**

5. _____
6. _____

silent **gh**

7. _____

silent **k**

8. _____
9. _____

silent **s**

10. _____

silent **w**

11. _____
12. _____
13. _____
14. _____

silent **l**

15. _____
16. _____

silent **d**

17. _____

silent **t**

18. _____
19. _____
20. _____

Rhyming

Write the List Word that rhymes with each word given.

1. bench _____

2. kite _____

3. decks _____

4. fist _____

5. bone _____

6. roast _____

Puzzle

Fill in the crossword puzzle by writing a
List Word to answer each clue.

ACROSS
2. day of the week
4. people
6. part of the way
10. a spirit
11. land in the middle
   of water
13. understood or
   realized
15. tool used on
   the hair
16. tiny bit
17. to make soft

DOWN
1. destroys
3. response to a
   question
5. many times
6. truthful
7. trip on a plane
8. one of the fingers
9. part of each finger
12. to try to hear
14. without feeling

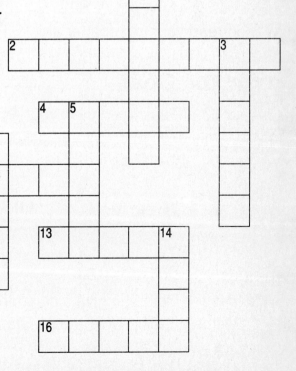

Flex Your Spelling Muscles

Writing

Imagine what it would be like to find a shipwreck full of treasure.
Write a newspaper article that reports the discovery.

Proofreading

This story has eight mistakes. Fix the mistakes with
the proofreading marks. Then write the misspelled
List Words correctly on the lines.

Proofreading Marks
⬭ spelling mistake
∧ add something

Imagine being on a haunted ship Well, lissen to
this. There may reportedly be more than one goast
on the Queen Mary, an ocean liner docked in Long
Beach, California. Several crew members say they
have sighted ghosts in different parts of the ship.
Others have heard noises, like the clanging of a
rentch banging on pipes. Some focks have seen
moving lights. How scary I would take flihte hafwaiy
out the door in a moment if I saw a ghost.

1. _____   4. _____

2. _____   5. _____

3. _____   6. _____

Now proofread your newspaper article. Fix any mistakes.

Go for the Goal

Take your Final Test. Then fill in your Scoreboard.
Send your mistakes to the Word Locker.

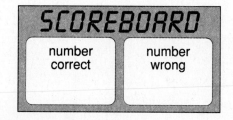

SCOREBOARD
number correct   number wrong

★ ★ ★ ★ ★ ★ ★ ★ ★ **All-Star Words** ★ ★ ★ ★ ★ ★ ★ ★ ★

daughter   bomb   knowledge   whistle   wrinkle

Draw a picture to give a clue for each All-Star Word. Trade drawings
with a partner. Write the All-Star Word that goes with each picture.

/f/ Sound

Warm Up

How do you move 230 elephants with a total weight of more than 600 tons?

Big Move

Can you imagine moving more than 600 tons? Actually, the 600 tons moved themselves. In Indonesia, 230 **elephants** had to be moved because there wasn't **enough** food. Eventually, the elephants would have destroyed nearby crops in their search for food. So the government relocated them to a place where they'd find enough food.

Moving was a tough job. The 30-mile trip took two months and one thousand people. The people first changed the **geography,** or surface, of the land. They cut roads into thick jungles and swamps. **After** the elephants traveled the roads, deep canals were dug behind them so the animals could not turn back. The work was rough, but worth it. The elephants are now happy and eating well.

The herders say they've always called the elephants by their proper name, "mbah." That means grandma or grandpa. Indonesian animal experts say this name keeps the elephants calm while moving. It appears that even elephants like respect!

Look back at the boldfaced words. Listen for the /f/ sound in each word. How many different spellings for the /f/ sound do you find?

On Your Mark

Take your Warm Up Test. Then check your spelling with the List Words on the next page.

Pep Talk

The sound /f/ is usually spelled with **f,** as in after. It can also be spelled with **ff,** as in stiff. Sometimes the /f/ sound is spelled with **ph,** as in photo and graphs. The /f/ sound can also be spelled with **gh,** as in cough and laughs.

LIST WORDS

1. photo
2. graphs
3. laughs
4. cough
5. trophy
6. roughly
7. enough
8. alphabet
9. shelf
10. after
11. stiff
12. elephants
13. giraffe
14. geography
15. nephew
16. phase
17. orphan
18. dolphin
19. phony
20. autograph

Game Plan

Spelling Lineup

Write each List Word under the correct heading.

/f/ spelled ph

1. _____
2. _____
3. _____
4. _____
5. _____
6. _____
7. _____
8. _____
9. _____
10. _____
11. _____
12. _____

/f/ spelled gh

13. _____
14. _____
15. _____
16. _____

/f/ spelled f

17. _____
18. _____

/f/ spelled ff

19. _____
20. _____

Dictionary

Write the List Word that would come between these entry words in the dictionary.

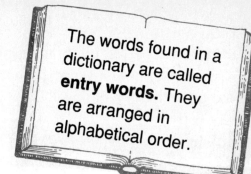

The words found in a dictionary are called **entry words.** They are arranged in alphabetical order.

1. monkey—open _____

2. rusty—spread _____

3. elk—garage _____

4. silver—taste _____

5. fresh—germ _____

6. glass—heavy _____

7. phonograph—question _____

8. other—pheasant _____

9. duty—elf _____

10. brand—desire _____

11. air—artist _____

12. attract—baby _____

Puzzle

This is a crossword puzzle without word clues. Study the length and the letters already done for each List Word. Then complete the puzzle.

Flex Your Spelling Muscles

Writing

Draw pictures of elephants, giraffes, dolphins, or other animals. Use your List Words to write captions that go with the pictures.

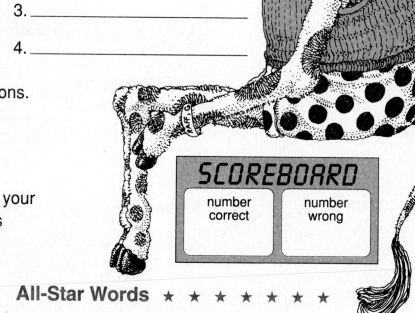

Giraffe is treated for Stiff neck

Proofreading

Look for the nine mistakes in this article. Use the proofreading marks to fix the mistakes. Then write the misspelled words on the lines.

Proofreading Marks
- ⬭ spelling mistake
- ≡ capital letter
- ∧ add something

how many wild animals are in trouble today Elefant herds have been greatly reduced and young elephants have been made orfans because of ivory hunting. some animals, like the jirafe, are forced out of their homes by people looking for new places to build and farm. Dolfins get caught in fishermen's nets along with the fish. when will people learn to share the earth with animals

1. _____
2. _____
3. _____
4. _____

Now proofread your picture captions. Fix any mistakes.

Go for the Goal

Take your Final Test. Then fill in your Scoreboard. Send your mistakes to the Word Locker.

SCOREBOARD

number correct	number wrong

★ ★ ★ ★ ★ ★ ★ ★ ★ **All-Star Words** ★ ★ ★ ★ ★ ★ ★ ★

affection   phrase   earmuffs   perfect   tough

Write a paragraph using the All-Star Words, but leave three or four letters out of each word. Trade papers with a partner. Fill in the missing letters.

Instant Replay • Lessons 7–11

Time Out

Take another look at consonant blends and digraphs, vowels with r, silent letters, and how to spell the sound /f/.

Check Your Word Locker

Look at the words in your Word Locker. Write your most troublesome words for Lessons 7 through 11.

_____

Practice writing your troublesome words with a partner. Try writing the letters for each word in a tray of sand, salt, or sugar. Your partner can check your spelling as you write.

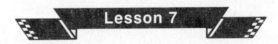

Lesson 7

In a **consonant blend,** you can hear the sound of each letter. A blend may be found anywhere in a word, as in <u>twister</u>, <u>colder</u>, and <u>sounds</u>.

List Words
crept
crunch
dusk
refund
skunk
milk
halt
stretch
blended
product

Write a List Word to complete each sentence.

1. Bob _____ the ingredients.

2. A _____ is black and white.

3. The sky begins to darken at _____ .

4. The store would not _____ my money.

5. Thin the batter with a cup of _____ .

6. Bike riders must _____ at stop signs.

7. The rabbit _____ into my garden.

8. Try to _____ the hat to fit.

9. My report was the _____ of hard work.

10. I heard the _____ of snow under my boots.

When the letter **r** comes after a vowel, it often changes the sound the vowel stands for.

cub—curb   spots—sports

List Words
heart
artist
dirty
sherbet
journal
garbage
organ
error
harbor
perfume

Write the List Word that belongs in each group.

1. diary, autobiography, _____

2. ice cream, pudding, _____

3. musician, dancer, _____

4. soiled, messy, _____

5. ocean, river, _____

6. valentine, love, _____

7. piano, violin, _____

8. trash, wastepaper, _____

9. mistake, blunder, _____

10. lipstick, powder, _____

Sometimes two consonants together form a consonant digraph, making a new sound, as in awhile, foolish, gather, and charge.

List Words
thunder
chicken
wheat
brother
chimney
leash
shipment
feathers
shovel
whiskers

Add a consonant digraph to each group of letters to form a List Word.

1. ___ ___ imney

2. fea ___ ___ ers

3. ___ ___ under

4. ___ ___ icken

5. bro ___ ___ er

6. ___ ___ iskers

7. ___ ___ ipment

8. lea ___ ___

9. ___ ___ eat

10. ___ ___ ovel

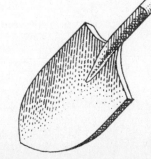

Some words contain silent letters. Be careful when you spell them.
Look for the silent letters in **ghost**, **numb**, and **Wednesday**.

List Words

known
folks
wrist
knuckle
comb
flight
wrench
crumb
soften
answer

Write each group of List Words in alphabetical order.

wrist flight soften wrench folks

known crumb comb knuckle answer

1. _____

2. _____

3. _____

4. _____

5. _____

6. _____

7. _____

8. _____

9. _____

10. _____

The sound /f/ can be spelled in four different ways, as in **after**,
stiff, **phony**, and **laughs**.

List Words

cough
trophy
roughly
enough
shelf
stiff
giraffe
nephew
orphan
dolphin

Build List Words by adding or subtracting letters.

1. knew – kn + neph _____

2. tough – t + c _____

3. stick – ck + ff _____

4. though – th + en _____

5. than – t + orp _____

6. girl – l + affe _____

7. thin – t + dolp _____

8. shed – d + lf _____

9. tropical – ical + hy _____

10. route – te + ghly _____

List Words

crept
crunch
dusk
heart
dirty
garbage
thunder
chicken
chimney
comb
flight
answer
trophy
giraffe
dolphin

Write a List Word to complete each song title or singing group.

1. "Take Out the _____," by the Trash Trio

2. "Let's Do the _____," by the Cluck Clucks

3. "Clean Up Your Act," by the _____ Shirts

4. "Take a _____ with Me," by the Airplanes

5. "Share My Popcorn," by the _____ Bunch

6. "True or False?" by the _____ Dancers

7. "Night Is Falling," by the _____ Duo

8. "My _____ Beats for You," by the Valentines

9. "_____ Your Hair," by the Brush Brothers

10. "_____ and Lightning," by the Boomers

11. "I'd Dive for You," by the _____ Duet

12. "Up in Smoke," by Jimmy _____

13. "Head in the Clouds," by Ginny _____

14. "A _____ for Sophie," by the Winners

15. "You _____ into My Heart," by the Sneakers

Go for the Goal

Take your Final Replay Test. Then fill in your Scoreboard. Send any misspelled words to the Word Locker.

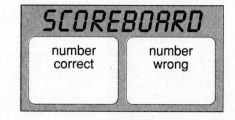

SCOREBOARD

number correct	number wrong

absent
journal
foolish
numb
phony

Clean Out Your Word Locker

Look in your Word Locker. Cross out each word you spelled correctly on your Final Replay Test. Circle the words you're still having trouble with. Add the words you circled to your Spelling Notebook. What do you notice about the words? Watch for those words as you write.

Suffixes <u>ed</u>, <u>er</u>, and <u>ing</u>

Warm Up

Who is the youngest person ever to enter America's space program?

Space Fever

Almost everyone knows that Neil Armstrong was the first person to walk on the moon and that Alan Shepard was the first American astronaut. Do you remember when Sally Ride became the first American woman in space?

There's another important first that should be **remembered.** That's the first teenager in America's space program, Jackie Parker. She became a flight controller for NASA when she was only 19 years old. Jackie was responsible for **watching** and **checking** computers during space launches.

In school, Jackie was a quick **learner, finishing** high school in only two years. Then she went on to college and studied computer science. She completed college in record time, too. **Following** college she went to flight school. After only one week she was flying solo.

Jackie Parker has some advice for those who'd like to follow in her footsteps. "If you believe in yourself, you can do anything."

NATIONAL AERONAUTICS & SPACE ADMINISTRATION
LYNDON B. JOHNSON SPACE CENTER

Look back at the boldfaced words. What do you notice about their spelling? Did the root words change when an ending, or suffix, was added?

On Your Mark

Take your Warm Up Test. Then check your spelling with the List Words on the next page.

You can add the suffixes **ed**, **er**, or **ing** to some words without changing the spelling of the root word. Study these examples:

clean + **ed** = cleaned
wish + **ing** = wishing
learn + **er** = learner
sing + **er** = singer

Find the unchanged root word in each List Word.

LIST WORDS

1. watching
2. checking
3. finishing
4. learner
5. bending
6. cleaned
7. sorted
8. missed
9. singer
10. guessed
11. teacher
12. walker
13. remembered
14. following
15. tossed
16. turning
17. wishing
18. landing
19. leading
20. catcher

Game Plan

Spelling Lineup

Write each List Word under the correct heading.

Root + **er**

1. _____
2. _____
3. _____
4. _____
5. _____

Root + **ed**

6. _____
7. _____
8. _____
9. _____
10. _____
11. _____

Root + **ing**

12. _____
13. _____
14. _____
15. _____
16. _____
17. _____
18. _____
19. _____
20. _____

Classification

Write the List Word that belongs in each group.

1. pitcher, batter, _____

2. hoping, wanting, _____

3. supposed, imagined, _____

4. runner, jogger, _____

5. seeing, looking, _____

6. dancer, actor, _____

7. threw, pitched, _____

8. divided, grouped, _____

9. thought of, recalled, _____

10. curving, stooping, _____

11. pupil, student, _____

12. avoided, escaped, _____

Dictionary

For each set of dictionary guide words, write two List Words that could be found on that page.

In a dictionary, **guide words** at the top of a page show the first and last entries on that page.

check/clue

lamp/leaf

1. _____

2. _____

film/fool

7. _____

8. _____

chance/click

3. _____

4. _____

tight/twelve

9. _____

10. _____

wake/wave

5. _____

6. _____

shore/soup

11. _____

12. _____

Flex Your Spelling Muscles

Writing

Imagine that you are the first astronaut to land on an unknown planet. Write a journal entry to describe what you see and hear. Use List Words.

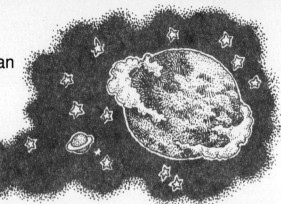

Proofreading

The paragraph below has ten mistakes. Use the proofreading marks to fix the mistakes. Then write the misspelled List Words correctly on the lines.

Proofreading Marks	
⬯	spelling mistake
≡	capital letter
ℒ	take out something

Yesterday I went to an air show with my friend david and his mother, who is a teachr. We were waching six jets jets streak across the sky, one folowing the other. Suddenly, the plane that was leeding began to turn. The others followed. we stared in amazement as the jets did loops and dips. When the pilots came in for the landng, the crowd cheered! We wouldn't have mised that that show for anything!

1. _____

2. _____

3. _____

4. _____

5. _____

6. _____

Now proofread your journal entry. Fix any mistakes.

Go for the Goal

Take your Final Test. Then fill in your Scoreboard. Send your mistakes to the Word Locker.

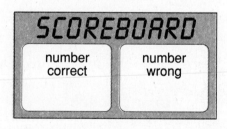

SCOREBOARD

number correct	number wrong

★ ★ ★ ★ ★ ★ ★ ★ ★ **All-Star Words** ★ ★ ★ ★ ★ ★ ★ ★ ★

gulped   performer   mending   sinking   soared

Write a paragraph using all five words, but leave a blank for each word's suffix. Then trade papers with a partner. Finish each other's words.

LESSON
14

Suffixes ed, er, and ing: Doubling Final Consonants

Warm Up

What kind of race uses giant canoes?

Blazing Paddles

The sky is bright and sunny. Light winds ripple the blue-green water. Six anxious competitors are **sitting** inside a giant canoe, ready to paddle. A gunshot pierces the silence. The blast marks the **beginning** of a 41-mile race from the Hawaiian island of Molokai to the island of Oahu. In moments, canoes are **skimming** across the water.

The Molokai Outrigger Canoe Race is not just a race. It has historical significance as well. Many years ago, hundreds of giant canoes could be seen in the Hawaiian Islands. Each boat was carved from a single tree—usually the Koa tree. The canoes were **outfitted** to be used as fishing boats, battleships, and even ferries. Over time, these giant boats were replaced by more efficient means of transportation.

Yet the tradition of the canoe continues with the annual outrigger race. Regardless of the outcome, all of us are **winners** because the race preserves an important part of Hawaiian culture.

Look back at the boldfaced words. What do you notice about the spelling of the root words?

On Your Mark

Take your Warm Up Test. Then check your spelling with the List Words on the next page.

Pep Talk

When a short-vowel word ends in a single consonant, the consonant is usually doubled before adding a suffix that begins with a vowel.

hum + **ing** = humming

When a word has more than one syllable, the final consonant is usually doubled if the last syllable has a short vowel followed by a single consonant.

outfit + **ed** = outfitted

LIST WORDS

1. beginning
2. humming
3. dropped
4. sitting
5. slipping
6. joggers
7. grabbing
8. bobbing
9. tripped
10. padded
11. skimming
12. scrubbing
13. winners
14. outfitted
15. wrapped
16. clapping
17. dragging
18. chatting
19. quitter
20. trimmer

Game Plan

Spelling Lineup

Write each List Word under the correct suffix. Then circle the root word in each List Word.

ing

1. _____
2. _____
3. _____
4. _____
5. _____
6. _____
7. _____
8. _____
9. _____
10. _____
11. _____

ed

12. _____
13. _____
14. _____
15. _____
16. _____

er or **ers**

17. _____
18. _____
19. _____
20. _____

Synonyms

Write the List Word that means the same or almost the same as the word or phrase given.

1. dressed   _____

2. washing   _____

3. covered   _____

4. starting   _____

5. let go of   _____

6. being seated   _____

7. runners   _____

8. not losers   _____

9. cushioned   _____

10. reaching for   _____

11. reading quickly   _____

12. floating   _____

13. singing   _____

14. applauding   _____

15. hair cutter   _____

16. stumbled   _____

Rhyming

Write the List Words whose root words rhyme with the words given.

that

1. _____

stop

2. _____

hit

3. _____

4. _____

5. _____

dim

6. _____

7. _____

strap

8. _____

9. _____

wag

10. _____

sum

11. _____

hip

12. _____

13. _____

Flex Your Spelling Muscles

Writing

Pretend that you are a newspaper reporter covering a canoe race in Hawaii. The canoes are <u>skimming</u> over the water. Who will the <u>winners</u> be? In your report, help people "see" what is happening.

Proofreading

The paragraphs below have eleven mistakes. Use the proofreading marks to fix the mistakes. Then write the misspelled List Words correctly on the lines.

Proofreading Marks	
⬭	spelling mistake
⊙	add period
¶	indent paragraph

Skeming along the ocean waters is a 50-foot-long cedar canoe Siting inside are seventeen people, who are testing the craft. It is the first canoe the people of their village have built in many years

The canoe is sliping into the bay while people on shore are claping and chattinge excitedly Draging the canoe onto land, the villagers feel proud. No other village has built such a magnificent canoe

1. _____

2. _____

3. _____

4. _____

5. _____

6. _____

Now proofread your news report. Fix any mistakes.

Go for the Goal

Take your Final Test. Then fill in your Scoreboard. Send your mistakes to the Word Locker.

SCOREBOARD

number correct	number wrong

★ ★ ★ ★ ★ ★ ★ ★ ★ **All-Star Words** ★ ★ ★ ★ ★ ★ ★ ★ ★

snapping   stepped   patrolling   dimmed   mugger

With a partner, identify the root word in each All-Star Word. Then look up the root words in a dictionary. Use the definitions to help you write each All-Star Word in a sentence.

Suffixes ed, er, and ing: Dropping the Final e

Warm Up

What snack food has been popular for hundreds of years?

Pop Quiz

What food explodes as it cooks? Do you give up? It's popcorn.

Long before the Pilgrims landed in the New World, the North American Indians had been **sharing** this explosive treat among themselves. For hundreds of years, people **loved** eating it plain and hot. In the 1900s, movie houses began selling it. The theater owners **served** it spiced with butter and salt. That made popcorn eaters so thirsty that they bought something to drink, too.

Today, popcorn can be bought in shops, flavored with anything from grapes to onions. Plain or fancy, it is becoming one of America's best loved treats—happily eaten by nearly everyone, from the ballet **dancer** to the furniture **mover.** Every year, we eat millions of pounds of the fluffy stuff! Unlike most snack foods, this one is good for you and very low in calories—as long as you eat it plain.

Look at the root words in the boldfaced words. What do you notice about their spelling?

On Your Mark

Take your Warm Up Test. Then check your spelling with the List Words on the next page.

Pep Talk

When a word ends in silent **e**, usually drop the **e** before adding a suffix that begins with a vowel.

trade + **ed** = traded
move + **er** = mover
surprise + **ing** = surprising

LIST WORDS

1. coming
2. loved
3. raking
4. served
5. proved
6. sharing
7. traded
8. mover
9. saved
10. giving
11. rider
12. dancer
13. promised
14. surprising
15. bouncing
16. writing
17. sliced
18. reduced
19. pictured
20. comparing

Game Plan

Spelling Lineup

Write the List Words that tell about action that is happening in the present. Circle the suffix in each word.

1. _____   5. _____

2. _____   6. _____

3. _____   7. _____

4. _____   8. _____

Write the List Words that tell about action that happened in the past. Circle the suffix in each word.

9. _____   14. _____

10. _____   15. _____

11. _____   16. _____

12. _____   17. _____

13. _____

Write the List Words that name people and what they do. Circle the suffix in each word.

18. _____   20. _____

19. _____

Suffixes

Write List Words by combining the root words and suffixes.

1. bounce + ing = _____

2. write + ing = _____

3. compare + ing = _____

4. prove + ed = _____

5. give + ing = _____

6. love + ed = _____

7. serve + ed = _____

8. ride + er = _____

9. share + ing = _____

Vocabulary

Write the List Word that best completes each sentence.

1. The _____ put furniture in the van.

2. Tom is _____ up the leaves in the yard.

3. Leah _____ twenty dollars to buy a new purse.

4. The magician was _____ everyone with magic tricks.

5. I _____ Pete I would help him paint the fence.

6. The football player _____ his weight by fifteen pounds.

7. My grandparents are _____ to visit us in July.

8. Mom _____ in her old car for a brand new one.

9. The _____ leaped gracefully.

10. I am _____ the two shirts to see which one I like better.

11. I never met Richard, but I _____ him to be tall and thin.

12. Anna _____ the loaf of bread into several pieces.

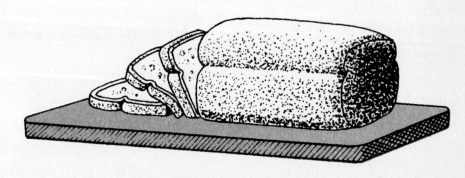

Flex Your Spelling Muscles

Writing

Some people love popcorn. What is your favorite snack? Write a description of it, using as many List Words as you can.

Proofreading

The advertisement below has twelve mistakes. Use the proofreading marks to fix the mistakes. Then write the misspelled List Words correctly on the lines.

Proofreading Marks

○ spelling mistake

∧ add something

⋎ add apostrophe

> A snack that's beyond compareing,
> One youre sure to enjoy shairing.
> Its a moveer in the store!
> You're sure to shout, "Lets have more "
> So if youve promisde yourself a treat,
> Or pichtured something great to eat,
> Go ahead and munch on our Yummies—
> What a thrill youll be giveing your tummies!

1. _____   4. _____

2. _____   5. _____

3. _____   6. _____

Now proofread your description of your favorite snack.
Fix any mistakes.

Go for the Goal

Take your Final Test. Then fill in your Scoreboard.
Send your mistakes to the Word Locker.

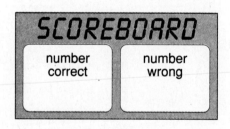

SCOREBOARD

number correct	number wrong

★ ★ ★ ★ ★ ★ ★ ★ ★   **All-Star Words**   ★ ★ ★ ★ ★ ★ ★ ★ ★

driving   stared   shaking   rising   skater

Write a sentence using each All-Star Word, but draw a picture clue where the word would be written. Trade papers with a partner. See if you can guess each other's words.

Name _____

Suffixes ed, es, and ing: Words Ending with y

Warm Up

Why would a scientist want to fly a kite during
a lightning storm?

Go Fly a Kite

Almost 250 years ago, Benjamin Franklin flew a kite in a lightning storm. His paper-and-string aircraft **carried** a key as part of an experiment with electricity. Franklin should have been full of **worries** and **petrified** with fright. We all know that his kite could have been **frying,** instead of flying!

Today, the kite is still being used as a scientific instrument. More and more, scientists are **relying** on kites to gather information. Satellites don't provide detailed pictures, and planes can't stay in one spot. But kites, which can remain stationary in the atmosphere, are often used to collect data about temperature, water vapor, radiation, and the ozone layer.

While Ben Franklin's key weighed only a few ounces, today's kites are being prepared to launch a much bigger cargo. Scientists are planning kites **supplied** with meteorological equipment weighing from twenty to thirty pounds! If you have any doubts about how remarkable that is, try to picture a kite carrying a couple of bowling balls, sailing as high as a jet. Rest easy though, the experiments will be held far out of the way of passing jets!

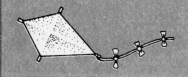

Look back at each boldfaced word. Identify the root word. Did it change when a suffix was added?

On Your Mark

Take your Warm Up Test. Then check your spelling with the List Words on the next page.

Pep Talk

When a word ends in **y** preceded by a consonant, change the **y** to **i** before adding a suffix other than **ing.**

worry + **es** = worries
dry + **ing** = drying
copy + **ed** = copied
fry + **ing** = frying

Game Plan

Spelling Lineup

Write each List Word under the correct suffix.

1. tries
2. carried
3. worries
4. buying
5. satisfied
6. relying
7. denies
8. copied
9. emptied
10. hurrying
11. cries
12. buries
13. multiplied
14. replies
15. supplied
16. drying
17. petrified
18. frying
19. applied
20. scurrying

es

1. _____
2. _____
3. _____
4. _____
5. _____
6. _____

ing

7. _____
8. _____
9. _____
10. _____
11. _____
12. _____

ed

13. _____
14. _____
15. _____
16. _____
17. _____
18. _____
19. _____
20. _____

Puzzle

Write the List Word that matches each clue. Then read
down the shaded boxes to solve the riddle.

1. puts a dead body in a tomb

2. imitated

3. sobs

K

4. transported

5. rushing

6. says something
   is not true

7. depending

8. feels anxious

9. answers

10. increased

Riddle: What kind of music do stone workers and bakers like?

Answer: _____   _____   _____

Root Words

Write the List Word formed from each root word below.

1. apply _____

2. petrify _____

3. bury _____

4. satisfy _____

5. dry _____

6. supply _____

7. buy _____

8. empty _____

9. try _____

10. fry _____

Flex Your Spelling Muscles

Writing

Do you know how to fly a kite? Have you ever made one? Write directions to a friend to tell how to make a kite or another kind of toy. Use List Words.

Proofreading

The article below has twelve mistakes. Use the proofreading marks to fix the mistakes. Then write the misspelled List Words correctly on the lines.

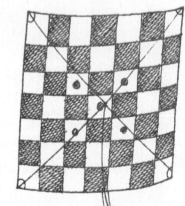

Proofreading Marks

◯ spelling mistake

∧ add something

⟑ take out something

What is a popular activity in Japan It's kite-flying! At different times of the year, children are hurryeing and skurying about, biyng supplies to to make kites. As the glue is driing, the children might be thinking about the colorful paints that will be applyied to their kites.

What happens after the children are satisfyed with their creations The kites are carryed to an open area area and flown. Sometimes one team of kite-flyers tryes to knock another team's kites out of the sky!

1. _____   5. _____

2. _____   6. _____

3. _____   7. _____

4. _____   8. _____

Now proofread your directions. Fix any mistakes.

Go for the Goal

Take your Final Test. Then fill in your Scoreboard. Send your mistakes to the Word Locker.

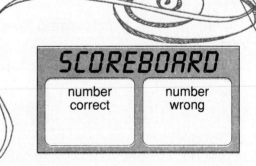

SCOREBOARD

number correct	number wrong

★ ★ ★ ★ ★ ★ ★ ★ ★ **All-Star Words** ★ ★ ★ ★ ★ ★ ★ ★ ★

dairies   horrified   pitying   magnifying   mysteries

With a partner, write a mystery story using all five words. Get together with another pair of students and compare stories.

Suffixes er and est: Words Ending with y

Warm Up

Which fruit is more than just a delicious food?

An Apple a Day

What do McIntosh, Granny Smith, and Cortland have in common? They're all apples. Some fruits may be **fancier.** Others may be **prettier,** but few can be enjoyed in more ways than the apple. Apples can be made into apple pie, applesauce, and apple butter. The **juiciest** ones can be squeezed into apple juice or apple cider. Of course, the **easiest** way to enjoy an apple is to eat it raw.

Apples are more than just a delicious food. They're part of our language. A person can describe someone special as "the apple of my eye." We call New York City "The Big Apple." We call the lump in a person's throat his or her "Adam's apple."

More than 100 years ago there were not many apple orchards in the United States. Then a man named John Chapman traveled across the country planting apple seeds. A **happier** or friendlier person than John Chapman would have been hard to find. People liked him and began to call him Johnny Appleseed. Thanks to John, apple picking is one of America's busiest farm industries.

Look back at the root word in each boldfaced word. How did each root word change?

On Your Mark

Take your Warm Up Test. Then check your spelling with the List Words on the next page.

Pep Talk

Adjectives ending in **er** compare two things. Adjectives ending in **est** compare three or more things. To add **er** or **est** to an adjective that ends in **y**, change the **y** to **i** first.

happy + **er** = happier

happy + **est** = happiest

Game Plan

Spelling Lineup

Write the List Words that compare two things. Circle the suffix at the end of each word.

1. _____   6. _____

2. _____   7. _____

3. _____   8. _____

4. _____   9. _____

5. _____   10. _____

Write the List Words that compare three or more things. Circle the suffix at the end of each word.

11. _____   19. _____

12. _____   20. _____

13. _____

14. _____

15. _____

16. _____

17. _____

18. _____

LIST WORDS

1. angrier
2. angriest
3. happier
4. happiest
5. easier
6. easiest
7. earlier
8. earliest
9. funnier
10. funniest
11. prettier
12. prettiest
13. lonelier
14. loneliest
15. heavier
16. heaviest
17. fancier
18. fanciest
19. juicier
20. juiciest

Suffixes

Fill in the chart by adding **er** and **est** to the root words to make List Words. Write the List Words on the lines.

	+ er	**+ est**
1. juicy	_____	_____
2. lonely	_____	_____
3. easy	_____	_____
4. angry	_____	_____
5. funny	_____	_____
6. early	_____	_____
7. heavy	_____	_____
8. pretty	_____	_____
9. fancy	_____	_____
10. happy	_____	_____

Synonyms

Write the List Word that means the same or almost the same as the phrase given.

1. more furious _____
2. most alone _____
3. more watery _____
4. least late _____
5. least light _____

6. most comical _____
7. less plain _____
8. less difficult _____
9. more pleased _____
10. least ugly _____

Flex Your Spelling Muscles

Writing

Some people eat an apple a day. Write a short poem to describe your favorite fruit. Is it <u>juicier</u> and <u>tastier</u> than an apple? Is it <u>prettier</u> than a strawberry or <u>heavier</u> than a cantaloupe?

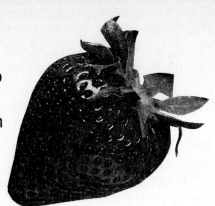

Proofreading

The paragraph below has ten mistakes. Use the proofreading marks to fix the mistakes. Then write the misspelled List Words correctly on the lines.

Proofreading Marks	
◯	spelling mistake
≡	capital letter
/	make small letter

The best apple pies are made with the juicyest apples, not with watery or mushy ones. making an apple pie will be easyer if the Crust is prepared ahead of time. But remember—the more shortening in a crust, the heaver it will be. A top crust can be made fansier and prettyer with cutouts. tough crusts make cooks the angrest. Flaky crusts make cooks—and pie-eaters—happyer.

Now proofread your poem. Fix any mistakes.

1. _____

2. _____

3. _____

4. _____

5. _____

6. _____

7. _____

Go for the Goal

Take your Final Test. Then fill in your Scoreboard. Send your mistakes to the Word Locker.

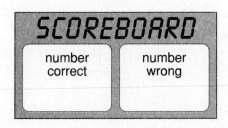

SCOREBOARD

number correct	number wrong

★ ★ ★ ★ ★ ★ ★ ★ ★ ★ **All-Star Words** ★ ★ ★ ★ ★ ★ ★ ★ ★ ★

tastier   loveliest   clumsier   luckiest   curlier

Write each All-Star Word and a clue to go with it. Then get together with a partner and read your clues aloud to each other. Can you guess the All-Star Word that goes with each clue?

Name _____

Instant Replay • Lessons 13–17

LESSON 18

Time Out

Take another look at root words and suffixes.

Check Your Word Locker

Look at the words in your Word Locker. Write your most troublesome words for Lessons 13 through 17.

_____

Practice spelling your troublesome words with a partner.
Take turns writing a word equation for each word.

apply − **y** + **i** + **ed** = applied

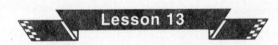
Lesson 13

You can add the suffixes **ed, er,** or **ing** to some words without changing the spelling of the root, as in sorted, learner, and checking.

List Words
watching
finishing
singer
guessed
teacher
walker
remembered
tossed
wishing
landing

Write a List Word that means the same or almost the same as each word or phrase.

1. vocalist _____

2. threw _____

3. touch down _____

4. recalled _____

5. viewing _____

6. ending _____

7. figured out _____

8. hoping _____

9. instructor _____

10. jogger _____

When a short-vowel word or final syllable ends in a single consonant, the consonant is usually doubled when a suffix that begins with a vowel is added, as in <u>slipping</u> and <u>quitter</u>.

List Words

beginning
humming
joggers
tripped
scrubbing
outfitted
wrapped
clapping
dragging
chatting

Write the List Word that belongs in each group.

1. talking, speaking, _____

2. stumbled, fell, _____

3. runners, racers, _____

4. opening, starting, _____

5. covered, sealed, _____

6. pulling, towing, _____

7. dressed, equipped, _____

8. cheering, applauding, _____

9. singing, whistling, _____

10. washing, rinsing, _____

When a word ends in silent **e,** the **e** is usually dropped before a suffix that begins with a vowel is added, as in <u>sharing</u> and <u>served</u>.

List Words

loved
proved
saved
dancer
promised
surprising
bouncing
sliced
pictured
comparing

Write each List Word under the correct category.

One Syllable	Two Syllables
1. _____	5. _____
2. _____	6. _____
3. _____	7. _____
4. _____	8. _____

Three Syllables

9. _____   10. _____

Lesson 16

When a word ends in a consonant and **y,** the **y** is changed to **i** before a suffix other than **ing** is added, as in <u>supplied</u> and <u>denies.</u>

List Words

worries
buying
satisfied
copied
emptied
cries
multiplied
replies
petrified
scurrying

Write a List Word to complete each sentence.

1. Four _____ by two is eight.

2. I saw Jo _____ a new baseball.

3. I expect the _____ to my letters to come soon.

4. The truck _____ a load of sand.

5. The delicious meal _____ my hunger.

6. Al _____ his story.

7. The baby _____ when she's tired.

8. Aunt Jan _____ if I'm late.

9. I watched a cat _____ up a tree.

10. _____ wood is as hard as rock.

Lesson 17

When the suffixes **er** or **est** are added to an adjective ending in **y,** the **y** changes to **i,** as in <u>prettier</u> and <u>earliest.</u>

List Words

angriest
happier
easiest
earlier
funnier
prettiest
lonelier
heaviest
fancier
juiciest

Write the List Word that contains the root word given.

1. early _____   8. juicy _____

2. angry _____   9. easy _____

3. happy _____   10. lonely _____

4. funny _____

5. heavy _____

6. pretty _____

7. fancy _____

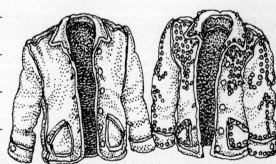

List Words

remembered
beginning
scrubbing
funnier
dancer
sliced
buying
replies
angriest
easiest

Write the List Word that matches each clue.

1. simplest _____

2. more humorous _____

3. brought back to mind _____

4. rubbing to remove dirt _____

5. answers _____

6. person who moves to music _____

7. cut into strips _____

8. the start, or first part _____

9. getting with money _____

10. maddest _____

Go for the Goal

Take your Final Replay Test. Then fill in your Scoreboard. Send any misspelled words to your Word Locker.

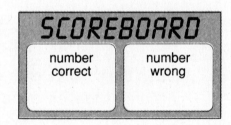

SCOREBOARD

number correct	number wrong

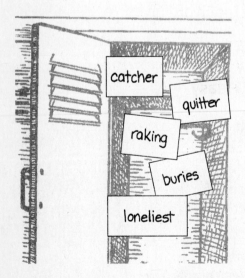

catcher
quitter
raking
buries
loneliest

Clean Out Your Word Locker

Look in your Word Locker. Cross out each word you spelled correctly on your Final Replay Test. Circle the words you're still having trouble with. Add the words you circled to your Spelling Notebook. What do you notice about the words? Watch for those words as you write.

Vowel Digraphs
<u>ee</u>, <u>ea</u>, <u>oa</u>, <u>oe</u>, and <u>ue</u>

LESSON
19

Warm Up

What is the "Great Outdoors" like?

Camping Anyone?

Millions of people go camping every year. Camping can cost a great deal of money, or it can cost very little. For example, you can make a simple tent by throwing a blanket over a line tied **between** two trees, or you can buy an expensive tent with double walls and screens. It doesn't matter how much or how little you spend. The most important thing is to have fun!

Sleeping bags are an important piece of camping equipment. There are many different kinds to choose from. Some sleeping bags are made to keep the chill off when there's a cool **breeze.** Others are lined with a special material that will keep you warm in freezing temperatures. Whatever kind of sleeping bag you choose, make sure it's appropriate for the climate.

It has been said that you haven't lived until you've **roasted** a marshmallow over a crackling fire, or smelled a fresh **meadow** in the early morning hours. It's all part of the camping experience. So, if you feel like **treating** someone you know to something special, take them camping. Remember, there's nothing better than the "Great Outdoors!"

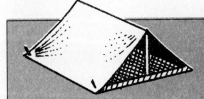

Say the boldfaced words in the selection. What sounds do the vowel pairs make in these words?

On Your Mark

Take your Warm Up Test. Then check your spelling with the List Words on the next page.

77

Vowel digraphs are two vowels together that stand for one vowel sound. The vowel digraphs **ee** and **ea** can make the /ē/ sound, as in <u>fleet</u> and <u>reason</u>. Sometimes the vowel digraph **ea** makes the /e/ sound, as in <u>measure</u>.

The vowel digraphs **oa** and **oe** make the /ō/ sound, as in <u>loaned</u> and <u>hoed</u>. The vowel digraph **ue** makes the /o͞o/ sound, as in <u>clues</u>.

LIST WORDS

1. between
2. eastern
3. breeze
4. clues
5. hoed
6. meaning
7. tiptoes
8. reason
9. treating
10. roasted
11. freedom
12. loaned
13. approach
14. measure
15. glued
16. instead
17. eagle
18. boasted
19. fleet
20. meadow

Game Plan

Spelling Lineup

Write each List Word under the correct heading.

/ē/ spelled **ee**

1. _____
2. _____
3. _____
4. _____

/o͞o/ spelled **ue**

5. _____
6. _____

/ē/ spelled **ea**

7. _____
8. _____
9. _____
10. _____
11. _____

/ō/ spelled **oa**

12. _____
13. _____
14. _____
15. _____

/ō/ spelled **oe**

16. _____
17. _____

/e/ spelled **ea**

18. _____
19. _____
20. _____

Dictionary

For each set of dictionary guide words, write two List Words that could be found on that page.

In a dictionary, **guide words** at the top of a page show the first and last entries on that page. **reason/reflect**

each/eat

1. _____

2. _____

hobble/invite

5. _____

6. _____

time/trip

3. _____

4. _____

feel/fuel

7. _____

8. _____

Vocabulary

Write the List Word that best completes each sentence.

1. At the play, I sat _____ Sue and Miguel.

2. I _____ my science book to Carter.

3. Use a ruler to _____ the size of the photograph.

4. Mel owns a farm with a beautiful, grassy _____.

5. When you _____ the corner, turn left.

6. Jen _____ the pictures into her scrapbook.

7. Mr. Hall _____ that he was the smartest man in town.

8. The _____ to the crossword puzzle were too hard.

Flex Your Spelling Muscles

Writing

Do you like to hike or camp? Write a persuasive paragraph that will convince people of the joys of the "Great Outdoors." Use as many List Words as you can.

Proofreading

This poem has twelve mistakes. Use the proofreading marks to fix the mistakes. Then write the misspelled List Words on the lines.

Proofreading Marks	
⬯	spelling mistake
⌃	add something

There's always a good reeson
To camp inany season.
To feel a forest breaze
To hearwind in the trees,
Gives freadom a new meisure,
To thosewho seek its treasure.
Be the one instede who bowsted
Of food that's gently rowsted
Ona fire burning bright
Near a meadoe green and light.

1. _____
2. _____
3. _____
4. _____
5. _____
6. _____
7. _____
8. _____

Proofread your persuasive paragraph about the outdoors. Fix any mistakes.

Go for the Goal

Take your Final Test. Then fill in your Scoreboard. Send your mistakes to the Word Locker.

SCOREBOARD

number correct	number wrong

★ ★ ★ ★ ★ ★ ★ ★ ★ **All-Star Words** ★ ★ ★ ★ ★ ★ ★ ★ ★

cheat   forehead   sneeze   groan   dues

Try to use all five All-Star Words in a single sentence. Then get together with a partner and compare sentences.

Vowel Digraphs ie and ei

Warm Up

What should runners do to take care of their feet?

Tenderfeet

It seems everywhere you look, people are running. You see them on smooth streets, rough roads, sandy beaches, and grassy **fields.** Running can be good for your health. Doctors **believe** it can strengthen your heart. However, running **amplifies** the wear and tear on your feet.

Pressure equal to three times what you **weigh** pushes on each foot as it hits the ground. This means that when a 90-pound person runs, each foot is being pushed to the ground by 270 pounds of pressure. That's quite a jolt for those bones and muscles! No wonder our feet may need help.

Here are some tips for tending your toes:
- Wash your feet every day. Make sure they are dried well before you put on your shoes.
- Wear socks made of cotton or wool.
- Make sure your running shoes fit well and give your feet good support.
- Make sure your shoes are tied snugly, but not tightly.
- If you notice any foot problems, see a doctor.

Pass these tips on to friends and **neighbors.** Their feet will be glad you did.

Look back at the boldfaced words. Notice that each word contains the vowel digraph **ie** or **ei.** Say each word. How many different vowel sounds do you hear?

On Your Mark

Take your Warm Up Test. Then check your spelling with the List Words on the next page.

LIST WORDS

1. died
2. fields
3. brief
4. relief
5. shriek
6. weigh
7. believe
8. sleigh
9. receive
10. eighteen
11. seize
12. neighbors
13. receipt
14. amplifies
15. chiefly
16. freighter
17. deceive
18. perceive
19. pies
20. diet

Game Plan

Spelling Lineup

Write each List Word under the correct heading.

/ā/ spelled ei

1. _____
2. _____
3. _____
4. _____
5. _____

/ē/ spelled ie

6. _____
7. _____
8. _____
9. _____
10. _____
11. _____

/ī/ spelled ie

12. _____
13. _____
14. _____

/ē/ spelled ei

15. _____
16. _____
17. _____
18. _____
19. _____

Write the List Word in which **ie** together has two sounds, the /ī/ sound and the /e/ sound.

20. _____

Missing Vowels

Add **ie** or **ei** to each group of letters to form a List Word.
Then write the whole word on the line.

1. p ___ ___ s _____

2. dec ___ ___ ve _____

3. ch ___ ___ fly _____

4. ___ ___ ghteen _____

Puzzle

Fill in the puzzle by writing a List Word to answer
each clue. Then read down the shaded boxes to
solve the riddle.

1. record of purchases

2. people who live close by

3. easing of pain

4. a vehicle to ride in snow

5. stopped living

6. stretches of open land

7. a ship for carrying freight

8. measure with a scale

9. makes stronger or louder

10. to accept as true and real

11. scream

Riddle: What wears shoes but has no feet?

Answer: _____ _____

Flex Your Spelling Muscles

Writing

Have you ever seen or heard about a bed race or a soap box derby? Use the List Words to describe an unusual or funny race that you may have seen or heard about.

Proofreading

The following article has nine mistakes. Use the proofreading marks to fix the mistakes. Then write the misspelled List Words on the lines.

Proofreading Marks
⬭ spelling mistake
∧ add something

If you perceev that you need more exercise, you probably do. Many people beleeve there are more choices in exercise programs today. Those who want to resieve the best in fitness can do walking running aerobics and step classes. When you combine exercise with dyet, you can be sure you will look and feel better. Some people feel better after a breif time, while others need a little longer because they want to lose weight, as well as feel fit. So sieze the moment. Get in shape!

1. _____

2. _____

3. _____

4. _____

5. _____

6. _____

Now proofread your description. Fix any mistakes.

Go for the Goal

Take your Final Test. Then fill in your Scoreboard. Send your mistakes to the Word Locker.

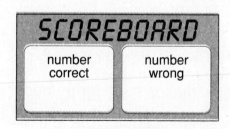

SCOREBOARD

number correct	number wrong

★ ★ ★ ★ ★ ★ ★ ★ ★ ★ **All-Star Words** ★ ★ ★ ★ ★ ★ ★ ★ ★ ★

ceiling   hygiene   veil   achieve   allies

With your partner, write a definition for each All-Star Word. Then look up the words in your dictionary. Do your definitions match?

Vowel Digraphs <u>au</u> and <u>aw</u>

Warm Up

How can a little animal build a dam?

Little Lumberjacks

The first time you see a beaver, you may think it looks a little strange. A beaver has a stout little body, small head, tiny **claws,** and a tail that looks like a ping-pong paddle. A beaver may look **awkward,** but in the water it is a fast, graceful, and strong swimmer.

Beavers are nature's best builders of dams. In spring and summer, the beavers **gnaw** on trees and branches. Their strong teeth can cut through a thick tree in minutes. They **launch** the cut logs into a stream. Then they push the logs into place. The wood is then packed with mud and **straw.**

Beavers usually make their homes in the ponds that form behind the dams. A beaver lodge has many underwater entrances. Inside is a dry place where the beavers live and store food inside for the winter. When the cold weather comes, they go inside and rest. But they must keep chewing on wood. If they don't, their teeth would keep growing and become too long, **causing** them harm. As soon as the spring thaw comes, the beavers go back to work. You can see why a busy person is often described as being "busy as a beaver."

Each boldfaced word in the selection is spelled with **au** or **aw.** Say each word. What do you notice about the sound each makes?

On Your Mark

Take your Warm Up Test. Then check your spelling with the List Words on the next page.

Pep Talk

Be careful when you spell words with the /ô/ sound you hear in <u>fault</u> and <u>dawn</u>. The vowel digraphs **au** and **aw** make the /ô/ sound, and sound alike.

Game Plan

Spelling Lineup

Write each List Word under the correct heading.

LIST WORDS

1. claws
2. fault
3. causing
4. dawn
5. straw
6. drawings
7. launch
8. sauce
9. jaw
10. haunt
11. yawn
12. fawns
13. awkward
14. gnaw
15. audience
16. scrawl
17. fraud
18. gaunt
19. restaurant
20. shawl

/ô/ spelled **aw**

1. _____
2. _____
3. _____
4. _____
5. _____
6. _____
7. _____
8. _____
9. _____
10. _____
11. _____

/ô/ spelled **au**

12. _____
13. _____
14. _____
15. _____
16. _____
17. _____
18. _____
19. _____
20. _____

Synonyms

Write the List Word that means the same or almost the
same as the word or phrase given.

1. sunrise _____

2. thin _____

3. pictures _____

4. eating
   place _____

5. baby deer _____

6. fake _____

7. scribble _____

8. scarf _____

Puzzle

Fill in the crossword puzzle by writing a List Word
to answer each clue.

ACROSS

2. a baby deer
3. liquid or soft mixture served with food
6. to send off a ship or spaceship
8. making happen
11. hollow stalks after grain is harvested
12. mouth part
13. sketches

DOWN

1. a sign you're tired
2. blame
4. animal's sharp nails
5. those who watch
7. to visit often
9. clumsy
10. to bite away bit by bit

Flex Your Spelling Muscles

Writing

Have you ever watched a wild animal at work or at play?
It might have been at the zoo, at the movies, or even in the
woods. Write a description of what you saw. Use as many
List Words as you can.

Proofreading

This description has twelve mistakes. Use the
proofreading marks to fix the mistakes. Then write
the misspelled List Words on the lines.

Proofreading Marks
◯ spelling mistake
≡ capital letter
∧ add something

Do you know what is fun to do Watch the
otters at the High desert museum. The museum
is not far from bend, Oregon. These otters love
an awdience. They are up at dahwn playing
and swimming. They lanche themselves down
hills and slide into the water, making people
laugh. can you guess what happens then They
do it all over again. it's also fun to watch an
otter eat. It floats, holding food in its claus. It's
like a show at a restawrant.

1. _____

2. _____

3. _____

4. _____

5. _____

Now proofread your animal description. Fix any mistakes.

Go for the Goal

Take your Final Test. Then fill in your Scoreboard.
Send your mistakes to the Word Locker.

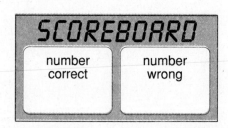

SCOREBOARD
number correct	number wrong

★ ★ ★ ★ ★ ★ ★ ★ ★ ★ **All-Star Words** ★ ★ ★ ★ ★ ★ ★ ★ ★ ★

drawn   saucer   automatic   author   lawyer

Write a sentence using each word, but leave a blank for the
All-Star Word that completes the sentence. Trade papers with
your partner. See if you can complete each other's sentences.

Vowel Digraphs ai, ay; Diphthongs oi, oy

Warm Up

How can a town be turned into a museum?

End of the Trail

The front door of Butch Cassidy's cabin stands open. A stagecoach is parked outside the General Store. No horses are restlessly pawing the gray dust. No **voices** can be heard from the well-traveled trail. In fact, the only **noises** that can be heard are the whispering breezes and chirping insects.

You may think this is a ghost town, but it's really a museum called Old Trail Town. It stands outside Cody, Wyoming. The town, which stands on five acres, was established by Bob and Terry Edgar. Among the **displays** are old cabins and treasures from the long-ago days of the Wild West.

Years ago, Bob noticed many old cabins standing empty on the range. "Some were falling in. Others were being **destroyed** by grazing cattle," he said. He decided to save them as a part of American history.

After working hard and sacrificing time and money, the Edgars' dream came to life. They should be **praised** for preserving a long-ago way of life. People are interested in seeing how cowhands and pioneers really lived. As Bob says, "The main thing is to enjoy the place and remember it."

Say each boldfaced word in the selection. How are the words with the /ā/ sound spelled? How are the words with the /oi/ sound spelled?

On Your Mark

Take your Warm Up Test. Then check your spelling with the List Words on the next page.

89

Pep Talk

The vowel digraphs **ai** and **ay** make the /ā/ sound you hear in <u>waist</u> and <u>fray</u>. Diphthongs are different from digraphs in that the two vowels blend together to make one sound. The diphthongs **oi** and **oy** make the /oi/ sound you hear in <u>voices</u> and <u>employ</u>.

Game Plan

Spelling Lineup
Write each List Word under the correct heading.

/ā/ spelled ai

1. _____
2. _____
3. _____
4. _____

/ā/ spelled ay

12. _____
13. _____
14. _____
15. _____

/oi/ spelled oi

5. _____
6. _____
7. _____
8. _____
9. _____
10. _____
11. _____

/oi/ spelled oy

16. _____
17. _____
18. _____
19. _____
20. _____

Rhyming

Write the List Word that rhymes with each word given.

1. train _____

2. grazed _____

3. day _____

4. annoy _____

5. toiled _____

6. playing _____

7. paste _____

8. replays _____

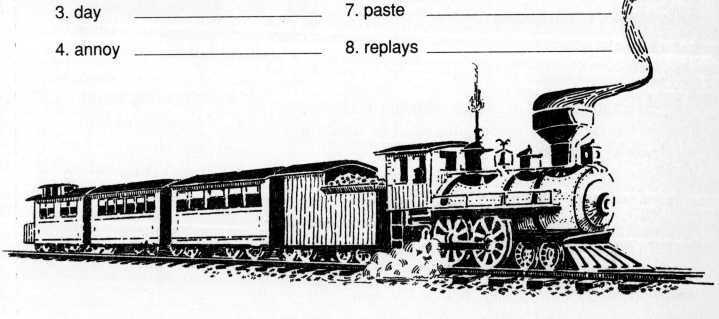

Classification

Write the List Word that belongs in each group.

1. pen, pencil, _____

2. baking, boiling, _____

3. bang, crash, _____

4. soprano, alto, _____

5. dissatisfy, fail, _____

6. rice, potato, _____

7. queens, kings, _____

8. untrue, unfaithful, _____

9. moving, rocking, _____

10. chosen, assigned, _____

Flex Your Spelling Muscles

Writing

Cowhands worked hard at herding cattle, and riding and mending fence. Yet, they had fun, too. Write a paragraph telling what you think it was like to be an Old West cowhand. Use as many List Words as you can.

Proofreading

The paragraph below has twelve mistakes. Fix the mistakes with the proofreading marks. Then write the misspelled List Words on the lines.

Proofreading Marks
◯ spelling mistake
⊙ add period
ℯ take out something

  The pioneers who came west in covered wagons are to be praysed Even with an appoynted leader, they had to use all all their skills just to survive. Long days were spent riding in in the swaiying wagons in boyling hot or icy cold weather. Accidents could and did happen! A wagon wheel could be destroied by by the rough terrain or someone could have a sprained ankle with with no one to treat it When the ralroad came, traveling west became easier, but still an adventure.

1. _____

2. _____

3. _____

4. _____

5. _____

6. _____

Now proofread your paragraph about cowhands. Fix any mistakes.

Go for the Goal

Take your Final Test. Then fill in your Scoreboard. Send your mistakes to the Word Locker.

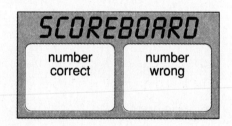

SCOREBOARD

number correct	number wrong

★ ★ ★ ★ ★ ★ ★ ★ ★ **All-Star Words** ★ ★ ★ ★ ★ ★ ★ ★ ★ ★

entertain delay embroider loyal raisin

Write a sentence for each word, but leave a blank in place of the All-Star Word. Then write a wrong All-Star Word in each blank. Trade papers with a partner. Try to write the correct All-Star Words in the sentences.

ou and ow

Warm Up

What bird can be as small as a sparrow or as big as a dog?

Night Prowlers

Owls may not be as well known to people as other birds. This may happen because owls prefer the night **hours.** Even if we don't see them often, owls can be found around the world. There are more than 130 different kinds. Some are as small as **sparrows,** like the elf or pygmy owls. Others are very large. The great horned owl stands two feet tall and has a four-foot wing span. That's about as big as an average dog!

Owls often live in nests left behind by other birds. Other times they use **hollow** trees or logs for homes. When they live near **towns,** owls may move into buildings, such as barns.

Most owls sleep during the day. When dusk comes, they glide silently through the air, looking around for food. Usually, a rat, mole, or field mouse will do. Owls can see even in a small **amount** of light. They can spot food in the darkest places. Their keen eyes are fixed in their sockets and do not move. But owls have long, thin necks that allow them to turn their heads in almost a complete circle. Owls' hearing is as sharp as their sight, **although** some people may not believe this. After all, if owls can hear so well, why do they always say "who"?

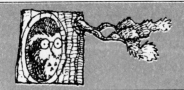 Look back at the boldfaced words. Say each word. Listen for the /ō/ and /ou/ sounds. What do you notice about the way these sounds are spelled?

On Your Mark

Take your Warm Up Test. Then check you spelling with the List Words on the next page.

Pep Talk

The diphthongs **ou** and **ow** can make the /ou/ sound, as in <u>without</u> and <u>towns</u>.
The letters **ow** can also be a vowel digraph, making the /ō/ sound, as in <u>hollow</u>.
The letters **ou** can make the /ō/ sound in <u>although</u>, the /ô/ sound in <u>thought</u>, or the /u/ sound, as in <u>southern</u>.

LIST WORDS

1. hours
2. sparrows
3. towns
4. powerful
5. amount
6. without
7. allows
8. shower
9. brought
10. sought
11. hollow
12. swallowed
13. southern
14. thousand
15. thought
16. trouble
17. bouquet
18. although
19. mountain
20. chowder

Game Plan

Spelling Lineup

Write each List Word under the correct heading.

/ou/ spelled **ou**

1. _____
2. _____
3. _____
4. _____
5. _____

/ou/ spelled **ow**

6. _____
7. _____
8. _____
9. _____
10. _____

/ō/ spelled **ou**

11. _____
12. _____

/ō/ spelled **ow**

13. _____
14. _____
15. _____

/ô/ spelled **ou**

16. _____
17. _____
18. _____

/u/ spelled **ou**

19. _____
20. _____

Puzzle

Read each clue. Write the List Word that means the same or almost the same as each word given. Then read down the shaded boxes to solve the riddle.

1. minus

2. problem

3. rain

4. permits

5. 1,000

6. sum

7. idea

8. empty

9. soup

10. hill

Riddle: Did you hear about the joke the owl told?

Answer: _____ _____ ___ _____ .

Dictionary

For each set of dictionary guide words, write the List Words that could be found on that page. Write the words in alphabetical order.

In a dictionary, **guide words** at the top of a page show the first and last entries on that page. **maybe/mountain**

alter/cat

1. _____

2. _____

3. _____

4. _____

skip/thorn

5. _____

6. _____

7. _____

8. _____

Flex Your Spelling Muscles

Writing

Write a poem about two kinds of birds, such as sparrows and hawks. Tell how they are alike and how they are different. Use some List Words in your poem.

Proofreading

Look for thirteen mistakes in this nature paragraph. Use the proofreading marks to fix the mistakes. Then write the misspelled List Words on the lines.

Proofreading Marks	
⬭	spelling mistake
⸜	add apostrophe
⋀	add something

Even people who live in touns may see an eagle during daylight howrs when eagles hunt. The golden eagle is found mainlyin mowntain areas. The bald eagle canbe seen in some sowthern states inthe winter. Althowgh the bald eagle hasbeen in trauble in the past, conservationists efforts to help these pouwerful birds have brooght some success.

Now proofread your poem about birds.
Fix any mistakes.

1. _____

2. _____

3. _____

4. _____

5. _____

6. _____

7. _____

8. _____

Go for the Goal

Take your Final Test. Then fill in your Scoreboard.
Send your mistakes to the Word Locker.

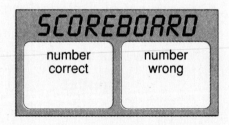

★ ★ ★ ★ ★ ★ ★ ★ ★ **All-Star Words** ★ ★ ★ ★ ★ ★ ★ ★ ★

scouts   drowned   marshmallow   couple   fought

Work with your partner to write a story using the All-Star Words. Trade stories with other students. How were the words used in the story?

Name_____

Instant Replay • Lessons 19–23

Time Out

Take another look at vowel digraphs and diphthongs.

Check Your Word Locker

Look at the words in your Word Locker. Write your most troublesome words for Lessons 19 through 23.

_____

Practice writing your troublesome words with a partner. Form the letters of each word using clay or pipe cleaners, while your partner spells the words aloud.

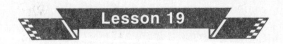
Lesson 19

The vowel digraphs **ee** and **ea** can spell /ē/, as in <u>fleet</u> and <u>reason</u>; **ea** can spell /e/, as in <u>instead</u>; **oa** and **oe** spell /ō/, as in <u>boasted</u> and <u>tiptoes</u>; and **ue** spells /o͞o/, as in <u>dues</u>.

List Words
breeze
hoed
meaning
roasted
freedom
approach
measure
glued
eagle
meadow

Add and subtract letters to form List Words.

1. fued – f + gl = _____

2. tasted – t + ro = _____

3. each – ch + gle = _____

4. house – use + ed = _____

5. approve – ve + ach = _____

6. freeze – f + b = _____

7. lining – li + mea = _____

8. meant – nt + dow = _____

9. random – ran + free = _____

10. treasure – tr + m = _____

The vowel digraph **ie** can spell /ī/, as in <u>died</u> or /ē/, as in <u>fields</u>. The digraph **ei** can spell /ē/, as in <u>seize</u> or /ā/, as in <u>weigh</u>.

List Words

brief
shriek
believe
sleigh
receive
neighbors
receipt
amplifies
chiefly
freighter

Write the List Word that belongs in each group.

1. canoe, sailboat, _____

2. scream, yell, _____

3. sled, ski, _____

4. friends, partners, _____

5. mainly, mostly, _____

6. short, small, _____

7. feel, think, _____

8. increases, boosts, _____

9. get, obtain, _____

10. check, ticket, _____

The vowel digraphs **au** and **aw** both spell /ô/, as in <u>haunt</u> and <u>claws</u>.

Write each List Word under the correct category.

List Words

fault
drawings
launch
sauce
awkward
gnaw
audience
scrawl
gaunt
restaurant

one syllable

1. _____

2. _____

3. _____

4. _____

5. _____

6. _____

two syllables

7. _____

8. _____

three syllables

9. _____

10. _____

Vowel digraphs **ai** and **ay** spell /ā/, as in <u>waist</u> and <u>fray</u>.
Diphthongs **oi** and **oy** spell /ȯi/, as in <u>voices</u> and <u>employ</u>.

List Words

sprain
disloyal
employ
destroyed
displays
disappoint
railroad
royalty
soybean
spoiled

Write each group of List Words in alphabetical order.

sprain royalty railroad soybean spoiled

disloyal employ destroyed displays disappoint

1. _____

2. _____

3. _____

4. _____

5. _____

6. _____

7. _____

8. _____

9. _____

10. _____

Lesson 23

The diphthongs **ou** and **ow** spell /ou/, as in <u>amount</u> and <u>towns</u>.
These letters can also be vowel digraphs. Listen for the /ō/ sound
in <u>hollow</u> and <u>although</u> and the /u/ sound in <u>trouble</u>.

List Words

hours
sparrows
powerful
shower
brought
hollow
swallowed
bouquet
mountain
chowder

Write a List Word to match each definition.

1. a very high hill _____

2. units of sixty minutes _____

3. strong or forceful _____

4. a light rainfall _____

5. carried or delivered _____

6. having empty space inside _____

7. a thick soup _____

8. gray and brown songbirds _____

9. a bunch of flowers _____

10. passed down the throat _____

List Words

breeze
roasted
eagle
believe
neighbors
freighter
drawings
scrawl
restaurant
employ
railroad
royalty
hours
mountain
chowder

Write a List Word to complete each book title or author's name.

1. "_____ in Yourself" by Faith Builder

2. "Famous _____ Trips" by Choo Choos

3. "At Sea on a _____" by C. U. Later

4. "A Cook's Guide to Soups" by Clem _____

5. "Make Better _____" by U. B. Artist

6. "_____ Chicken Recipes" by Chef Cluck

7. "Flying High" by I. M. N. _____

8. "Counting the _____" by Telly Time

9. "Visit Your _____" by N. E. Juan Home

10. "Improve Your Handwriting" by I. _____

11. "Great Meals at a _____" by Bertha D. Diner

12. "Swaying in the _____" by Leaves R. Falling

13. "My Life in the _____" by Ima King

14. "People Want to Work for You!" by U. _____

15. "Climb the Tallest _____" by Hi Hills

Go for the Goal

Take your Final Replay Test. Then fill in your
Scoreboard. Send any misspelled words to your
Word Locker.

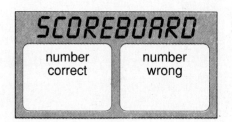

SCOREBOARD

number correct	number wrong

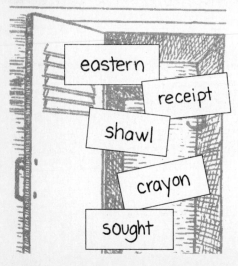

eastern
receipt
shawl
crayon
sought

Clean Out Your Word Locker

Look in your Word Locker. Cross out each word you
spelled correctly on your Final Replay Test. Circle the
words you're still having trouble with. Add the words
you circled to your Spelling Notebook. What do you
notice about the words? Watch for those words as
you write.

Plurals

Warm Up

How do you keep a bike in tip-top shape?

Clean Machine

You have to work hard to keep a bike in tip-top shape. The best time to care for a bike is before anything goes wrong. Wash your bike with soap and water and dry it with towels. Pay attention to the reflectors. The cleaner they are, the easier they are for a driver of a car to see. To protect the shine, apply a coat of car wax. Some **waxes** can be applied in the sun.

To keep your bike safe, keep its chain in good condition. Old **toothbrushes** are great for removing grime. Oil the chain with bike chain oil. Don't use too much oil! Oily **chains** become gummy and collect dirt. If your bike has hand brakes, check each brake shoe. These are the rubber pads that grip the tires. Use rubbing alcohol to wipe the **shoes** clean. Make sure the brakes work well too, so you won't ride into any **ditches** and can avoid **crashes.**

Once your bike is in good working order, take it out for a test run.

Look back at the boldfaced words. What letter or letters are added to each word to make it plural?

On Your Mark

Take your Warm Up Test. Then check your spelling with the List Words on the next page.

You make most singular words plural by adding just **s** to the singular form.

shoe + **s** = shoes

If a singular word ends in **x, ss, sh,** or **ch,** you usually add **es** to make it mean more than one.

fox + **es** = foxes

Game Plan

Spelling Lineup

Finish spelling each List Word.

LIST WORDS

1. axes
2. chains
3. bosses
4. shoes
5. kisses
6. waxes
7. foxes
8. splashes
9. ashes
10. crashes
11. matches
12. sandwiches
13. toothbrushes
14. eyelashes
15. sashes
16. ditches
17. flashes
18. churches
19. paces
20. clashes

1. ki _____
2. as _____
3. wa _____
4. ax _____
5. di _____
6. cha _____
7. ma _____
8. sas _____
9. sh _____
10. sand _____
11. tooth _____

12. cr _____
13. bo _____
14. fl _____
15. eye _____
16. fo _____
17. pa _____
18. chu _____
19. cla _____
20. spl _____

Classification

Write the List Word that belongs in each group.

1. dentists, teeth, _____

2. ribbons, bows, _____

3. wolves, rabbits, _____

4. holes, tunnels, _____

5. candles, wicks, _____

6. noses, lips, _____

7. schools, libraries, _____

8. hotdogs, soups, _____

9. accidents, collisions, _____

10. managers, owners, _____

Definitions

Write the List Word that matches each clue. Then read down the shaded boxes to solve the riddle.

1. used to chop trees
2. used to light candles
3. conflicts; disagreements
4. links or loops joined together

5. bright bursts of light
6. steps
7. worn on feet
8. used to show love
9. dust of burned wood

Riddle: How did the bicycle wheels communicate?

Answer: _____ _____.

Flex Your Spelling Muscles

Writing

Bicycles are not the only things that need special care. Write a paragraph that tells how to take care of something else, such as a favorite toy, a pet, your teeth, or books. Use as many List Words as you can.

Proofreading

The following poem has twelve mistakes. Use the proofreading marks to fix the mistakes. Then write the misspelled List Words on the lines.

Proofreading Marks
⬯ spelling mistake
∧ add something
℮ take out something

We ride bicycles onthe street.
We wave to to all the friends we meet.
We hit puddles to make splashis
And now andthen we have krashes.
We we jump dichtes in a bunch,
And eat sandwechs forlunch.
Even in the the hardest rains
We always stopto fix our chayns.

1. _____
2. _____
3. _____
4. _____
5. _____

Now proofread your paragraph. Fix any mistakes.

Go for the Goal

Take your Final Test. Then fill in your Scoreboard. Send your mistakes to the Word Locker.

SCOREBOARD

number correct	number wrong

★ ★ ★ ★ ★ ★ ★ ★ ★ **All-Star Words** ★ ★ ★ ★ ★ ★ ★ ★ ★

pardons   witnesses   taxes   purses   scratches

Write a short story using the All-Star Words in their singular form. Trade papers with a partner. See if you can write the correct plural form of each All-Star Word in the story.

Plurals of Words That End in y

LESSON

26

Warm Up

When is it okay to "pig out?"

Pig Out

Most of the time, "pigging out" is considered bad manners and unhealthy. There is one day a year, however, when not pigging out is impolite. That day is March 1, National Pig Day.

Most **holidays** were begun to recall historic events. This one, though, was begun by two sisters from Texas who happened to love pigs. When these girls were very young, they had read many children's stories about pigs and piglets. For **birthdays,** they exchanged such gifts as glass piggybanks. **Stories** of their pig-presents spread. Soon, friends, families, and neighboring **communities** began to share in the celebration. Their pig **parties** got larger and larger. Finally, the sisters were able to have their Pig Day registered as a real holiday.

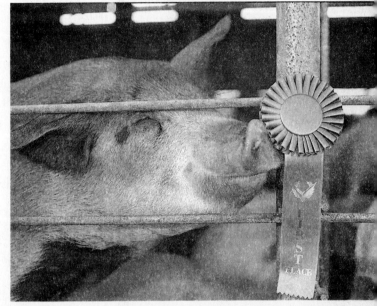

Today, the holiday is celebrated by pig lovers everywhere. Some people bake pig-shaped cookies or cakes. Others have piggyback races or play pig-tail. That's a game in which each player races to braid a piece of rope. You may even want to think of a special way to celebrate National Pig Day.

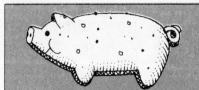
The singular form of each boldfaced word in the selection ends with the same letter. Which letter is it? How are the plurals spelled?

On Your Mark

Take your Warm Up Test. Then check your spelling with the List Words on the next page.

Pep Talk

If a word ends in **y** preceded by a vowel, add **s** to make the plural.

holiday + **s** = holidays

If a word ends in **y** preceded by a consonant, change **y** to **i** and add **es**.

copy + **es** = copies

Game Plan

Spelling Lineup

Complete each List Word by writing **y** and adding **s** to make the plural or by changing the **y** to **i** and adding **es** to make the plural.

LIST WORDS

1. holidays
2. parties
3. stories
4. flies
5. birthdays
6. copies
7. duties
8. ladies
9. counties
10. valleys
11. groceries
12. hobbies
13. libraries
14. highways
15. batteries
16. injuries
17. cherries
18. melodies
19. surveys
20. communities

1. grocer _____
2. fl _____
3. stor _____
4. dut _____
5. highwa _____
6. cop _____
7. birthda _____
8. hobb _____
9. batter _____
10. valle _____
11. holida _____
12. part _____
13. injur _____
14. surve _____
15. melod _____
16. communit _____
17. cherr _____
18. lad _____
19. count _____
20. librar _____

Rhyming

Write the plural List Word whose singular form rhymes
with the word given.

1. lobby _____

2. byway _____

3. rally _____

4. fruity _____

5. shy _____

6. sloppy _____

Classification

Write the List Word that belongs in each group.

1. stamps, baseball cards, _____

2. tunes, songs, _____

3. books, shelves, quiet, _____

4. flashlights, radios, _____

5. grapes, strawberries, _____

6. houses, neighborhoods, _____

7. ants, spiders, bees, _____

8. mysteries, adventures, _____

9. Thanksgiving,
   New Year's Day, _____

10. cuts, broken bones, _____

11. streets, turnpikes, _____

12. canned beans, cereals, _____

13. hills, rivers, _____

14. towns, cities, _____

15. women, females, _____

Flex Your Spelling Muscles

Writing

What event or day do you think should be celebrated? Use the List Words to write a paragraph to convince people that your holiday is important.

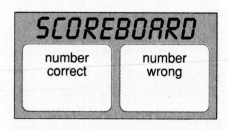

Proofreading

The article below has eleven mistakes. Use the proofreading marks to fix the mistakes. Then write the misspelled List Words on the lines.

Proofreading Marks	
◯	spelling mistake
≡	capital letter
∧	add something

you've probably read or heard a lot of storys about pigs. Did any of them suggest having a pig as a pet Although pigs are often thought to be filthy and dumb, survays have shown that they can be smart and clean. people in many communitees have even been able to teach their pet pigs to do tricks. The squeals of these pigs are melodeys to pig lovers everywhere and their birthdais are big partees. now that you know more about pigs, would you like a pet pig

1. _____

2. _____

3. _____

4. _____

5. _____

6. _____

Now proofread your paragraph. Fix any mistakes.

Go for the Goal

Take your Final Test. Then fill in your Scoreboard. Send your mistakes to the Word Locker.

SCOREBOARD

number correct	number wrong

★ ★ ★ ★ ★ ★ ★ ★ ★ ★ **All-Star Words** ★ ★ ★ ★ ★ ★ ★ ★ ★ ★

grizzlies   universities   deliveries   convoys   essays

Write a sentence for each word, but leave a blank for the All-Star Word that completes the sentence. Trade papers with your partner. Write the correct word in each sentence.

Name _____

Irregular Plurals: Plurals of Words That End in <u>f</u> or <u>fe</u>

Warm Up

How can you help keep your teeth healthy?

Smile!

Babies are usually born without **teeth.** By the time children are about three years old, they have 28 teeth. One by one, these fall out and are replaced by 32 adult teeth. These should last people all their **lives.** Over half of the men and **women** in this country, however, lose some of their teeth because they haven't taken good care of them. Take care of **yourselves!** Follow these dental health rules today to give you a better chance of having your teeth tomorrow.

- Brush after meals.
- Drink lots of water.
- Use dental floss. Floss is a specially made string that helps remove food from between teeth.
- Avoid sugar, especially the kind that comes in cookies, in caramel, and in sugar-coated cereals.
- Visit your dentist regularly.

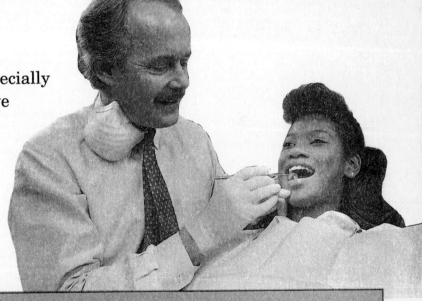

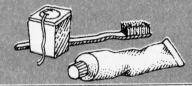 Look back at the boldfaced words. Notice that all the words are plurals. What is the singular form of each word?

On Your Mark

Take your Warm Up Test. Then check your spelling with the List Words on the next page.

LIST WORDS

1. teeth
2. mice
3. women
4. knives
5. leaves
6. halves
7. loaves
8. lives
9. calves
10. moose
11. sheep
12. oxen
13. yourselves
14. geese
15. chiefs
16. buffaloes
17. handkerchiefs
18. scarves
19. hoofs
20. bison

Game Plan

Spelling Lineup

Write the List Word that is the plural form of each word given.

1. hoof _____
2. knife _____
3. sheep _____
4. chief _____
5. ox _____
6. half _____
7. bison _____
8. leaf _____
9. life _____
10. handkerchief _____
11. buffalo _____
12. yourself _____
13. moose _____
14. mouse _____
15. loaf _____
16. goose _____
17. scarf _____
18. tooth _____
19. calf _____
20. woman _____

Comparing Words

The first two underlined words in each sentence are
related. Write a List Word that has the same relationship
to the third underlined word.

1. Snow is to shovel as _____ are to rake.

2. Feet are to people as _____ are to horses.

3. Patties are to hamburgers as _____ are to bread.

4. Walk is to legs as chew is to _____ .

5. Men are to boys as _____ are to girls.

6. Scissors are to paper as _____ are to meat.

7. Calf is to calves as life is to _____ .

8. Belts are to waists as _____ are to necks.

9. Hay is to horses as cheese is to _____ .

10. Puppies are to dogs as lambs are to _____ .

Vocabulary

Write the List Word that matches each clue.

1. leaders of a group _____

2. two parts of a whole _____

3. birds that fly south in winter _____

4. pieces of cloth used to blow your nose _____

5. the plural of yourself _____

6. baby cows _____

Flex Your Spelling Muscles

Writing

How do you feel about going to the dentist? Use the List Words to write a paragraph sharing your feelings.

Proofreading

This informational article has nine mistakes. Use the proofreading marks to fix the mistakes. Then write the misspelled List Words on the lines.

Look at the teeth of people dogs, sheep, and other animals. They differ because they chew different kinds of food. Sheep, oxin, bisen, buffalows, and mooses have flat teeth for eating twigs, leavss grass, and hay. Dogs, cats and tigers have sharp teeth for eating meat. People have both kinds of teeth. Sharks, whose teeth are as sharp as knifes, never run out of teeth because new ones grow in place of lost teeth.

Now proofread your paragraph. Fix any mistakes.

Proofreading Marks

⬭ spelling mistake

⌃ add something

1. _____

2. _____

3. _____

4. _____

5. _____

6. _____

Go for the Goal

Take your Final Test. Then fill in your Scoreboard. Send your mistakes to the Word Locker.

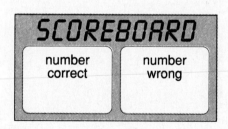

SCOREBOARD

| number correct | number wrong |

★ ★ ★ ★ ★ ★ ★ ★ ★ **All-Star Words** ★ ★ ★ ★ ★ ★ ★ ★ ★

beliefs   wives   patios   broccoli   deer

Use the All-Star Words to create a crossword puzzle. Then write a clue for each word. Swap papers with a partner. Can you fill in the puzzle with the correct All-Star Words?

Possessives and Contractions

LESSON 28

Warm Up

What is a geoglyph?

Grand Designs

If you ever fly over **Arizona's** deserts, look down. You may see block-long carvings of a rattlesnake or any of a dozen other designs. These carvings cover many flat areas between the Colorado River and Mexico. **They'll** be easier to figure out from above, in a plane. Some show horses, pumas, lizards, or people. Some carvings look more like doodles—just swirls and squares.

Wouldn't you like to know who made these grand designs on the **desert's** floor? Scientists don't know for sure. Yet more than 250 of them exist. They're called geoglyphs by the scientists. Some people think the 1,000-year-old geoglyphs are examples of ancient Native American art. Perhaps we'll never know for sure just where they came from or what they mean.

Look back at the boldfaced words. Notice that each word has an apostrophe. Can you identify which words are possessives and which words are contractions?

On Your Mark

Take your Warm Up Test. Then check your spelling with the List Words on the next page.

Pep Talk

Use an apostrophe to show where letters have been left out in a contraction.

she will—she'll   how is—how's

Use an apostrophe and **s** to show singular ownership.

the bike of my uncle—my uncle's bike

LIST WORDS

1. she'll
2. wouldn't
3. they'll
4. how's
5. let's
6. where's
7. we're
8. desert's
9. person's
10. sister's
11. bicycle's
12. Arizona's
13. child's
14. aunt's
15. cousin's
16. Florida's
17. uncle's
18. doctor's
19. hasn't
20. season's

Game Plan

Spelling Lineup

Write the List Word that is a contraction for each pair of words given.

1. has not _____

2. how is _____

3. she will _____

4. we are _____

5. would not _____

6. where is _____

7. they will _____

8. let us _____

we are
we're

Write the List Words that show ownership.

9. _____   15. _____

10. _____   16. _____

11. _____   17. _____

12. _____   18. _____

13. _____   19. _____

14. _____   20. _____

Vocabulary

Write the List Word that goes with the underlined phrase
in each sentence.

1. The hat that <u>the child owns</u> is pretty. _____

2. The clothes <u>of my sister</u> are too big for me. _____

3. The house <u>of my aunt</u> is painted yellow. _____

4. I know <u>they will</u> enjoy meeting you. _____

5. The nickname <u>of Arizona</u> is the Grand Canyon State. _____

6. <u>Let us</u> see if we can find some orange juice. _____

7. The newspaper <u>has not</u> arrived yet. _____

8. I can't remember the name <u>of the person</u>. _____

9. The office <u>belonging to the doctor</u> is on Elm Street. _____

10. <u>Where is</u> the new playground being built? _____

11. The 30,000 lakes <u>Florida has</u> are different sizes. _____

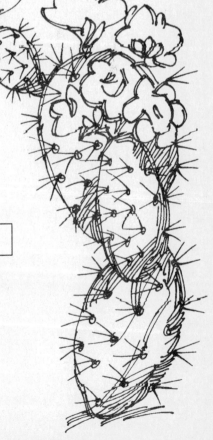

Puzzle

Fill in the crossword puzzle by writing a
List Word to answer each clue. The
apostrophes have been filled in for you.

ACROSS
1. how is
4. belonging to a bicycle
5. we are
6. of the desert

DOWN
2. she will
3. of the uncle

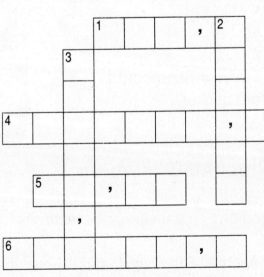

Flex Your Spelling Muscles

Writing

Imagine that you've discovered how the designs in Arizona's deserts came to be. Share your ideas in a news report. Use as many List Words as you can.

Proofreading

This article has eleven mistakes. Use the proofreading marks to fix the mistakes. Then write the List Words correctly on the lines.

Proofreading Marks
⍁ add apostrophe
∧ add something
≡ capital letter

   Wouldnt you know it, arizona was a big surprise I went to visit my cousins ranch near flagstaff. I asked, "Wheres the desert?" He said, "Below us. Flagstaff is too high for a desert climate. We're in forests where each seasons weather is different." What a beautiful place It should be on every persons list of places to go. some people like Florida's palm trees. I, however, like Arizonas pine trees.

1. _____   4. _____

2. _____   5. _____

3. _____   6. _____

Now proofread your news report. Fix any mistakes.

Go for the Goal

Take your Final Test. Then fill in your Scoreboard.
Send your mistakes to the Word Locker.

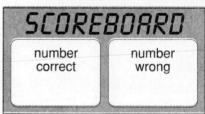

SCOREBOARD

number correct	number wrong

★ ★ ★ ★ ★ ★ ★ ★ ★   **All-Star Words**   ★ ★ ★ ★ ★ ★ ★ ★ ★

doesn't   shouldn't   principal's   factory's   there's

Write a sentence for each All-Star Word, and then erase the apostrophe. Trade papers with a partner, and add the apostrophe to the words.

Plurals and Plural Possessives

Warm Up

What fabric never goes out of style?

Durable Denim

There is a kind of fabric that never goes out of style, and almost everyone has worn it at least once. Some people wear it every day. It's denim. This sturdy cloth has been meeting **families'** clothing needs for more than one hundred years.

In 1873, when Levi Strauss began making **men's** work clothes for miners, he needed a fabric that would be strong, and yet comfortable to wear. Cotton denim was the answer. It was a basic durable fabric that looked good.

Jeans, which are made of demin, have become an almost necessary piece of everyday clothing today. Denim is used not only for men's clothing, but women's clothing and **children's** clothing as well. Levi Strauss probably had no idea that after a century, denim would be the center of his **businesses'** success.

You might think that denim is strictly American, but the word *denim* comes from French. Weavers in Nîmes, a city in France, created this sturdy twilled cloth, woven so that the cloth's ribs were diagonal and parallel. This made the cloth strong, but flexible. The name denim comes from the twilled cloth of Nîmes, or as the French say *de Nîmes*. Somehow over time, the "de" and "Nîmes" were blended together to form the word denim.

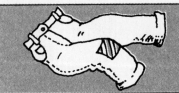

Look back at the boldfaced words. Notice that all the words are plural. How is the possessive of each word formed?

On Your Mark

Take your Warm Up Test. Then check your spelling with the List Words on the next page.

Pep Talk

Form the possessive of a plural ending in **s** by adding just an apostrophe, as in <u>armies—armies'</u>.

If the plural does not end in **s**, form its possessive by adding an apostrophe and **s,** as in <u>men—men's</u>.

Game Plan

Spelling Lineup

Write each List Word that was formed by adding an apostrophe and **s** to a plural word.

1. _____   2. _____

Write each List Word that was formed by adding just an apostrophe to a plural word.

3. _____   15. _____

4. _____   16. _____

5. _____   17. _____

6. _____   18. _____

7. _____   19. _____

8. _____   20. _____

9. _____

10. _____

11. _____

12. _____

13. _____

14. _____

Vocabulary

Write the List Word that best completes each sentence.

1. The cattle of the ranches are the _____ cattle.

2. The strings of the banjos are the _____ strings.

3. The barracks of the armies are the _____ barracks.

4. The uniforms of the hostesses are the _____ uniforms.

5. The parts of our bodies are our _____ parts.

6. The families of the passengers are the _____ families.

7. The pictures on the televisions are the _____ pictures.

8. The keys of the pianos are the _____ keys.

9. The paint of the benches is the _____ paint.

10. The prices of the dresses are the _____ prices.

11. The stems of the daisies are the _____ stems.

Possessives

Circle the word in each pair of sentences that needs
an apostrophe. Then write the word correctly.

1. The airlines have friendly attendants.
   Those airlines attendants have a lot of experience.   _____

2. The decisions of the umpires are final.
   The umpires uniforms protect them from injury.   _____

3. The businesses need more workers.
   The businesses workers put in long hours.   _____

4. The members dues are paid every month.
   The club's members will all vote in the election.   _____

Flex Your Spelling Muscles

Writing

Imagine you are having a fashion show to exhibit the latest denim clothing. Use the List Words to write an ad telling people what you're showing.

Proofreading

Find the eleven mistakes in the article below. Use the proofreading marks to fix the mistakes. Then write the List Words correctly on the lines.

Proofreading Marks	
⚓	add apostrophe
∧	add something
/	make small letter

Thousands of years ago, Only the Chinese knew that silkworms spin the silk threads needed for making silk fabric. For a longtime, Several governments officials guarded thesecret. When other countries discovered this wonderful cloth, they wanted to make it themselves. Soon some traders discovered how to sneak silkworms out of China. The thieves idea was to carry the creatures out inthe hollows of bamboo canes. The idea worked! Soon other countries could Make silk fabric and produce mens, women's, and childrens clothing. Many families wardrobes could now include this fabric.

1. _____

2. _____

3. _____

4. _____

5. _____

Now proofread your fashion ad. Fix any mistakes.

Go for the Goal

Take your Final Test. Then fill in your Scoreboard. Send your mistakes to the Word Locker.

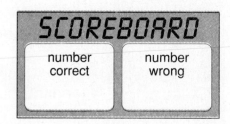

SCOREBOARD

number correct	number wrong

★ ★ ★ ★ ★ ★ ★ ★ ★ **All-Star Words** ★ ★ ★ ★ ★ ★ ★ ★ ★

diaries'   fish's   classes'   spies'   species'

Work with your partner to write a short story, leaving blanks in place of the All-Star Words. Trade stories with other students. Write the All-Star Words in the appropriate places.

Instant Replay • Lessons 25–29

LESSON

30

Time Out

Take another look at plurals, contractions, and possessives.

Check Your Word Locker

Look at the words in your Word Locker. Write your troublesome words for Lessons 25–29.

_____

_____

Practice writing your troublesome words with a partner. Form the letters of each word using clay. Your partner can spell the word aloud as you form the letters.

Lesson 25

Most plurals are formed by adding **s** to the singular form, as in <u>chains</u>. If a word ends in **x, ss, sh,** or **ch,** add **es** to form the plural, as in <u>foxes</u> and <u>bosses</u>.

List Words
axes
waxes
matches
sandwiches
eyelashes
sashes
ditches
flashes
churches
paces

Write a List Word to match each definition.

1. bright bursts of light _____

2. cloths worn at waists _____

3. sticks to light a fire _____

4. hairs on eyelids _____

5. tools to chop wood _____

6. holes in the ground _____

7. meals between bread _____

8. makes surfaces shiny _____

9. places of worship _____

10. steps taken _____

If a word ends in **vowel-y,** add **s,** as in <u>valleys</u>. If it ends in **consonant-y,** chang**e** y to **i** and add **es,** as in <u>duties</u>.

List Words

holidays
flies
groceries
libraries
batteries
injuries
cherries
melodies
surveys
communities

Write a List Word to complete each sentence.

1. _____ loan books.

2. _____ are common insects.

3. School is closed on _____ .

4. Portable radios run on _____ .

5. I made a pie with fresh _____ .

6. _____ are made up of families.

7. Don sang three new _____ .

8. We were told to fill out _____ .

9. Helmets have prevented _____ .

10. Those _____ will feed us for a week.

If a word ends in **f** or **fe,** usually change the **f** or **fe** to **v** and add **es,** as in <u>scarves</u>. Some words change their vowel sound or spelling to make the plural form, as in <u>teeth</u>. Others have the same form for singular and plural, as in <u>bison</u>.

List Words

mice
knives
halves
calves
sheep
oxen
geese
chiefs
buffaloes
hoofs

Write the List Words in alphabetical order.

1. _____

2. _____

3. _____

4. _____

5. _____

6. _____

7. _____

8. _____

9. _____

10. _____

Use apostrophes in contractions, as in <u>where's</u> and <u>wouldn't</u>. Singular possessives and those made from irregular plurals take **'s,** as in <u>sister's</u> and <u>children's</u>.

List Words

she'll
they'll
we're
bicycle's
Arizona's
cousin's
Florida's
uncle's
doctor's
hasn't

Write the List Word that is a part of each word given.

1. has _____

2. Arizona _____

3. bicycle _____

4. cousin _____

5. she _____

6. Florida _____

7. we _____

8. uncle _____

9. doctor _____

10. they _____

Form the possessive of a plural word that ends in **s** by adding an apostrophe, as in <u>dresses'</u>.

List Words

passengers'
umpires'
airlines'
hostesses'
families'
banjos'
men's
children's
members'
businesses'

Circle the correct form of the List Word in each group. Then write the List Word on the line.

1. banjose'   banjos'   _____

2. businesses'   business'es   _____

3. mens'   men's   _____

4. hostes's   hostesses'   _____

5. umpirs'   umpires'   _____

6. members'   membors'   _____

7. children's   childrens'   _____

8. familie's   families'   _____

9. passengers'   pasengers'   _____

10. airlines'   airlineses'   _____

Lesson 30 ▪ Instant Replay   123

List Words

waxes
sandwiches
umpires'
communities
oxen
hostesses'
uncle's
doctor's

Write the List Word that matches each clue. Then read down the shaded boxes to solve the riddle.

1. lunch foods

2. belonging to sports figures

3. polishes

4. towns or cities

5. farm animals

6. belonging to a relative

7. belonging to a medical person

8. belonging to party givers

Riddle: What do a baseball umpire and a jeweler have in common?

Answer: Each works on _____ !

Go for the Goal

Take your Final Replay Test. Then fill in your Scoreboard. Send any misspelled words to your Word Locker.

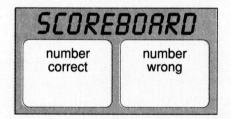

SCOREBOARD

number correct	number wrong

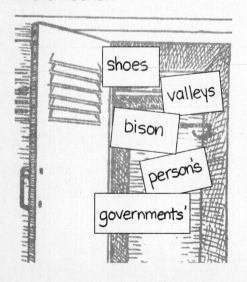

Clean Out Your Word Locker

Look in your Word Locker. Cross out each word you spelled correctly on your Final Replay Test. Circle the words you're still having trouble with. Add the words you circled to your Spelling Notebook. What do you notice about the words? Watch for those words as you write.

Prefixes pre, re, im, non, and con

Warm Up

How can the sun light up the night?

Night Light

What if we could harness the sunlight and use it to light the night? It may seem like **nonsense,** but scientists **report** that they are trying to figure out a way to use the sun as a giant night light.

The idea is to **construct** a giant mirror, position it in space, and reflect light back to the dark side of the earth. Since the sun is always shining somewhere on the earth, reflecting light to the darkened side is possible. Put simply, it's the same as using a hand mirror to reflect sunlight to a dark corner of a room.

Russian scientists have considered this possibility for many years. In an experiment called Banner (*Znamya* in Russian), they are determining whether or not the idea is an **impractical** one. If successful, scientists **predict** that the extra light could save billions of dollars in electricity. Farmers with longer daylight hours could have more efficient planting and harvesting seasons. Building projects could be completed more quickly by working at night.

Of course, those of us who like to sleep will probably be calling the Russians to ask them to turn out that night light!

Say the boldfaced words in the selection. These words have word parts that are added to the front of the words to make new words. These word parts are called **prefixes.** Can you name the prefix in each word?

On Your Mark

Take your Warm Up Test. Then check your spelling with the List Words on the next page.

Pep Talk

A **prefix** is a word part that is added to the beginning of a root to make a new word. Every prefix has a meaning, and it changes the meaning of the root.

pre means <u>before</u>, as in <u>pre</u>view
re means <u>again</u> or <u>back</u>, as in <u>re</u>fills
im and **non** mean <u>not</u>, as in <u>im</u>perfect
con means <u>with</u> or <u>together</u>, as in <u>con</u>struct

LIST WORDS

1. nonsense
2. prepaid
3. control
4. returned
5. impractical
6. nonstop
7. conduct
8. preview
9. report
10. imperfect
11. nonprofit
12. refills
13. construct
14. immovable
15. precaution
16. predict
17. convince
18. impersonal
19. impure
20. reaction

Game Plan

Spelling Lineup

Write each List Word under the correct heading.

words with the prefix **pre**

1. _____
2. _____
3. _____
4. _____

words with the prefix **re**

13. _____
14. _____
15. _____
16. _____

words with the prefix **im**

5. _____
6. _____
7. _____
8. _____
9. _____

words with the prefix **con**

17. _____
18. _____
19. _____
20. _____

words with the prefix **non**

10. _____
11. _____
12. _____

Antonyms

Write the List Word that means the opposite of the word or words given.

1. personal   _____

2. movable   _____

3. sense   _____

4. with stops   _____

5. perfect   _____

6. for profit   _____

Puzzle

Fill in the crossword puzzle by writing the List Words that contain the roots given.

ACROSS
2. port   9. fills
5. pure   10. caution
7. dict

DOWN
1. trol   4. view
2. action   6. paid
3. turned   8. duct

Flex Your Spelling Muscles

Writing

A giant space mirror that creates more hours of daylight would be an amazing news story. Use the List Words to write a brief news report on this new invention.

Proofreading

Look for nine mistakes in this informational article. Use the proofreading marks to fix the mistakes. Then write the misspelled List Words on the lines.

Proofreading Marks
- ⬭ spelling mistake
- ⚲ take out something
- ⊙ add period

A practical way to use the heat from the sun is is already in use. People construkt flat metal plates on their roofs to collect and store energy from the sun in in the form of heat They can conduck the stored heat into their homes to warm themselves on cold or cloudy days. Some people predikt this energy method will will become even more popular in the future if we can convinse more people to try it

1. _____   3. _____

2. _____   4. _____

Now proofread your news report. Fix any mistakes.

Go for the Goal

Take your Final Test. Then fill in your Scoreboard. Send your mistakes to the Word Locker.

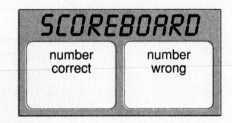

SCOREBOARD

number correct	number wrong

★ ★ ★ ★ ★ ★ ★ ★ **All-Star Words** ★ ★ ★ ★ ★ ★ ★ ★

nonfiction   contact   preset   recount   impatient

Write a sentence for each All-Star Word. Trade sentences with a partner. Circle the prefixes in the All-Star Words.

Prefixes ex, de, dis, un, and ad

Warm Up

How can you avoid catching a cold?

Don't Catch It!

With all the advances in medicine today, doctors still have not found a cure for an **unpleasant** illness that affects more of us than any other—the common cold. Every year, North Americans spend over a billion dollars on medicines to battle colds, but we still catch over 500 million colds a year! Most of those colds happen to children. But there are ways to **defend** ourselves. Let's **explore** one of them—knowing in **advance** how colds are spread.

Colds are not caused by going out without a hat or working too hard. Although many will **disagree,** people rarely catch colds by being near someone who is sneezing or coughing. Colds are caused by viruses, and there are at least 200 different types! These viruses almost always travel from the nose of a person with a cold to their hands. From there it goes to anything they touch. If someone else touches that same object, and then touches their nose or eyes, the virus can infect them.

The average person touches his or her eyes or nose about three times every hour! So it is very good **advice** to wash your hands often, and try not to touch your face. With your help, the common cold could become a little less common!

Take a look at the boldfaced words in the selection. What prefixes do you find?

On Your Mark

Take your Warm Up Test. Then check your spelling with the List Words on the next page.

Pep Talk

Here are more **prefixes** to add to the beginning of roots or root words. Each prefix has a meaning, and it changes the meaning of the root.

ex means <u>out of</u> or <u>from</u>, as in <u>express</u>

de means <u>down</u> or <u>away from</u>, as in <u>defend</u>

dis and **un** mean <u>not</u> or <u>the opposite of</u>, as in <u>unclear</u>

ad means <u>to</u>, <u>at</u>, or <u>toward</u>, as in <u>advice</u>

LIST WORDS

1. express
2. design
3. unknown
4. admit
5. unclear
6. explore
7. disagree
8. defend
9. unreal
10. adventure
11. unwise
12. disclose
13. advice
14. excuse
15. disinterested
16. dishonest
17. unprepared
18. unpleasant
19. advance
20. adverb

Game Plan

Spelling Lineup

Write each List Word under the correct heading.

words with the prefix un

1. _____
2. _____
3. _____
4. _____
5. _____
6. _____

words with the prefix ex

7. _____
8. _____
9. _____

words with the prefix dis

10. _____
11. _____
12. _____
13. _____

words with the prefix ad

14. _____
15. _____
16. _____
17. _____
18. _____

words with the prefix de

19. _____
20. _____

Word Parts

Write List Words by adding prefixes to the roots or root words given.

1. fend _____

2. verb _____

3. plore _____

4. vice _____

5. vance _____

6. press _____

7. venture _____

8. agree _____

9. close _____

10. honest _____

11. mit _____

12. clear _____

13. cuse _____

14. sign _____

Vocabulary

Write a List Word with the prefix **un** to complete each sentence. Use each word only once.

1. Some _____ jewels look just like the real ones.

2. Tell whether you understood the directions

   or if you think they are _____ .

3. Dr. Holmes is an _____ person who rarely smiles.

4. We felt _____ for the difficult test.

5. The identity of the masked stranger is still _____ .

6. We knew it would be _____ to skate on the thin ice.

CAUTION!
DO NOT SKATE
BEYOND THIS POINT!
THIN ICE AHEAD!

Flex Your Spelling Muscles

Writing

What should you do to take care of a cold? Use the List Words to write a paragraph advising people how to take care of their colds.

Proofreading

The article below has eight mistakes. Use the proofreading marks to fix the mistakes. Then write the misspelled List Words on the lines.

Proofreading Marks	
⬭	spelling mistake
¶	indent paragraph
∧	add something

Having a cold is certainly unpleesant— especially if you are unpropared for that sudden sneeze. Here's some good advies, "Keep a handkerchief close by."

Handkerchiefs havebeen used for a long time. At first, they were madefrom grass mats. In China, silk tissue, or paper was used. In the 1600s, handkerchiefs of every size shape, and dezin could be found. Imagine using a handkerchief decorated with gem stones! Toward the 1800s, people became disintarested in these fancy pieces of cloth and began to use tissues.

1. _____

2. _____

3. _____

4. _____

5. _____

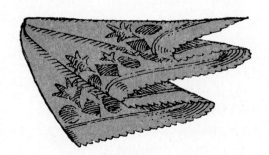

Now proofread your paragraph. Fix any mistakes.

Go for the Goal

Take your Final Test. Then fill in your Scoreboard. Send your mistakes to the Word Locker.

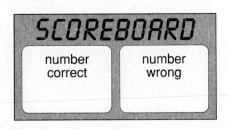

SCOREBOARD

number correct	number wrong

★ ★ ★ ★ ★ ★ ★ ★ ★ ★ **All-Star Words** ★ ★ ★ ★ ★ ★ ★ ★ ★ ★

define   unrelated   disgrace   advantage   exchange

Write a sentence for each word, and then erase the prefix. Trade papers with a partner, and add the correct prefix to the All-Star Words so that they make sense in the sentence.

Compound Words

Warm Up

What is *birling*?

Falling Off a Log

What's the favorite sport of lumberjacks? Its official name is *birling*. Most people know it as *logrolling*. Every year **outstanding** logrollers from all over North America come to Historyland in Hayward, Wisconsin, to take part in the world logrolling championship.

In the contest, two contestants step onto a floating log. They start the log rolling, then spin it rapidly with their feet. They can stop the log or start it spinning in the other direction. The idea is to throw your opponent off balance without falling off the log yourself. When the loser falls into the water, it's called "a wetting." The contest always ends with a big splash for **everybody!** It could even be called a **waterfall.**

Logrolling started in New England in the 1800s. The practice spread to the U.S. **northwest** and Canada. Lumberjacks would roll logs to break up jams. Then the logs could float freely down the river. Rolling logs was part of a lumberjack's everyday life. Today it is a popular sport played **outdoors** by both men and women. It's as easy as falling off a log, but it's a lot more fun!

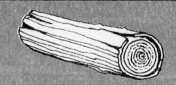

Look back at the boldfaced words. What two words make up each word?

On Your Mark

Take your Warm Up Test. Then check your spelling with the List Words on the next page.

Pep Talk

A **compound word** is made up of two or more words joined together to make a new word. A <u>sidewalk</u> is a place to <u>walk</u> near the <u>side</u> of the road. Study the List Words to find the words that make up each compound word.

LIST WORDS

1. northwest
2. outdoors
3. everybody
4. teaspoon
5. waterfall
6. downtown
7. schoolhouse
8. southeast
9. supermarket
10. therefore
11. homework
12. sidewalk
13. breakfast
14. outstanding
15. overcoat
16. typewriter
17. horseshoes
18. toothache
19. aircraft
20. knapsack

Game Plan

Spelling Lineup

Add a word to each word given to write a List Word.

1. knap

2. out

3. down

4. north

5. air

6. over

7. tea

8. home

9. every

10. tooth

11. out

12. type

13. horse

14. break

15. water

16. there

17. school

18. super

19. south

20. side

Definitions

Write the List Word that matches each clue. Then read down the shaded boxes to solve the riddle.

1. a walkway next to the street

2. work done at home

3. a machine that makes printed letters

4. business section of a city

5. as a result

6. a canvas or leather bag

7. water that falls from a steep height

8. a place to learn

Riddle: What did the king find on the stairs?

Answer: his _____

Classification

Write the List Word that belongs in each group.

1. lunch, dinner, _____

2. headache, earache, _____

3. river, lake, _____

4. great, terrific, _____

5. cup, tablespoon, _____

6. saddle, reins, _____

7. store, shop, _____

8. all, everyone, _____

9. jacket, parka, _____

10. helicopter, plane, _____

Flex Your Spelling Muscles

Writing

What exciting contests or events have you seen? Write a paragraph to describe the event. Use as many List Words as you can.

Proofreading

Find the ten mistakes in the poster below. Use the proofreading marks to fix the mistakes. Then write the misspelled List Words on the lines.

<table>
<tr><td colspan="2">Proofreading Marks</td></tr>
<tr><td>◯</td><td>spelling mistake</td></tr>
<tr><td>⊙</td><td>add period</td></tr>
<tr><td>/</td><td>make a small letter</td></tr>
</table>

Come one, come all to Idaho Spud Day Visit dountown Shelley, Idaho, for The best potatoes in the narthwest. There will be free spuds for everebody Enjoy a fine breckfast, lunch, or dinner served outdores Join us on the Third Saturday in September for a super day of fun.

1. _____

2. _____

3. _____

4. _____

5. _____

Now proofread your paragraph. Fix any mistakes.

Go for the Goal

Take your Final Test. Then fill in your Scoreboard. Send your mistakes to the Word Locker.

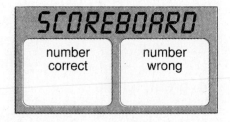

SCOREBOARD

number correct	number wrong

★ ★ ★ ★ ★ ★ ★ ★ ★ **All-Star Words** ★ ★ ★ ★ ★ ★ ★ ★ ★

taxpayer   easygoing   sweatshirt   breakdown   westward

Write a sentence for each All-Star Word. Replace each All-Star Word with an equation that shows the two parts that make up a compound word. Trade papers with your partner and solve each other's equations.

Synonyms and Antonyms

LESSON 34

Warm Up

Why was the Pony Express in business for only two years?

The Mail Must Go Through!

It's been over a hundred years since the Pony Express delivered mail. The Express was started in 1860 between Missouri and California. Riders made the **journey** on horseback. It was a **difficult** ride for both horse and rider so relay stations were set up ten to fifteen miles apart. Riders would pick up fresh horses at each station. The **lengthy** trip took eight days. Because it was so **expensive,** the Pony Express had only a brief life. Railroads could offer cheap rates and quicker delivery. After only two years, the Pony Express went out of business.

However, years later the Express was in business again but only for a short time. In California, a huge mud slide had closed the road to a mountain town called Little Norway. The only way mail could be delivered was by horseback. Each morning, the postmaster gave the first rider a pouch of mail. It took ten riders to make the long, forty-mile trip. Riders ranged in age from teenagers to a 72-year-old. Eventually the road was **repaired,** but for a brief time the Pony Express rode once again.

Look back at the boldfaced words in the selection. Can you name the word that means almost the same as trip? Can you name the word that means the opposite of easy?

On Your Mark

Take your Warm Up Test. Then check your spelling with the List Words on the next page.

Pep Talk

A **synonym** is a word that means the same or almost the same as another word.
The word <u>long</u> is a synonym for <u>lengthy</u>.
An **antonym** is a word that means the opposite or almost the opposite of another word.
The word <u>brief</u> is an antonym for <u>lengthy</u>.

Game Plan

Spelling Lineup

Write the List Word that best completes each sentence.

LIST WORDS

1. difficult
2. tender
3. lengthy
4. sturdy
5. expensive
6. repaired
7. enormous
8. journey
9. weary
10. tense
11. cautious
12. sorrow
13. vague
14. ancient
15. courage
16. drowsy
17. disbelief
18. current
19. descend
20. rapidly

1. A hard problem is

_____

2. A long book is

_____

3. A huge elephant is

_____

4. A sleepy baby is

_____

5. A costly ring is

_____

6. Sadness is also

_____

7. An uptight person is

_____

8. A long trip is a

_____

9. A brave person has

_____

10. A fixed watch is

_____

11. Go slowly, not

_____

12. Don't be tough, be

_____

13. Climb up, don't

_____

14. Be energetic, not

_____

15. A modern desk is not

_____

16. A weak floor is not

_____

17. A clear idea is not

_____

18. It isn't trust, it's

_____

19. Reckless people aren't

_____

20. A past issue is not

_____

Puzzle

Fill in the crossword puzzle by writing a List Word to answer each clue. Write antonyms ACROSS. Write synonyms DOWN.

ACROSS (antonyms)
- 3. clear
- 6. happiness
- 9. broken
- 11. fear
- 13. modern
- 14. short

DOWN (synonyms)
- 1. recent
- 2. strong
- 4. nervous
- 5. costly
- 7. tired
- 8. hard
- 10. trip

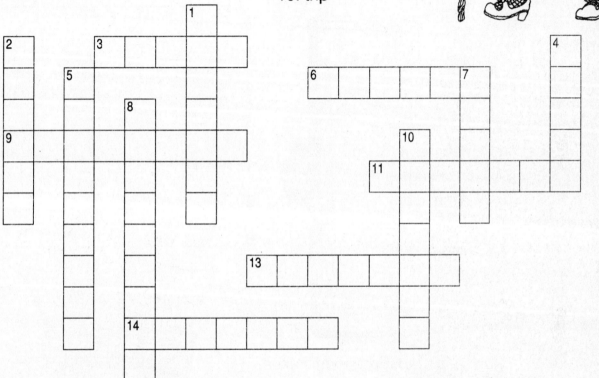

Dictionary

Write the List Word for each sound-spelling given.

1. (ē nôr´ məs) _____

2. (kô´ shəs) _____

3. (dis bə lēf´) _____

4. (dē send´) _____

5. (drou´ zē) _____

6. (sär´ ō) _____

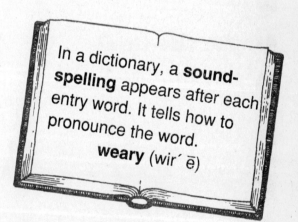

In a dictionary, a **sound-spelling** appears after each entry word. It tells how to pronounce the word.
weary (wir´ ē)

Flex Your Spelling Muscles

Writing

The Pony Express riders faced many dangers on their long rides. Use the List Words to write a newspaper ad asking for riders to sign up. Include some special skills or qualities a Pony Express rider might need.

Proofreading

There are eleven mistakes in this diary entry. Use the proofreading marks to fix the mistakes. Then write the misspelled List Words on the lines.

September 23, 1847

This journey seems more lengthee than I thought it would be be. Emmas horse has tennder feet and may have to to be left behind. Johns wagon has been repayred, but the delay was espensive. We cant waste any more time because winter is rapidlee approaching.

1. _____

2. _____

3. _____

4. _____

5. _____

6. _____

Now proofread your newspaper ad. Fix any mistakes.

Go for the Goal

Take your Final Test. Then fill in your Scoreboard. Send your mistakes to the Word Locker.

SCOREBOARD

number correct	number wrong

★ ★ ★ ★ ★ ★ ★ ★ ★ **All-Star Words** ★ ★ ★ ★ ★ ★ ★ ★ ★ ★

smooth   regular   familiar   intelligent   brilliant

With your partner, write a paragraph using an antonym for each All-Star Word. Trade papers with another team. Rewrite their paragraph, using the All-Star Words.

Homonyms

Warm Up

Who holds the record for the world's tallest hair style?

A Hair-Raising Tale

It may seem like a tall tale, but according to the *Guinness Book of World Records,* in 1989, a woman named Colinda Sirls broke the record for the world's tallest hair style. Colinda's hair measured eight feet over her head! She called it the "flagpole" style. It's not clear exactly who she was trying to flag down, but it was definitely a signal to someone!

Hair as a transmitter of signals is common in the animal kingdom. Moose have hairs between **their** toes that turn green when sending signals to other moose during the mating season.

There are many animals **whose** hair serves as insulation, not only for the animals themselves, but also for their young. For example, the polar bear has a thick coat of fur that keeps it warm. A mother **hare** (rabbit) makes a nest of her own **hair** to shelter her young! Hair is also used as protection from enemies. A porcupine's quills are a type of hair. Porcupines are able to stick their quills into the bodies of attackers.

Look back at the boldfaced words. Which words sound the same, but have different spellings and meanings? Do you know another word that sounds the same as <u>tale</u> or <u>whose</u>?

On Your Mark

Take your Warm Up Test. Then check your spelling with the List Words on the next page.

Pep Talk

Homonyms are words that sound the same, but have different meanings and spellings.

<u>heel</u>—the back of the foot

<u>heal</u>—to make someone well

The meaning of a sentence helps you know which homonym to use.

Game Plan

Spelling Lineup

Write the List Words that rhyme with each word given.

LIST WORDS

1. *tale*
2. *tail*
3. *heel*
4. *heal*
5. *peace*
6. *piece*
7. *plain*
8. *plane*
9. *there*
10. *their*
11. *sense*
12. *scents*
13. *which*
14. *witch*
15. *whose*
16. *who's*
17. *break*
18. *brake*
19. *hair*
20. *hare*

take

1. _____

2. _____

mail

3. _____

4. _____

tents

5. _____

6. _____

bear

7. _____

8. _____

9. _____

10. _____

chain

11. _____

12. _____

shoes

13. _____

14. _____

feel

15. _____

16. _____

pitch

17. _____

18. _____

grease

19. _____

20. _____

142   Lesson 35 ■ Homonyms

Synonyms and Antonyms

Write the List Word that means the same or almost the same as each word given.

1. rabbit _____

2. portion _____

3. story _____

4. smells _____

5. smash _____

6. cure _____

Write the List Word that means the opposite of each word given.

1. fancy _____   3. foolishness _____

2. here _____   4. war _____

Homonyms

Write two List Words that are homonyms to complete each sentence.

1. _____ _____ fell off her broom?

2. _____ the lucky kid _____ pony we can ride?

3. The bike won't stop if you _____ the _____ .

4. _____ seats for the game are over _____ .

5. Soaking my hurt _____ should help it _____ .

6. The _____ we flew in was very _____ .

7. The _____ all over the floor is from my pet _____ .

8. One folk _____ tells how

   the bear lost its _____ .

Flex Your Spelling Muscles

Writing

Do you think hair fashions are funny, great, or not a subject you think about? Write your opinion in a paragraph and state your reasons. Use as many List Words as you can.

Proofreading

There are ten mistakes in this article. Use the proofreading marks to fix the mistakes. Circle the List Words that are used incorrectly. Then write the correct List Words on the lines.

Proofreading Marks	
≡	capital letter
∧	add something

This tail of the history of the beard will raise your hare. did you know that at one time, all men wore beards Then Alexander the Great thought it made scents for soldiers to shave there beards so enemies could not grab them. Did you know that the Vandyke beard, witch was pointed, was popular in the 1600s In the 1830s in america, men were not allowed to wear beards. Joseph Palmer, who's beard was bushy, was jailed for that reason. Newspaper stories forced his release to keep the piece.

1. _____   4. _____

2. _____   5. _____

3. _____   6. _____

Now proofread your opinion paragraph. Fix any mistakes.

Go for the Goal

Take your Final Test. Then fill in your Scoreboard. Send your mistakes to the Word Locker.

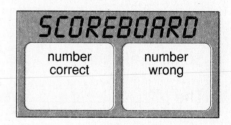

SCOREBOARD

number correct	number wrong

★ ★ ★ ★ ★ ★ ★ ★ ★ **All-Star Words** ★ ★ ★ ★ ★ ★ ★ ★ ★

flew   flue   flu   knead   need

Write a paragraph using each word. Then mix up the All-Star Words. Trade papers with a partner. Rewrite each other's paragraph, using the All-Star Words correctly.

Name_____

Instant Replay • Lessons 31–35

Time Out

Take another look at prefixes, compound words, synonyms and antonyms, and homonyms.

Check Your Word Locker

Look at the words in your Word Locker. Write your troublesome words for Lessons 31 through 35.

_____

Practice writing your troublesome words with a partner. Take turns dividing the words into syllables as your partner spells them aloud.

Lesson 31

Prefixes

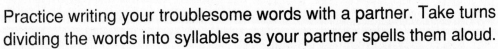

pre = <u>before</u>, as in <u>preview</u>   **re** = <u>again</u> or <u>back</u>, as in <u>refills</u>
im = <u>not</u>, as in <u>impure</u>   **non** = <u>not</u>, as in <u>nonprofit</u>
con = <u>with</u> or <u>together</u>, as in <u>control</u>

Add a prefix to each word or word part to make a List Word.

List Words
nonsense
prepaid
impractical
nonstop
nonprofit
construct
immovable
predict
convince
reaction

1. _____ movable _____

2. _____ vince _____

3. _____ sense _____

4. _____ profit _____

5. _____ action _____

6. _____ stop _____

7. _____ paid _____

8. _____ struct _____

9. _____ dict _____

10. _____ practical _____

Prefixes

ex = <u>out of</u> or <u>from</u>, as in <u>express</u>　　　**de** = <u>down</u> or <u>away from</u>, as in <u>defend</u>

dis = <u>opposite</u> or <u>not</u>, as in <u>dishonest</u>　　**un** = <u>not</u>, as in <u>unreal</u>

ad = <u>to</u>, <u>at</u>, or <u>towards</u>, as in <u>admit</u>

List Words
express
design
unknown
explore
disagree
adventure
unwise
excuse
unprepared
admit

Write a List Word to match each definition.

1. to be against an idea _____

2. not ready _____

3. not showing good sense _____

4. to state or say _____

5. decoration or pattern _____

6. to search carefully _____

7. to take or accept as true _____

8. undiscovered _____

9. to free from blame _____

10. an exciting experience _____

 Lesson 33

A **compound word** is made up of two or more words, as in <u>homework</u> and <u>downtown</u>.

List Words
outdoors
everybody
supermarket
sidewalk
breakfast
outstanding
typewriter
toothache
aircraft
knapsack

Combine each word in the first box with a word in the second box to make a compound List Word. Then write the List Word.

out	type	every	side
super	break	out	tooth
	air	knap	

doors	fast	standing	body
walk	market	writer	ache
	sack	craft	

1. _____　　6. _____

2. _____　　7. _____

3. _____　　8. _____

4. _____　　9. _____

5. _____　　10. _____

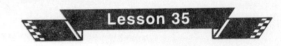

Lesson 34

A **synonym** means the same or almost the same as another word.
An **antonym** means the opposite or almost opposite of another word.

List Words
lengthy
expensive
repaired
enormous
journey
cautious
vague
ancient
courage
descend

Write a List Word to match each clue.

Synonyms

1. careful _____

2. bravery _____

3. fixed _____

4. voyage _____

5. old _____

Antonyms

6. go up _____

7. brief _____

8. cheap _____

9. small _____

10. clear _____

Lesson 35

Homonyms are words that sound alike, but have different meanings and spellings.

List Words
tale
tail
peace
piece
there
their
whose
who's
break
brake

Underline the List Word that completes each sentence. Then write that List Word on the line.

1. The dog wagged its (tale, tail). _____

2. Grandma told us a (tale, tail). _____

3. (Whose, Who's) coat is this? _____

4. (Whose, Who's) the best singer? _____

5. I'd like a (peace, piece) of toast. _____

6. We work for world (peace, piece). _____

7. Please put my books (there, their). _____

8. Put (their, there) books on the table. _____

9. Use the (break, brake) to stop. _____

10. The cup could (break, brake). _____

List Words

nonsense
nonstop
construct
design
adventure
admit
supermarket
breakfast
toothache
expensive
repaired
ancient
tale
tail
brake

Write the List Words in alphabetical order.

1. _____

2. _____

3. _____

4. _____

5. _____

6. _____

7. _____

8. _____

9. _____

10. _____

11. _____

12. _____

13. _____

14. _____

15. _____

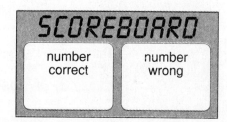

Go for the Goal

Take your Final Replay Test. Then fill in your Scoreboard. Send any misspelled words to your Word Locker.

SCOREBOARD

number correct	number wrong

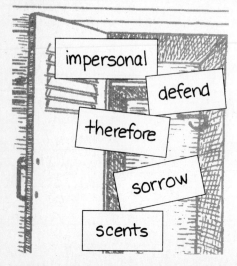

impersonal
defend
therefore
sorrow
scents

Clean Out Your Word Locker

Look in your Word Locker. Cross out each word you spelled correctly on your Final Replay Test. Circle the words you're still having trouble with. Add the words you circled to your Spelling Notebook. What do you notice about the words? Watch for those words as you write.

Writing and Proofreading Guide

1. Choose a topic to write about.
2. Write your ideas. Don't worry about mistakes.
3. Now organize your writing so that it makes sense.
4. Proofread your work.
   Use these proofreading marks to make changes.

Proofreading Marks	
⬭	spelling mistake
≡	capital letter
⊙	add period
∧	add something
⌄	add apostrophe
ℒ	take out something
¶	indent paragraph
/	make small letter

Isnt a ⬭dolfin⬭ one of the ~~the~~ most /intelligent sea mammals ?

5. Write your final copy.

   Isn't a dolphin one of the most intelligent sea mammals?

6. Share your writing.

Dolphins use sound to communicate with each other.

Using Your Dictionary

The Spelling Workout Dictionary shows you
many things about your spelling words.

The **sound-spelling or respelling**
tells how to pronounce the word.

The **entry word** listed in
alphabetical order is the
word you are looking up.

The **part of speech** is
given as an abbreviation.

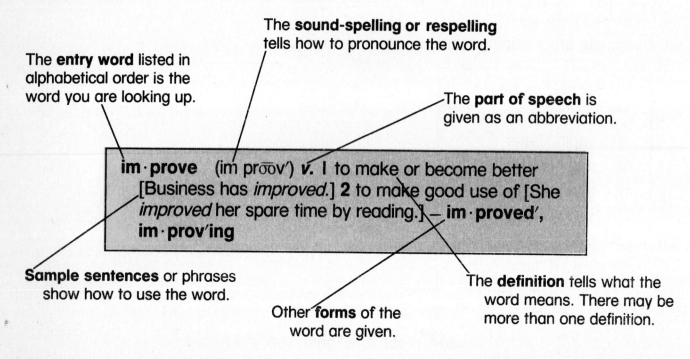

im·prove (im pr͞oov′) **v.** 1 to make or become better
[Business has *improved*.] 2 to make good use of [She
improved her spare time by reading.] — im·**proved**′,
im·**prov**′ing

Sample sentences or phrases
show how to use the word.

Other **forms** of the
word are given.

The **definition** tells what the
word means. There may be
more than one definition.

Pronunciation Key

SYMBOL	KEY WORDS	SYMBOL	KEY WORDS	SYMBOL	KEY WORDS	SYMBOL	KEY WORDS
a	ask, fat	o͡o	look, pull	b	bed, dub	t	top, hat
ā	ape, date	o͞o	ooze, tool	d	did, had	v	vat, have
ä	car, lot	ou	out, crowd	f	fall, off	w	will, always
				g	get, dog	y	yet, yard
e	elf, ten	u	up, cut	h	he, ahead	z	zebra, haze
ē	even, meet	ʉ	fur, fern	j	joy, jump		
				k	kill, bake	ch	chin, arch
i	is, hit	ə	a in ago	l	let, ball	ŋ	ring, singer
ī	ice, fire		e in agent	m	met, trim	sh	she, dash
			e in father	n	not, ton	th	thin, truth
			i in unity	p	put, tap	*th*	then, father
ō	open, go		o in collect	r	red, dear	zh	s in pleasure
ô	law, horn		u in focus	s	sell, pass		
oi	oil, point						

An Americanism is a word or usage of a word that was born in this country. An open star before an
entry word or definition means that the word or definition is an Americanism.

These dictionary entries are taken, by permission, in abridged or modified form from *Webster's New World
Dictionary*. Copyright © 1992 by Simon & Schuster Inc.

Aa

ab·sent (ab′sənt) *adj.* not present; away [No one in the class was *absent* that day.]

a·chieve (ə chēv′) *v.* 1 to do; succeed in doing; accomplish [She *achieved* a lot while she was mayor.] 2 to get or reach by trying hard; gain [He *achieved* his goal of graduating.] —**a·chieved′, a·chiev′ing**

ad·just (ə just′) *v.* 1 to change or move so as to make fit [You can *adjust* the piano bench to suit your size.] 2 to arrange the parts of to make work correctly; regulate [My watch needs *adjusting*.] 3 to settle or put in order [We *adjust* our accounts at the end of the month.]

ad·mit (ad mit′) *v.* 1 to permit or give the right to enter [One ticket *admits* two persons.] 2 to have room for [The hall *admits* 500 people.] 3 to take or accept as being true; confess [Lucy will not *admit* her mistake.] —**ad·mit′ted, ad·mit′ting**

a·dopt (ə däpt′) *v.* 1 to choose and take into one's family by a legal process [They *adopted* their daughter when she was four months old.] 2 to take and use as one's own [He *adopted* her teaching methods for his own classroom.] 3 to choose or follow [We must *adopt* a new plan of action.] —**a·dop′tion** *n.*

ad·vance (ad vans′) *v.* 1 to go or bring forward; move ahead [On first down they *advanced* the football two yards.] 2 to cause to happen earlier [The test date was *advanced* from May 10 to May 5.] —**ad·vanced′, ad·vanc′ing** ◆*n.* a moving forward or ahead; progress [new *advances* in science.]

ad·van·tage (ad van′tij) *n.* a more favorable position; better chance [My speed gave me an *advantage* over them.]

ad·ven·ture (ad ven′chər) *n.* 1 an exciting and dangerous happening [He told of his *adventures* in the jungle.] 2 an unusual experience that is remembered [Going to a circus is an *adventure* for a child.]

ad·verb (ad′vurb) *n.* a word used with a verb, adjective, or another adverb to tell when, where, how, what kind, or how much [In the sentence, "She runs fast," the word "fast" is an *adverb*.]

ad·vice (ad vīz′) *n.* opinion given as to what to do or how to do something [We followed her *advice* in selecting a new home.]

af·fec·tion (ə fek′shən) *n.* fond or tender feeling; warm liking.

af·ter (af′tər) *adv.* 1 behind; coming next [You go on ahead, and we'll follow *after*.] 2 following in time; later [They came at noon and left three hours *after*.] ◆*prep.* 1 behind [The soldiers marched one *after* the other.] 2 in search of [What are you *after*?] 3 later than [It's ten minutes *after* four.] 4 as a result of; because of [*After* what has happened, he won't go.]

air·craft (er′kraft) *n.* any machine or machines for flying [Airplanes, dirigibles, and helicopters are all *aircraft*.] —*pl.* **air′craft**

☆**air·line** (er′līn) *n.* a system or company for moving freight and passengers by aircraft.

al·low (ə lou′) *v.* 1 to let be done; permit; let [*Allow* us to pay. No smoking *allowed*.] 2 to let have [She *allows* herself no sweets.] 3 to let enter or stay [Dogs are not usually *allowed* on buses.] 4 to admit to be true or right [His claim for $50 was *allowed*.]

al·ly (al′ī) *n.* a country or person joined with another for a special purpose [England was our *ally* during World War II.] —*pl.* **al′lies**

al·pha·bet (al′fə bet) *n.* 1 the letters of a language, given in the regular order [The English *alphabet* goes from A to Z.] 2 any system of symbols used in writing [the Braille *alphabet*].

al·though (ôl thō′) *conj.* in spite of the fact that; even if; though: *sometimes spelled* **altho** [*Although* the sun is shining, it may rain later.]

al·ti·tude (al′tə tōōd *or* al′tə tyōōd) *n.* 1 height; especially, the height of a thing above the earth's surface or above sea level. 2 a high place.

a·mount (ə mount′) *v.* to add up; total [The bill *amounts* to $4.50.] ◆*n.* 1 the sum; total [The bill was $50, but he paid only half that *amount*.] 2 a quantity [a small *amount* of rain].

am·pli·fy (am′plə fī′) *v.* to make larger, stronger, louder, etc. —**am′pli·fied, am′pli·fy·ing**

an·cient (ān′chənt *or* ān′shənt) *adj.* 1 of times long past; belonging to the early history of people, before about 500 A.D. 2 having lasted a long time; very old [their *ancient* quarrel].

An·go·ra (aŋ gôr′ə) *n.* 1 a kind of cat with long, silky fur. 2 a kind of goat with long, silky hair. This hair, called **Angora wool**, is used in making mohair. 3 a long-eared rabbit (**Angora rabbit**) with long, silky hair. This hair is used to make a soft yarn which is woven into sweaters, mittens, etc.

an·gry (aŋ′grē) *adj.* 1 feeling or showing anger [*angry* words; an *angry* crowd]. 2 wild and stormy [an *angry* sea]. —**an′gri·er, an′gri·est**

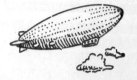

aircraft

a	ask, fat
ā	ape, date
ä	car, lot
e	elf, ten
ē	even, meet
i	is, hit
ī	ice, fire
ō	open, go
ô	law, horn
oi	oil, point
oo	look, pull
ōō	ooze, tool
ou	out, crowd
u	up, cut
ʉ	fur, fern
ə	a in ago
	e in agent
	e in father
	i in unity
	o in collect
	u in focus
ch	chin, arch
ŋ	ring, singer
sh	she, dash
th	thin, truth
th	then, father
zh	s in pleasure

an·swer (an'sər) **n. 1** something said, written, or done in return to a question, argument, letter, action, etc.; reply; response [The only *answers* required for the test were "true" or "false." His *answer* to the insult was to turn his back.] **2** a solution to a problem, as in arithmetic. ◆**v. 1** to give an answer; reply or react, as to a question or action. **2** to be responsible [You must *answer* for the children's conduct.]

Ant·arc·ti·ca (ant ärk'ti kə *or* ant är'ti kə) a large area of land, completely covered with ice, around the South Pole: *also called* **Antarctic Continent**.

an·to·nym (an'tə nim) **n.** a word opposite in meaning to another word ["Sad" is an *antonym* of "happy."]

a·part·ment (ə pärt'mənt) **n.** a group of rooms, or a single large room, to live in. It is usually a single suite in a building (called an **apartment house**) of several or many suites.

ap·pe·tiz·er (ap'ə tīz ər) **n.** a small bit of a tasty food or a drink for giving one a bigger appetite at the beginning of a meal [Olives, tomato juice, etc. are used as *appetizers*.]

ap·ply (ə plī') **v. 1** to put or spread on [*Apply* glue to the surface.] **2** to put into use [*Apply* your knowledge to this problem.] **3** to work hard and steadily [He *applied* himself to his studies.] **4** to have to do with or be suitable to [This rule *applies* to all of us.] —**ap·plied', ap·ply'ing**

ap·point (ə point') **v. 1** to fix or set; decide upon [Let's *appoint* a time for our meeting.] **2** to name or choose for an office or position [Federal judges are *appointed* by the President.]

ap·proach (ə prōch') **v. 1** to come closer or draw nearer [We saw three riders *approaching*. Vacation time *approaches*.] **2** to go to someone with a plan or request [Have you *approached* the bank about a loan?] ◆**n.** a coming closer or drawing nearer [The first robin marks the *approach* of spring.]

A·pril (ā'prəl) **n.** the fourth month of the year, which has 30 days: abbreviated **Apr.**

a·rith·me·tic (ə rith'mə tik) **n.** the science or skill of using numbers, especially in adding, subtracting, multiplying, and dividing.

Ar·i·zo·na (ər'ə zō'nə) a State in the southwestern part of the U.S.: abbreviated **Ariz., AZ**

ar·mor (är'mər) **n. 1** covering worn to protect the body against weapons [The knight's suit of *armor* was made of metal plate.] **2** any covering that protects, as the shell of a turtle or the metal plates on a warship.

astronaut

ar·my (är'mē) **n. 1** a large group of soldiers trained for war, especially on land; also, all the soldiers of a country. **2** a large group of persons organized to work for some cause [the Salvation *Army*]. **3** any large group of persons or animals [An *army* of workers was building the bridge.] —*pl.* **ar'mies**

ar·riv·al (ə rī'vəl) **n. 1** the act of arriving [to welcome the *arrival* of spring]. **2** a person or thing that has arrived [They are recent *arrivals* to the U.S. from South America.]

ar·rive (ə rīv') **v. 1** to come to a place after a journey [When does the bus from Chicago *arrive* here?] **2** to come [The time has *arrived* to say goodbye.] —**ar·rived', ar·riv'ing**

art·ist (ärt'ist) **n. 1** a person who works in any of the fine arts, especially in painting, drawing, sculpture, etc. **2** a person who does anything very well.

ash·es (ash'əz) **n.pl.** the grayish powder or fine dust that is left after something has been burned.

A·sia (ā'zhə) the largest continent, about 17,000,000 square miles in area. The Pacific Ocean is on its east and it is separated from northern Europe by the Ural Mountains.

as·tro·naut (as'trə nôt *or* as'trə nät) **n.** a person trained to make rocket flights in outer space.

as·tron·o·my (ə strän'ə mē) **n.** the science that studies the motion, size, and makeup of the stars, planets, comets, etc.

au·di·ence (ô'dē əns *or* ä'dē əns) **n. 1** a group of persons gathered together to hear and see a speaker, a play, a concert, etc. **2** all those persons who are tuned in to a radio or TV program.

aunt (ant *or* änt) **n. 1** a sister of one's mother or father. **2** the wife of one's uncle.

Aus·tral·ia (ô strāl'yə *or* ä strāl'yə) **1** an island continent in the Southern Hemisphere, southeast of Asia. **2** a country made up of this continent and Tasmania.

au·thor (ôthər *or* a'ther) **n.** a person who writes something, as a book or story [She is the *author* of many mystery stories.]

au·to·graph (ôt'ə graf) **n.** something written in a person's own handwriting, especially that person's name. ◆**v.** to write one's name on [Please *autograph* this baseball.]

au·to·mat·ic (ôt'ə mat'ik *or* ät'ə mat'ik) **adj. 1** done without thinking about it, as if mechanically or from force of habit; unconscious [Breathing is usually *automatic*.] **2** moving or working by itself [*automatic* machinery].

a·vi·a·tor (ā'vē āt'ər) **n.** a person who flies airplanes; pilot.

a·while (ə hwīl' *or* ə wīl') **adv.** for a while; for a short time [Sit down and rest *awhile*.]

awk·ward (ôk′wərd *or* äk′wərd) *adj.* **1** not having grace or skill; clumsy; bungling [an *awkward* dancer; an *awkward* writing style] . **2** hard to use or manage; not convenient [an *awkward* tool]. **3** uncomfortable; cramped [sitting in an *awkward* position]. **4** embarrassed or embarrassing [an *awkward* remark]. —**awk′ward·ly** *adv.* —**awk′ward·ness** *n.*

ax or **axe** (aks) *n.* a tool for chopping or splitting wood. It has a long wooden handle and a metal head with a sharp blade. —*pl.* **ax′es**

bag·gage (bag′ij) *n.* the trunks, suitcases, etc. that a person takes on a trip; luggage.

bait (bāt) *n.* **1** food put on a hook or trap to attract and catch fish or animals. **2** anything used to tempt or attract a person. ◆*v.* **1** to put bait on a hook or trap. **2** to torment or tease by saying annoying or cruel things [They *baited* me by calling me "Fatty."]

bal·co·ny (bal′kə nē) *n.* **1** a platform with a low wall or railing, that juts out from the side of a building. **2** an upper floor of rows of seats, as in a theater. It often juts out over the main floor. —*pl.* **bal′co·nies**

bal·lot (bal′ət) *n.* **1** a piece of paper on which a person marks a choice in voting. **2** the act or a way of voting.

band·age (ban′dij) *n.* a strip of cloth, gauze, etc. used to cover a sore or wound or to bind up an injured part of the body. ◆*v.* to bind or cover with a bandage. —**band′aged, band′ag·ing**

☆**ban·jo** (ban′jō) *n.* a stringed musical instrument with a long neck and a round body covered on top with tightly stretched skins. It has, usually, four or five strings that are plucked with the fingers or a pick. —*pl.* **ban′jos or ban′joes**

ban·ner (ban′ər) *n.* **1** a piece of cloth with an emblem or words on it [The *banner* behind the President's desk bears the seal of the U.S.] **2** a flag [the Star-Spangled *Banner*]. **3** a headline across a newspaper page. ◆*adj.* top; leading [Our company had a *banner* year in sales.]

barge (bärj) *n.* a large boat with a flat bottom, for carrying goods on rivers or canals. ◆*v.* to enter in a clumsy or rude way [They *barged* in without knocking.] —**barged, barg′ing**

ba·rom·e·ter (bə räm′ə tər) *n.* **1** an instrument that measures the pressure of the air around us. It is used in forecasting changes in the weather and finding the height above sea level. **2** anything that shows changes in conditions [The stock market is a *barometer* of business.] —**bar·o·met·ric** (bar′ə met′rik) *adj.*

bar·rel (bar′əl) *n.* **1** a large, round container that has bulging sides and a flat top and bottom. It is usually made of wooden slats bound together by metal hoops. **2** the amount a barrel will hold: the standard barrel in the U.S. holds 31 1/2 gallons (119.2275 liters). ◆*v.* to put in barrels. —**bar′reled** or **bar′relled, bar′rel·ing** or **bar′rel·ling**

bask (bask) *v.* to warm oneself pleasantly [to *bask* in the sun].

bass (bas) *n.* a fish with spiny fins, found in both fresh and salt water and used for food. —*pl.* **bass** or **bass′es**

bat·ter·y (bat′ər ē) *n.* an electric cell or a group of connected cells that furnishes an electric current [*Batteries* are used in automobiles and flashlights.] —*pl.* **bat′ter·ies**

be·gin (bē gin′) *v.* to start being, doing, acting, etc.; get under way [Work *begins* at 8:00 A.M. My cold *began* with a sore throat.] —**be·gan′, be·gun′, be·gin′ning**

be·gin·ning (bē gin′iŋ) *n.* a start or starting; first part or first action [We came in just after the *beginning* of the movie. Going to the dance together was the *beginning* of our friendship.]

be·lief (bē lēf′) *n.* a feeling that something is true or real; faith [You cannot destroy my *belief* in the honesty of most people.] —*pl.* **be·liefs**

be·lieve (bē lēv′) *v.* **1** to accept as true or real [Can we *believe* that story?] **2** to have trust or confidence [I know you will win; I *believe* in you.] **3** to suppose; guess. —**be·lieved′, be·liev′ing** —**be·liev′a·ble** *adj.* —**be·liev′er** *n.*

bench (bench) *n.* **1** a long, hard seat for several persons, with or without a back. **2** a strong table on which work with tools is done [a carpenter's *bench*]. **3** the place where judges sit in a courtroom. **4** a seat where sports players sit when not on the field. —*pl.* **bench′es**

bend (bend) *v.* **1** to pull or press something hard or stiff into a curve or angle [*Bend* the branch down so we can reach the plums.] **2** to be curved in this way [The trees *bent* under the weight of the snow.] **3** to stoop [*Bend* over and touch your toes.] —**bent, bend′ing** ◆*n.* **1** the act of bending. **2** a bent or curving part.

banjo

a	ask, fat
ā	ape, date
ä	car, lot
e	elf, ten
ē	even, meet
i	is, hit
ī	ice, fire
ō	open, go
ô	law, horn
oi	oil, point
oo	look, pull
o͞o	ooze, tool
ou	out, crowd
u	up, cut
ʉ	fur, fern
ə	a in ago
	e in agent
	e in father
	i in unity
	o in collect
	u in focus
ch	chin, arch
ŋ	ring, singer
sh	she, dash
th	thin, truth
th	then, father
zh	s in pleasure

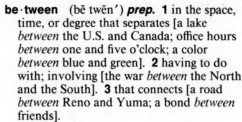

be·tween (bē twēn′) *prep.* **1** in the space, time, or degree that separates [a lake *between* the U.S. and Canada; office hours *between* one and five o'clock; a color *between* blue and green]. **2** having to do with; involving [the war *between* the North and the South]. **3** that connects [a road *between* Reno and Yuma; a bond *between* friends].

bev·er·age (bev′ər ij *or* bev′rij) *n.* any kind of drink (except water), as milk, coffee, or lemonade.

bi·cy·cle (bī′si kəl) *n.* a vehicle to ride on that has two wheels, one behind the other. It is moved by foot pedals and steered by a handlebar. ◆*v.* to ride a bicycle. —**bi′cy·cled, bi′cy·cling**

birth·day (burth′dā) *n.* **1** the day on which a person is born or something is begun. **2** the anniversary of this day.

bi·son (bī′sən) *n.* a wild animal of the ox family, with a shaggy mane, short, curved horns, and a humped back. The American bison is often called a *buffalo*. —*pl.* **bi′son**

blend (blend) *v.* **1** to mix different kinds together in order to get a certain flavor, color, etc. [to *blend* tea or paint]. **2** to come together or mix so that the parts are no longer distinct [The sky *blended* with the sea at the horizon.] **3** to go well together; be in harmony [Her blue sweater *blends* well with her gray skirt.] ◆*n.* a mixture of different kinds [a *blend* of coffee].

☆**bliz·zard** (bliz′ərd) *n.* a heavy snowstorm with very strong, cold winds.

board (bôrd) *n.* **1** a long, flat, broad piece of sawed wood, used in building. **2** a flat piece of wood or other hard material made for a special use [a checker*board*; a bulletin *board*; an ironing *board*]. **3** a group of people who manage or control a business, school, department, etc. [*board* of education]. ◆*v.* **1** to cover up with boards [The windows of the old house were *boarded* up.] **2** to get on a ship, airplane, bus, etc.

boast (bōst) *v.* **1** to talk about with too much pride and pleasure; praise too highly; brag [We tired of hearing him *boast* of his bravery.] **2** to be proud of having [Our city *boasts* a fine new zoo.]

bob (bäb) *v.* **1** to move with short, jerky motions [Our heads *bobbed* up and down as our car bounced over the ruts.] **2** to cut off short [to *bob* a dog's tail]. —**bobbed, bob′bing** ◆*n.* **1** a short, jerky movement [She greeted us with a *bob* of her head.] **2** a style of short haircut for women or girls. **3** a hanging weight at the end of a plumb line. **4** a cork on a fishing line.

bison

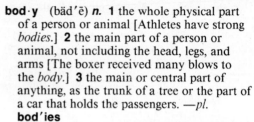

bod·y (bäd′ē) *n.* **1** the whole physical part of a person or animal [Athletes have strong *bodies*.] **2** the main part of a person or animal, not including the head, legs, and arms [The boxer received many blows to the *body*.] **3** the main or central part of anything, as the trunk of a tree or the part of a car that holds the passengers. —*pl.* **bod′ies**

boil (boil) *v.* **1** to bubble up and become steam or vapor by being heated [Water *boils* at 100°C.] **2** to heat a liquid until it bubbles up in this way [to *boil* water]. **3** to cook in a boiling liquid [to *boil* potatoes]. **4** to be stirred up, as with rage. ◆*n.* the condition of boiling [Bring the soup to a *boil*.]

bomb (bäm) *n.* a hollow case filled with an explosive or a poisonous gas: bombs are blown up by a fuse or timing device or by being dropped or thrown against something with force.

☆**boss** (bôs *or* bäs) *n.* **1** a person who is in charge of workers, as an employer, a manager, or a foreman. **2** a person who controls a political group, as in a county. —*pl.* **bosses.** ◆*v.* to act as boss of.

both·er (bä*th*′ər) *v.* **1** to annoy; cause worry or trouble to; pester [Does the noise *bother* you?] **2** to take the time or trouble [Don't *bother* to answer this letter.] ◆*n.* something that annoys or causes worry or trouble [Flies are a *bother*.]

bot·tle (bät′l) *n.* **1** a container, especially for liquids, usually made of glass or plastic. Bottles generally have a narrow neck and no handles. **2** the amount that a bottle holds [The baby drank a *bottle* of milk.] ◆*v.* **1** to put into a bottle or into bottles. **2** to store under pressure in a tank [*bottled* gas]. —**bot′tled, bot′tling**

bounce (bouns) *v.* **1** to hit against a surface so as to spring back; bound or rebound [to *bounce* a ball against a wall; to *bounce* up and down on a sofa]. **2** to move suddenly; jump; leap [I *bounced* out of bed when the alarm went off.] —**bounced, bounc′ing** ◆*n.* **1** a springing or bounding; leap. **2** the ability to bound or rebound [This ball has lost its *bounce*.]

bounc·ing (boun′siŋ) *adj.* big, healthy, strong, etc. [It's a *bouncing* baby boy.]

bou·quet (boo kā′ *or* bō kā′) *n.* **1** a bunch of flowers. **2** (boo kā′) a fragrant smell.

☆**box·car** (bäks′kär) *n.* a railroad car for carrying freight, with a roof and closed sides.

brain (brān) *n.* **1** the gray and white tissue inside the skull of a person or of any animal with a backbone. It is the main part of the nervous system, by which one thinks and feels. **2** *often* **brains**, *pl.* intelligence; understanding.

brake (brāk) *n.* a device used to slow down or stop a car, machine, etc. It is often a block or band that is pressed against a wheel or other moving part. ◆*v.* to slow down or stop with a brake. —**braked, brak′ing**

branch (branch) *n.* any part of a tree growing from the trunk or from a main limb.

break (brāk) *v.* **1** to come or make come apart by force; split or crack sharply into pieces [*Break* an egg into the bowl. The rusty hinge *broke*.] **2** to force one's way [A firefighter *broke* through the door.] **3** to get out of working order; make or become useless [You can *break* your watch by winding it too tightly.] **4** to fail to carry out or follow [to *break* an agreement; to *break* the law] —**broke, bro′ken, break′ing** ◆*n.* **1** a broken place [The X-ray showed a *break* in the bone.] **2** an interruption [Recess is a relaxing *break* in our school day.]

break·down (brāk′doun) *n.* a failure to work properly [*breakdown* of a machine].

break·fast (brek′fəst) *n.* the first meal of the day. ◆*v.* to eat breakfast.

breeze (brēz) *n.* **1** a light and gentle wind. **2** a thing easy to do: *used only in everyday talk* [The test was a *breeze*.] ◆*v.* to move or go quickly, briskly, etc.: *slang in this meaning.* —**breezed, breez′ing**

brief (brēf) *adj.* **1** not lasting very long; short in time [a *brief* visit]. **2** using just a few words; not wordy; concise [a *brief* news report]. ◆*v.* to give the main points or necessary facts to [to *brief* pilots before a flight]. —**brief′ly** *adv.* —**brief′ness** *n.*

bril·liant (bril′yənt) *adj.* **1** very bright; glittering or sparkling [the *brilliant* sun on the water]. **2** outstanding or distinguished [a *brilliant* performance]

bring (briŋ) *v.* **1** to carry or lead here or to the place where the speaker will be [*Bring* it to my house tomorrow.] **2** to cause to happen or come [War *brings* death and hunger.]

broc·co·li (bräk′ə lē) *n.* a plant whose tender shoots and loose heads of tiny green buds are eaten as a vegetable.

broil (broil) *v.* **1** to cook or be cooked close to a flame or other high heat [to *broil* steaks over charcoal]. **2** to make or be very hot [a *broiling* summer day]. ◆*n.* the act or state of broiling.

broth·er (bru*th*′ər) *n.* **1** a boy or man as he is related to the other children of his parents. **2** a person who is close to one in some way; especially, a fellow member of the same race, religion, club, etc. —*pl.* **broth′ers**

brought (brôt *or* brät) *past tense and past participle of* **bring**.

buf·fa·lo (buf′ə lō) *n.* a wild ox, sometimes tamed as a work animal, as the water buffalo of India. The American bison is also commonly called a *buffalo.* —*pl.* **buf′fa·loes** *or* **buf′fa·los** *or* **buf′fa·lo**

bump (bump) *v.* **1** to knock against something; hit with a jolt [The bus *bumped* the car ahead of it. Don't *bump* into the wall.] **2** to move with jerks or jumps; jolt [The car *bumped* over the railroad tracks.] ◆*n.* **1** a knock or blow; light jolt. **2** a part that bulges out, causing an uneven surface. **3** a swelling caused by a blow.

bur·y (ber′ē) *v.* **1** to put a dead body into the earth, a tomb, or the sea [The Egyptians *buried* the Pharaohs in pyramids.] **2** to cover up so as to hide [He *buried* his face in his hands.] **3** to put away and forget [Let's *bury* our feud.] **4** to put oneself deeply into [She *buried* herself in her work.] —**bur′ies, bur′ied, bur′y·ing**

busi·ness (biz′nəs) *n.* **1** what one does for a living; one's work or occupation [Shakespeare's *business* was writing plays.] **2** what one has a right or duty to do [You had no *businesses* telling her I was here.] **3** the buying and selling of goods and services; commerce; trade. **4** a place where things are made or sold; store or factory [Nino owns three *businesses*.]—*pl.* **bus′i·ness·es**

but·ter·milk (but′ər milk) *n.* the sour liquid left after churning butter from milk.

buy (bī) *v.* to get by paying money or something else [The Dutch *bought* Manhattan Island for about $24.] —**bought, buy′ing**

byte (bīt) *n.* a series of computer bits, usually eight, used as a single piece of information.

Cc

cab·in (kab′in) *n.* **1** a small house built in a simple, rough way, usually of wood [Lincoln was born in a log *cabin*.] **2** a room on a ship, especially one with berths for sleeping. **3** the space in an airplane where the passengers ride.

ca·boose (kə bō͞os′) *n.* ☆a car for the crew on a freight train. It is usually the last car.

cac·tus (kak′təs) *n.* a plant with fleshy stems that bear spines or scales instead of leaves. Cactuses grow in hot, dry places and often have showy flowers. —*pl.* **cac′tus·es** *or* **cac·ti** (kak′tī)

cal·cu·la·tor (kal′kyoo lāt′ər) *n.* **1** a person who calculates. **2** a machine that adds, subtracts, etc. rapidly, now often by electronic means.

calf¹ (kaf) *n.* **1** a young cow or bull. **2** a young elephant, whale, hippopotamus, seal, etc. **3** *a shorter word for* **calfskin**. —*pl.* **calves**

cactus

a	ask, fat
ā	ape, date
ä	car, lot
e	elf, ten
ē	even, meet
i	is, hit
ī	ice, fire
ō	open, go
ô	law, horn
oi	oil, point
o͝o	look, pull
o͞o	ooze, tool
ou	out, crowd
u	up, cut
ʉ	fur, fern
ə	a in ago
	e in agent
	e in father
	i in unity
	o in collect
	u in focus
ch	chin, arch
ŋ	ring, singer
sh	she, dash
th	thin, truth
th	then, father
zh	s in pleasure

calf² (kaf) *n.* the fleshy back part of the leg between the knee and the ankle. —*pl.* **calves**

cam·el (kam′əl) *n.* a large, cud-chewing animal with a humped back, that is commonly used for riding and for carrying goods in Asian and North African deserts. When food and drink are scarce, it can keep going for a few days on the fat and water stored in its body tissue. The **Arabian camel** has one hump and the **Bac·tri·an** (bak′trē ən) **camel** has two.

can·di·date (kan′di dāt′) *n.* a person who seeks, or who has been suggested for, an office or award [a *candidate* for mayor].

car·di·nal (kärd′n əl) *adj.* **1** of most importance; chief [The *cardinal* points of the compass are north, south, east, and west.] **2** bright-red. ◆*n.* ☆ an American songbird that is bright red and has a black face.

car·go (kär′gō) *n.* the load of goods carried by a ship, airplane, truck, etc. —*pl.* **car′goes** or **car′gos**

car·ry (ker′ē) *v.* **1** to take from one place to another; transport or conduct [Please help me *carry* these books home. The large pipe *carries* water. Air *carries* sounds.] **2** to cause to go; lead [A love of travel *carried* them around the world.] **3** to bring over a figure from one column to the next in adding a row of figures. —**car′ried, car′ry·ing**

car·ton (kärt′n) *n.* a box or other container made of cardboard, plastic, etc.

cast (kast) *v.* **1** to throw out or down; toss; fling; hurl [to *cast* stones into the water; to *cast* a line in fishing]. **2** to deposit a ballot or vote. ◆*n.* a stiff plaster form for keeping a broken arm or leg in place while it is healing. —**cast, cast′ing**

catch·er (kach′ər *or* kech′ər) *n.* **1** one who catches. ☆**2** in baseball, the player behind home plate, who catches pitched balls that are not hit away by the batter.

camel

cat·e·go·ry (kat′ə gôr′ē) *n.* a division of a main subject or group; class [Biology is divided into two *categories*, zoology and botany.] —*pl.* **cat′e·go′ries**

cause (kôz *or* käz) *n.* **1** a person or thing that brings about some action or result [A spark from the wire was the *cause* of the fire.] **2** a reason for some action, feeling, etc. [We had *cause* to admire the coach.] ◆*v.* to be the cause of; make happen; bring about [The icy streets *caused* some accidents.] —**caused, caus′ing** —**cause′less adj.**

cau·tious (kô′shəs *or* kä′shəs) *adj.* careful not to get into danger or make mistakes [a *cautious* chess player]. —**cau′tious·ly adv.**

ceil·ing (sēl′iŋ) *n.* the inside top part of a room, opposite the floor.

cel·e·ry (sel′ər ē) *n.* a plant whose crisp, long stalks are eaten as a vegetable.

ce·ment (sə ment′) *n.* **1** a powder made of lime and clay, mixed with water and sand to make mortar or with water, sand, and gravel to make concrete. It hardens like stone when it dries. **2** any soft substance that fastens things together when it hardens, as paste or glue ◆*v.* to fasten together or cover with cement [to *cement* the pieces of a broken cup].

cen·ter (sen′tər) *n.* **1** a point inside a circle or sphere that is the same distance from all points on the circumference or surface. **2** the middle point or part; place at the middle [A vase of flowers stood at the *center* of the table.] ◆*v.* to place in or at the center [Try to *center* the design on the page.]

chain (chān) *n.* **1** a number of links or loops joined together in a line that can be bent [a *chain* of steel; a *chain* of daisies]. **2 chains**, *pl.* anything that binds or holds someone prisoner, as bonds or shackles. **3** a series of things joined together [a mountain *chain*; a *chain* of events]. ◆*v.* **1** to fasten or bind with chains [The prisoner was *chained* to the wall.] **2** to hold down; bind [I was *chained* to my job.]

cham·pi·on (cham′pē ən) *n.* a person, animal, or thing that wins first place or is judged to be best in a contest or sport [a tennis *champion*].

change (chānj) *v.* **1** to make or become different in some way; alter [Time *changes* all things. His voice began to *change* at the age of thirteen.] **2** to put or take one thing in place of another; substitute [to *change* one's clothes; to *change* jobs]. **3** to give or take one thing in return for another; substitute [Let's *change* seats. Can you *change* this dollar bill for four quarters?] —**changed, chang′ing** ◆*n.* **1** the act of changing in some way [There will be a *change* in the weather tomorrow.] **2** something put in place of something else [a fresh *change* of clothing]. **3** the money returned when one has paid more than the amount owed [If it costs 70 cents and you pay with a dollar, you get back 30 cents as *change*.]

charge (chärj) *v.* **1** to load or fill [to *charge* a gun with ammunition]. ☆**2** to supply with electrical energy [to *charge* a battery]. **3** to give a task, duty, etc. to; make responsible for [The nurse was *charged* with the care of the child.] **4** to set as a price; ask for payment [Barbers once *charged* a quarter for a haircut. We do not *charge* for gift wrappings.] —**charged, charg′ing**

chat (chat) *v.* to talk in an easy, relaxed way. —**chat′ted, chat′ting** ◆*n.* an easy, relaxed talk or conversation.

cheat (chēt) *v.* to act in a dishonest or unfair way in order to get what one wants [to *cheat* on a test].

check (chek) *n.* **1** a test to find out if something is as it should be [Add the column of numbers again as a *check* on your answer.] **2** the mark ✓, used to show that something is right, or to call attention to something. **3** a piece of paper telling how much one owes, as for a meal at a restaurant. **4** a written order to a bank to pay a certain amount of money from one's account to a certain person. **5** a pattern of small squares like a checkerboard; also, any of the squares in such a pattern. ◆*v.* to prove to be right or find what is wanted by examining, comparing, etc. [These figures *check* with mine. *Check* the records for this information.]

cheer·ful (chir′fəl) *adj.* **1** full of cheer; glad; joyful [a *cheerful* smile]. **2** bright and gay [a *cheerful* room]. **3** willing; glad to help [a *cheerful* worker]. —**cheer′ful·ly** *adv.* —**cheer′ful·ness** *n.*

chee·tah (chēt′ə) *n.* an animal found in Africa and southern Asia that is like the leopard but smaller. It can be trained to hunt.

cher·ry (cher′ē) *n.* **1** a small, round fruit with sweet flesh covering a smooth, hard seed. Cherries are bright red, dark red, or yellow. **2** the tree that this fruit grows on. **3** bright red. —*pl.* **cher′ries**

Chi·ca·go (shi kä′gō) a city in northeastern Illinois, on Lake Michigan.

chick·en (chik′ən) *n.* **1** a common farm bird raised for its eggs and flesh; hen or rooster, especially a young one. **2** the flesh of a chicken.

chief (chēf) *n.* the leader or head of some group [an Indian *chief*; the *chief* of a hospital staff]. —*pl.* **chiefs** ◆*adj.* **1** having the highest position [the *chief* foreman]. **2** main; most important [Jill's *chief* interest is golf.]

chief·ly (chēf′lē) *adv.* most of all; mainly; mostly [A watermelon is *chiefly* water.]

child (chīld) *n.* **1** a baby; infant. **2** a young boy or girl. **3** a son or daughter [Their *children* are all grown up.] —*pl.* **chil′dren**

chil·dren (chil′drən) *n. plural of* **child**.

chim·ney (chim′nē) *n.* **1** a pipe or shaft going up through a roof to carry off smoke from a furnace, fireplace, or stove. Chimneys are usually enclosed with brick or stone. **2** a glass tube around the flame of a lamp. —*pl.* **chim′neys**

Chi·na (chī′nə) a country in eastern Asia. It has the most people of any country in the world.

☆**chow·der** (chou′dər) *n.* a thick soup made of fish or clams with onions, potatoes, milk or tomatoes, etc.

church (church) *n.* **1** a building for holding religious services, especially one for Christian worship. **2** religious services [*Church* will be at 11 on Sunday.]—*pl.* **church′es**

cir·cle (sur′kəl) *n.* **1** a closed curved line forming a perfectly round, flat figure. Every point on this line is the same distance from a point inside called the center. **2** the figure formed by such a line. **3** anything round like a circle or ring [a *circle* of children playing a game].

clap (klap) *v.* **1** to make the sudden, loud sound of two flat surfaces being struck together **2** to strike the palms of the hands together, as in applauding. —**clapped, clap′ping** ◆*n.* **1** the sudden, loud sound of clapping [a *clap* of thunder]. **2** a sharp blow; slap.

clash (klash) *n.* **1** a loud, harsh noise, as of metal striking against metal with great force [the *clash* of a sword on a shield]. **2** a sharp disagreement; conflict [a *clash* of ideas]. —*pl.* **clash′es** ◆*v.* to strike with a clash [He *clashed* the cymbals together.]

clasp (klasp) *n.* **1** a fastening, as a hook or catch, for holding two things or parts together [The *clasp* on my pocketbook is loose.] **2** a holding in the arms; embrace. **3** a holding with the hand; grip. ◆*v.* to fasten with a clasp.

class (klas) a group of students meeting together to be taught [Half the *class* missed school today.] —*pl.* **clas·ses**

claw (klô *or* klä) *n.* **1** a sharp, curved nail on the foot of an animal or bird. **2** a foot with such nails [The eagle holds its victims in its *claws*.] **3** the grasping part on each front leg of a lobster, crab, or scorpion.

clean (klēn) *adj.* **1** without dirt or impure matter [*clean* dishes; *clean* oil]. **2** without evil or wrongdoing [to lead a *clean* life]. **3** neat and tidy [to keep a *clean* desk]. ◆*v.* to make clean. [Please *clean* the oven.]

clerk (klurk) *n.* **1** an office worker who keeps records, types letters, etc. [Some *clerks*, as a *clerk* of courts or a city *clerk*, have special duties.] ☆**2** a person who sells in a store; salesperson.

Cleve·land (klēv′lənd) a city in northeastern Ohio.

cli·mate (klī′mət) *n.* **1** the average weather conditions of a place over a period of years [Arizona has a mild, dry *climate*, but its weather last week was stormy.] **2** a region with particular weather conditions [They went south to a warmer *climate*.]

clo·ver (klō′vər) *n.* a low-growing plant with leaves in three parts and small, sweet-smelling flowers. *Red clover* is grown for fodder; *white clover* is often found in lawns.

clue (klōō) *n.* a fact or thing that helps to solve a puzzle or mystery [Muddy footprints were a *clue* to the man's guilt.]

clum·sy (klum′zē) *adj.* not having good control in moving the hands or feet; awkward [The *clumsy* waiter dropped the dish.] —**clum′si·er, clum′si·est**

cheetah

a	ask, fat
ā	ape, date
ä	car, lot
e	elf, ten
ē	even, meet
i	is, hit
ī	ice, fire
ō	open, go
ô	law, horn
oi	oil, point
σο	look, pull
ōο	ooze, tool
ou	out, crowd
u	up, cut
u	fur, fern
ə	a in ago
	e in agent
	e in father
	i in unity
	o in collect
	u in focus
ch	chin, arch
ŋ	ring, singer
sh	she, dash
th	thin, truth
th	then, father
zh	s in pleasure

cock·pit (käk′pit) *n.* in a small airplane, the space where the pilot and passengers sit. In a large plane, it is the space for the pilot and copilot.

col·an·der (kul′ən dər *or* käl′ən dər) *n.* a pan with holes in the bottom for draining off liquids, as in washing vegetables.

cold (kōld) *adj.* **1** having a temperature much lower than that of the human body; very chilly; frigid [a *cold* day; a *cold* drink]. **2** without the proper heat or warmth [Your bath will get *cold*.] **3** feeling chilled [If you are *cold*, put on your coat.] **4** without any feeling; unkind, unfriendly, or gloomy [a *cold* welcome; a *cold* stare]. **—cold′er, cold′est**

colander

col·lege (käl′ij) *n.* a school that one can go to after high school for higher studies.

Co·lum·bus (kə lum′bəs) the capital of Ohio.

comb (kōm) *n.* a thin strip of hard rubber, plastic, metal, etc. with teeth. A comb is passed through the hair to arrange or clean it, or is put in the hair to hold it in place. ◆*v.* **1** to smooth, arrange, or clean with a comb. **2** to search carefully through [I *combed* the house for that book.]

come (kum) *v.* **1** to move from "there" to "here" [*Come* to me. Will you *come* to our party?] **2** to arrive or appear [Help will *come* soon.] **—came, come, com′ing**

com·ing (kum′iŋ) *adj.* that will come; approaching; on the way [Let's go this *coming* Friday.] ◆*n.* arrival; approach [Cold mornings warn of the *coming* of winter.]

com·mon (käm′ən) *adj.* **1** belonging equally to each or all [England, Canada, and the U.S. share a *common* language.] **2** belonging to all the people; public [a *common* park]. **3** of, from, by, or to all [the *common* good]. **4** often seen or heard; widespread; usual [Squirrels are *common* in these woods. That's a *common* saying.]

com·mu·ni·ty (kə myoo′ni tē) *n.* **1** all the people who live in a particular district, city, etc. [The new swimming pool is for the use of the entire *community*.] **2** a group of people living together and having similar interests and work [a college *community*]. **—pl. com·mu′ni·ties**

☆**com·mut·er** (kə myoot′ər) *n.* a person who travels daily by train, bus, car, etc. between home and work or school.

constellation

com·pare (kəm per′) *v.* **1** to describe as being the same; liken [The sound of thunder can be *compared* to the roll of drums.] **2** to examine certain things in order to find out how they are alike or different [How do the two cars *compare* in size and price?] **3** to equal or come close to by comparison [Few dogs can *compare* with the Great Dane in size.] **—com·pared′, com·par′ing**

com·put·er (kəm pyoot′ər) *n.* **1** a person who computes. **2** an electronic device used as a calculator or to store and select data.

con·duct (kän′dukt) *n.* the way one acts or behaves; behavior [The teacher praised the students for their good *conduct* in class.] ◆*v.* (kən dukt′) **1** to manage; direct; be the leader of [to *conduct* a meeting; to *conduct* an orchestra]. **2** to behave [They *conducted* themselves like adults.] **3** to be a means for carrying; transmit [Copper *conducts* electricity.]

cone (kōn) *n.* a solid object that narrows evenly from a flat circle at one end to a point at the other.

con·stel·la·tion (kän′stə lā′shən) *n.* a group of stars, usually named after something that it is supposed to suggest [Orion is a *constellation* seen in the winter sky.]

con·struct (kən strukt′) *v.* to make or build with a plan [to *construct* a house or a theory].

con·tact (kän′takt) *v.* to get in touch with; communicate with [*Contact* my cousin as soon as possible.]

con·test (kən test′) *v.* **1** to try to prove that something is not true, right, or lawful; dispute [to *contest* a will]. **2** to fight for; struggle to win or keep [to *contest* a prize]. ◆*n.* (kän′test) **1** a fight, struggle, or argument. **2** a race, game, etc. in which there is a struggle to be the winner.

con·ti·nent (kän′ti nənt) *n.* any of the main large land areas of the earth. The continents are Africa, Asia, Australia, Europe, North America, South America, and, sometimes, Antarctica. **—the Continent,** all of Europe except the British Isles.

con·tin·ue (kən tin′yoo) *v.* **1** to keep on being or doing [The rain *continued* for five days.] **2** to stay in the same place or position [The chairman will *continue* in office for another year.] **3** to go on or start again after a stop; resume [After a sip of water, the speaker *continued*.] **4** to go on or extend; stretch **—con·tin′ued, con·tin′u·ing**

con·trol (kən trōl′) *v.* **1** to have the power of ruling, guiding, or managing [A thermostat *controls* the heat.] **2** to hold back; curb [*Control* your temper!] **—con·trolled′, con·trol′ling** ◆*n.* power to direct or manage [He's a poor coach, with little *control* over the team.]

con·vince (kən vins′) *v.* to make feel sure; persuade [I'm *convinced* they are telling the truth.] **—con·vinced′, con·vinc′ing**

con·voy (kän′voi) *n.* a group of ships or vehicles traveling together in order to protect one another.

cop·y (käp′ē) *n.* **1** a thing made just like another; imitation or likeness [four carbon *copies* of a letter]. **2** any one of a number of books, magazines, pictures, etc. with the same printed matter [a library with six *copies* of *Tom Sawyer*]. **3** a piece of writing that is to be set in type for printing [Reporters must write clear *copy*.] —*pl.* **cop′ies** ◆*v.* **1** to make a copy or copies of [*Copy* the questions that are on the chalkboard.] **2** to act or be the same as; imitate. —**cop′ied, cop′y·ing**

cor·al (kôr′əl) *n.* **1** a hard, stony substance made up of the skeletons of many tiny sea animals. Reefs of coral are found in tropical seas. **2** a piece of coral. ◆*adj.* **1** made of coral. **2** yellowish-red in color.

cor·ner (kôr′nər) *n.* **1** the place where two lines or surfaces come together to form an angle. **2** the space between such lines or surfaces [a lamp in the *corner* of a room]. **3** the place where two streets meet. **4** a place or region; quarter [every *corner* of America].

cos·tume (käs′tŏŏm *or* käs′tyŏŏm) *n.* **1** the way or style of dressing of a certain place or time or for a certain purpose [a Japanese *costume*; an eighteenth-century *costume*; a riding *costume*]. **2** clothing worn by an actor in a play or by a person at a masquerade [a pirate *costume*].

cot·tage (kät′ij) *n.* a small house [a peasant's *cottage*; a summer *cottage* at the beach].

cou·gar (kŏŏ′gər) *n.* a large animal of the cat family, with a slender, tan body and a long tail.

cough (kôf *or* käf) *v.* **1** to force air from the lungs with a sudden, loud noise, as to clear the throat. **2** to get out of the throat by coughing [to *cough* up phlegm]. ◆*n.* **1** the act or sound of coughing. **2** a condition of coughing often [I have a bad *cough*.]

coun·ty (koun′tē) *n.* ☆**1** in the U.S., any of the sections into which a State is divided. Each county has its own officials. **2** any of the districts into which Great Britain and Ireland are divided. —*pl.* **coun′ties**

cou·ple (kup′əl) *n.* two things of the same kind that go together; pair [a *couple* of bookends].

cour·age (kur′ij) *n.* the quality of being able to control one's fear and so to face danger, pain, or trouble willingly; bravery.

cous·in (kuz′ən) *n.* **1** the son or daughter of one's uncle or aunt: *also called* **first cousin.** You are a *second cousin* to the children of your parents' first cousins, and you are a *first cousin once removed* to the children of your first cousins. **2** a distant relation.

crack (krak) *v.* **1** to make or cause to make a sudden, sharp noise, as of something breaking [The lion tamer *cracked* his whip.] **2** to break or split, with or without the parts falling apart [The snowball *cracked* the window. *Crack* the coconut open.] **3** to become harsh or change pitch suddenly [Her voice *cracked* when she sang the highest note.]

craft (kraft) *n.* **1** special skill or ability. **2** work that takes special skill, especially with the hands [the *craft* of weaving]. **3** the members of a skilled trade. **4** skill in fooling or tricking others; slyness.

crash (krash) *v.* **1** to fall, hit, or break with force and with a loud, smashing noise. **2** to fall to the earth so as to be damaged or smashed [The airplane *crashed*.] ◆*n.* **1** a loud, smashing noise. **2** the crashing of a car, airplane, etc.

cray·on (krā′ən *or* krā′än) *n.* a small stick of chalk, charcoal, or colored wax, used for drawing or writing. ◆*v.* to draw with crayons.

cra·zy (krā′zē) *adj.* mentally ill; insane. —**cra′zi·er, cra′zi·est**

cream (krēm) *n.* **1** the oily, yellowish part of milk that rises to the top and contains the butterfat. **2** any food that is made of cream or is like cream [ice *cream*]. **3** a smooth, oily substance used to clean and soften the skin.

creep (krēp) *v.* **1** to move along with the body close to the ground, as a baby on hands and knees. **2** to move in a slow or sneaking way [The cars *crept* along in the heavy traffic. The thieves *crept* into the store at night.] **3** to come on almost without being noticed [Old age *crept* up on her.] —**crept, creeping**

crept (krept) *v.* *past tense and past participle of* **creep.**

cries (krīz) **1** *the form of the verb* **cry** *used in the present with* he, she, *or* it. **2** *the plural of the noun* **cry.**

crime (krīm) *n.* **1** the doing of something that is against the law; serious wrongdoing that breaks the law. **2** an evil or foolish act; sin [It would be a *crime* to waste this food.]

cruise (krŏŏz) *v.* **1** to sail or drive about from place to place, as for pleasure or in searching for something. **2** to move smoothly at a speed that is not strained [The airplane *cruised* at 300 miles per hour.] —**cruised, cruis′ing** ◆*n.* a ship voyage from place to place for pleasure.

crumb (krum) *n.* **1** a tiny piece broken off, as of bread or cake. **2** any bit or scrap [*crumbs* of knowledge].

crunch (krunch) *v.* **1** to chew with a noisy, crackling sound [to *crunch* raw carrots]. **2** to grind or move over with a noisy, crushing sound [The wheels *crunched* the pebbles in the driveway.]

costume

a	ask, fat
ā	ape, date
ä	car, lot
e	elf, ten
ē	even, meet
i	is, hit
ī	ice, fire
ō	open, go
ô	law, horn
oi	oil, point
oo	look, pull
o͞o	ooze, tool
ou	out, crowd
u	up, cut
u	fur, fern
ə	a in ago
	e in agent
	e in father
	i in unity
	o in collect
	u in focus
ch	chin, arch
ŋ	ring, singer
sh	she, dash
th	thin, truth
th	then, father
zh	s in pleasure

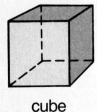

cube

crush (krush) *v.* **1** to press or squeeze with force so as to break, hurt, or put out of shape [She *crushed* the flower in her hand. His hat was *crushed* when he sat on it.] **2** to grind or pound into bits [This machine *crushes* rocks.] **3** to bring to an end by force; subdue; suppress [The government *crushed* the revolt.] ◆*n.* a crushing or squeezing; strong pressure.

cry (krī) *v.* **1** to make a loud sound with the voice; call out or shout [Lou *cried* out in fright when a face appeared at the window.]   **2** to show sorrow, pain, etc. by sobbing or shedding tears. **3** to say loudly; shout; exclaim ["Help! Help!" the victim *cried*.] —**cried, cry′ing** ◆*n.* **1** a loud sound made by the voice; shout or call [I heard your *cry* for help.] **2** a fit of sobbing and weeping [I had a good *cry* and fell asleep.] **3** the sound an animal makes [the *cry* of a lost sheep]. —*pl.* **cries**

cube (kyōōb) *n.* **1** a solid with six square sides, all the same size. **2** anything with more or less this shape [an ice *cube*]. **3** the result got by multiplying a number by itself and then multiplying the product by the same number [The *cube* of 3 is 27 (3 × 3 × 3 = 27).] ◆*v.* to cut into cubes [I *cubed* the fruit for salad.] —**cubed, cub′ing**

curb (kurb) *n.* **1** a chain or strap passed around a horse's jaw and attached to the bit. It holds back the horse when the reins are pulled. **2** anything that checks or holds back [Fear of punishment is often a *curb* to wrongdoing.] **3** the stone or concrete edging along a street. ◆*v.* to hold back; keep in check [to *curb* one's appetite].

curl·y (kur′lē) *adj.* full of curls [*curly* hair]. —**curl′i·er, curl′i·est**

cur·rent (kur′ənt) *adj.* **1** of the present time; now going on; most recent [the *current* decade; *current* events]. **2** commonly known, used, or accepted [*current* gossip; a belief *current* in earlier times]. ◆*n.* **1** a flow of water or air in a definite direction; stream. **2** the flow of electricity in a wire or other conductor. **3** the general movement or drift, as of opinion. —**cur′rent·ly** *adv.*

dair·y (der′ē) *n.* **1** a building where milk and cream are kept and butter and cheese are made. **2** a farm (**dairy farm**) on which milk, butter, cheese, etc. are produced. **3** a store that sells milk, butter, cheese, etc. —*pl.* **dair′ies**

dai·sy (dā′zē) *n.* ☆**1** a common plant with flowers that have white or pink petals around a yellow center. **2** such a flower. —*pl.* **dai′sies**

dam·age (dam′ij) *n.* injury or harm to a person or thing that results in a loss of health, value, and so on [A poor diet can cause *damage* to your heart.]

danc·er (dan′sər) *n.* a person who dances.

daugh·ter (dôt′ər *or* dät′ər) *n.* a girl or woman as she is related to a parent or to both parents.

dawn (dôn *or* dän) *v.* **1** to begin to grow light as the sun rises [Day is *dawning*.] **2** to come into being; begin to develop [With the discovery of electricity, a new age *dawned*.]   **3** to begin to be understood or felt [The meaning suddenly *dawned* on me.] ◆*n.* **1** the beginning of day; daybreak. **2** the beginning of anything [the *dawn* of the Space Age]

de·ceive (dē sēv′) *v.* to make someone believe what is not true; fool or trick; mislead [The queen *deceived* Snow White by pretending to be her friend.]

de·cide (dē sīd′) *v.* **1** to choose after some thought; make up one's mind [I can't *decide* what suit to wear.] **2** to end a contest or argument by giving one side the victory; settle [A jury will *decide* the case.] —**de·cid′ed, de·cid′ing**

deer (dir) *n.* a swift-running, hoofed animal. —*pl.* **deer** or **deers**

de·fend (dē fend′) *v.* **1** to keep safe from harm or danger; guard; protect [She learned karate to *defend* herself.] **2** to uphold something that is under attack; especially, to be the lawyer for a person accused or sued in a law court.

de·fine (dē fīn′) *v.* to tell the meaning or meanings of; explain [The dictionary *defines* "deficient" as "not having enough."]

de·lay (dē lā′) *v.* to put off to a later time; postpone [The bride's illness will *delay* the wedding.]

de·liv·er·y (dē liv′ər ē) *n.* the act of transferring or distributing [daily *deliveries* to customers]. —*pl.* **de·liv′er·ies**

den·tist (den′tist) *n.* a doctor whose work is preventing and taking care of diseased or crooked teeth, or replacing them with artificial teeth.

de·ny (dē nī′) *v.* **1** to say that something is not true or right; contradict [They *denied* that they had broken the window.] **2** to refuse to grant or give [We were *denied* permission to see the movie.] —**de·nies′, de·nied′, de·ny′ing**

de·scend (dē send′) *v.* **1** to move down to a lower place [to *descend* from a hilltop; to *descend* a staircase]. **2** to become lesser or smaller [Prices have *descended* during the past month.] **3** to come from a certain source [They are *descended* from pioneers.]

des·ert (dez′ərt) *n.* a dry sandy region with little or no plant life. ◆*adj.* **1** of or like a desert. **2** wild and not lived in [a *desert* island].

de·sign (dē zīn′) *v.* **1** to think up and draw plans for [to *design* a new model of a car]. **2** to arrange the parts, colors, etc. of [Who *designed* this book?] **3** to set apart for a certain use; intend [This chair was not *designed* for hard use.] ◆*n.* **1** a drawing or plan to be followed in making something [the *designs* for a house]. **2** the arrangement of parts, colors, etc.; pattern or decoration [the *design* in a rug]. **3** a plan or purpose [It was my *design* to study law.]

de·stroy (dē stroi′) *v.* to put an end to by breaking up, tearing down, ruining, or spoiling [The flood *destroyed* 300 homes.]

di·a·ry (dī′ə rē) *n.* a record written day by day of some of the things done, seen, or thought by the writer. —*pl.* **di′a·ries**

die (dī) *v.* **1** to stop living; become dead. **2** to stop going, moving, acting, etc. [The motor sputtered and *died*.] **3** to lose force; become weak, faint, etc. [The sound of music *died* away.] **4** to want greatly: *used only in everyday talk* [She's *dying* to know my secret.] —**died, dy′ing**

di·et (dī′ət) *n.* **1** what a person or animal usually eats or drinks; usual food [Rice is a basic food in the *diet* of many Asian peoples.] **2** a special choice as to kinds and amounts of food eaten, as for one's health or to gain or lose weight [a sugar-free *diet*; a reducing *diet*]. ◆*v.* to eat certain kinds and amounts of food, especially in order to lose weight.

dif·fer·ent (dif′ər ənt *or* dif′rənt) *adj.* **1** not alike; unlike [Cottage cheese is quite *different* from Swiss cheese.] **2** not the same; separate; distinct [There are three *different* colleges in the city.] **3** not like most others; unusual [Their house is really *different*.] —**dif′fer·ent·ly** *adv.*

dif·fi·cult (dif′i kult) *adj.* **1** hard to do, make, or understand; that takes much trouble, thought, or skill [This arithmetic problem is *difficult*.] **2** hard to please; not easy to get along with [a *difficult* employer].

dim (dim) *v.* to make or grow somewhat dark [Cars approaching each other should *dim* their headlights.] —**dimmed, dim′ming**

dirt·y (durt′ē) *adj.* **1** having dirt on or in it; not clean; soiled. **2** foul or indecent; not nice; mean [a *dirty* trick]. —**dirt′i·er, dirt′i·est** ◆*v.* to make or become dirty; soil. —**dirt′ied, dirt′y·ing** —**dirt′i·ness** *n.*

dis·a·gree (dis ə grē′) *v.* **1** to differ in opinion; often, to quarrel or argue [to *disagree* on politics]. **2** to be different; differ [His story of the accident *disagreed* with hers.] —**dis·a·greed′, dis·a·gree′ing**

dis·ap·point (dis ə point′) *v.* to fail to give or do what is wanted, expected, or promised; leave unsatisfied [I am *disappointed* in the weather. You promised to come, but *disappointed* us.]

dis·be·lief (dis bə lēf′) *n.* the state of not believing; lack of belief [The guide stared at me in *disbelief*.]

dis·close (dis klōz′) *v.* **1** to bring into view; uncover [I opened my hand and *disclosed* the new penny.] **2** to make known; reveal [to *disclose* a secret]. —**dis·closed′, dis·clos′ing**

dis·grace (dis grās′) *n.* loss of favor, respect, or honor; dishonor; shame [in *disgrace* for cheating]

dis·hon·est (dis än′əst) *adj.* not honest; lying, cheating, stealing, etc. —**dis·hon′est·ly** *adv.* —**dis·hon′es·ty** *n.*

dis·in·ter·est·ed (dis in′trəs təd) *adj.* **1** not having a selfish interest in the matter; impartial [A *disinterested* judge picked the winner.] **2** not interested; uninterested: *an older meaning that is being used again.*

dis·loy·al (dis loi′əl) *adj.* not loyal or faithful; faithless. —**dis·loy′al·ty** *n.*

dis·play (di splā′) *v.* **1** to put or spread out so as to be seen; exhibit [to *display* a collection of stamps]. **2** to do something that is a sign or example of; show; reveal [to *display* one's courage]. ◆*n.* a displaying or showing; exhibition [a *display* of jewelry; a *display* of strength].

ditch (dich) *n.* a long, narrow opening dug in the earth, as for carrying off water; trench [a *ditch* along the road]. —*pl.* **ditch′es** ◆*v.* **1** to dig a ditch in or around. **2** to throw into a ditch.

doc·tor (däk′tər) *n.* **1** a person trained to heal the sick; especially, a physician or surgeon. **2** a person who has received the highest degree given by a university [*Doctor* of Philosophy]. ◆*v.* to try to heal [to *doctor* oneself].

does·n't (duz′ənt) does not.

dol·lar (däl′ər) *n.* ☆**1** a United States coin or piece of paper money, equal to 100 cents. The dollar is our basic unit of money; its symbol is $. **2** a unit of money in certain other countries, as Canada.

dol·phin (dôl′fin) *n.* a water animal related to the whale but smaller. The common dolphin has a long snout and many teeth.

☆**down·town** (doun′toun) *adj., adv.* in or toward the lower part or the main business section of a city or town. ◆*n.* this section of a city or town.

drag (drag) *v.* **1** to pull in a slow, hard way, especially along the ground; haul [He *dragged* the sled up the hill.] **2** to be pulled along the ground, floor, etc. [Her skirt *dragged* in the mud.] **3** to move or pass too slowly [Time *dragged* as we waited for recess.] **4** to search for something in a river, lake, etc. by dragging a net or hooks along the bottom. —**dragged, drag′ging**

a	ask, fat
ā	ape, date
ä	car, lot
e	elf, ten
ē	even, meet
i	is, hit
ī	ice, fire
ō	open, go
ô	law, horn
oi	oil, point
o͝o	look, pull
o͞o	ooze, tool
ou	out, crowd
u	up, cut
ʉ	fur, fern
ə	a in ago
	e in agent
	e in father
	i in unity
	o in collect
	u in focus
ch	chin, arch
ŋ	ring, singer
sh	she, dash
th	thin, truth
th	then, father
zh	s in pleasure

draw (drô *or* drä) *v.* to make a picture or design with a pencil, pen, or chalk. —**drew** (drōō), **draw′ing**

draw·ing (drô′iŋ *or* drä′iŋ) *n.* **1** the making of pictures, designs, etc., as with a pencil or pen. **2** such a picture, design, etc. **3** a lottery.

drawn (drôn *or* drän) *past participle of* **draw.**

dream (drēm) *n.* **1** a series of thoughts, pictures, or feelings that passes through the mind of a sleeping person. **2** a pleasant idea that one imagines or hopes for; daydream [to have *dreams* of glory]. ◆*v.* **1** to have a dream or dreams. **2** to imagine as possible; have any idea of [I wouldn't *dream* of going without you.] —**dreamed** or **dreamt** (dremt), **dream′ing** —**dream′er** *n.*

eagle

dress (dres) *n.* **1** the common outer garment worn by girls and women. It is usually of one piece with a skirt. **2** clothes in general [native *dress;* formal *dress*]. —*pl.***dress′es** ◆*v.* **1** to put clothes on; clothe. **2** to put medicine and bandages on a wound or sore. **3** to make ready for use; prepare [to *dress* a chicken; to *dress* leather]. ◆*adj.* worn on formal occasions [a *dress* suit].

drive (drīv) *v.* to control the movement of an automobile, horse and wagon, bus, or other vehicle [She *drives* a school bus.] —**drove, driv′ing**

drop (dräp) *n.* **1** a bit of liquid that is rounded in shape, as when falling [*drops* of rain]. **2** anything like this in shape [a chocolate *drop*]. **3** a very small amount [He hasn't a *drop* of courage.] ◆*v.* **1** to fall or let fall in drops [Tears *dropped* from the actor's eyes.] **2** to fall or let fall [Ripe fruit *dropped* from the trees. He *dropped* his lunch in the mud.] —**dropped** or *sometimes* **dropt, drop′ping**

drown (droun) *v.* to die from being under water, where the lungs can get no air [to fall overboard and *drown*]. —**drowned, drown′ing**

drow·sy (drou′zē) *adj.* **1** sleepy or half asleep. **2** making one feel sleepy [*drowsy* music]. —**drow′si·er, drow′si·est** —**drow′si·ly** *adv.* —**drow′si·ness** *n.*

dry (drī) *adj.* **1** not under water [*dry* land]. **2** not wet or damp; without moisture. **3** having little or no rain or water [a *dry* summer]. **4** with all its water or other liquid gone [a *dry* fountain pen; *dry* bread; a *dry* well]. —**dri′er, dri′est** —**dried, dry′ing** —**dry′ly** *adv.* —**dry′ness** *n.*

dues (dōōz *or* dyōōz) *pl.n.* money paid regularly for being a member of a club or institution [The *dues* are $25 per month.]

dusk (dusk) *n.* the dim part of twilight that comes before the dark of night.

du·ty (dōōt′ē *or* dyōōt′ē) *n.* **1** what a person should do because it is thought to be right, just, or moral [It is the *duty* of every citizen to vote.] **2** any of the things that are done as part of a person's work [the *duties* of a secretary]. —*pl.* **du′ties**

Ee

ea·gle (ē′gəl) *n.* a large, strong bird that captures and eats other birds and animals and has sharp eyesight. The **bald eagle** is the symbol of the U.S.

ear·ly (ur′lē) *adv., adj.* **1** near the beginning; soon after the start [in the *early* afternoon; *early* in his career]. **2** before the usual or expected time [The bus arrived *early.*] —**ear′li·er, ear′li·est** —**ear′li·ness** *n.*

ear·muffs (ir′mufs) *pl.n.* cloth or fur coverings worn over the ears to keep them warm in cold weather.

east·ern (ēs′tərn) *adj.* **1** in, of, or toward the east [the *eastern* sky]. **2** from the east [an *eastern* wind]. **3 Eastern,** of the East.

eas·y (ē′zē) *adj.* **1** not hard to do, learn, get, etc. [an *easy* job; an *easy* book]. **2** without worry, pain, or trouble [an *easy* life]. **3** restful or comfortable [an *easy* chair]. —**eas′i·er, eas′i·est**

eas·y·go·ing (ē′zē gō′iŋ) *adj.* not worried, rushed, or strict about things.

edge (ej) *n.* **1** the sharp, cutting part [the *edge* of a knife]. **2** the line or part where something begins or ends; border or margin [the *edge* of a plate; the *edge* of the forest]. **3** the brink [on the *edge* of disaster]. —**edged, edg′ing**

ed·i·tor (ed′it ər) *n.* **1** a person who edits. ☆**2** the head of a department of a newspaper, magazine, etc.

eight·een (ā′tēn′) *n., adj.* eight more than ten; the number 18.

el·e·phant (el′ə fənt) *n.* a huge animal with a thick skin, two ivory tusks, and a long snout, or trunk. It is found in Africa and India and is the largest of the four-legged animals.

e·lev·en (ē lev′ən) *n., adj.* one more than ten; the number 11.

em·broi·der (em broi′dər) *v.* to stitch designs on cloth with a needle and thread [Hal *embroidered* his initials on his shirt.]

e·mer·gen·cy (ē mur′jən sē) *n.* a sudden happening that needs action or attention right away [the *emergency* created by a hurricane]. —*pl.* **e·mer′gen·cies**

em·ploy (em ploi′) *v.* **1** to hire and pay for the work or services of; have working for one [That company *employs* 50 people.] **2** to use [The baby *employed* clever tricks to get attention.] ◆*n.* the condition of being employed [Chan is no longer in our *employ.*]

emp·ty (emp′tē) *adj.* **1** having nothing or no one in it; not occupied; vacant [an *empty* jar; an *empty* house]. —**emp′ti·er, emp′ti·est** ◆*v.* **1** to make or become empty [The auditorium was *emptied* in ten minutes.] **2** to take out or pour out [*Empty* the dirty water in the sink.] **3** to flow out; discharge [The Amazon *empties* into the Atlantic.] —**emp′tied, emp′ty·ing** —**emp′ti·ly** *adv.* —**emp′ti·ness** *n.*

en·e·my (en′ə mē) *n.* a person, group, or country that hates another or fights against another; foe. —*pl.* **en′e·mies**

en·er·gy (en′ər jē) *n.* **1** power to work or be active; force; vigor [Eleanor Roosevelt was a woman of great *energy*.] **2** the power of certain forces in nature to do work [Electricity and heat are forms of *energy*.] **3** resources, as coal, oil, etc., used to produce such power; also, the supply of such resources that can be got [an *energy* shortage]. —*pl.* **en′er·gies**

e·nor·mous (ē nôr′məs) *adj.* much larger than usual; huge [an *enormous* stadium]. —**e·nor′mous·ly** *adv.* —**e·nor′mous·ness** *n.*

e·nough (ē nuf′) *adj.* as much or as many as needed or wanted; sufficient [There is *enough* food for all.] ◆*n.* the amount needed or wanted [I have heard *enough* of that music.] ◆*adv.* **1** as much as needed; to the right amount [Is your steak cooked *enough*?] **2** fully; quite [Oddly *enough*, she never asked me.]

en·ter·tain (en tər tān′) *v.* to keep interested and give pleasure to [She *entertained* us by playing the organ.]

e·qual (ē′kwəl) *adj.* **1** of the same amount, size, or value [The horses were of *equal* height.] **2** having the same rights, ability, or position [All persons are *equal* in a court of law in a just society.] ◆*n.* any person or thing that is equal [As a sculptor, she has few *equals*.] ◆*v.* to be equal to; match [His long jump *equaled* the school record. Six minus two *equals* four.] —**e′qualed** or **e′qualled, e′qual·ing** or **e′qual·ling** —**e′qual·ly** *adv.*

e·qua·tor (ē kwāt′ər) *n.* an imaginary circle around the middle of the earth, at an equal distance from the North Pole and South Pole.

er·ror (er′ər) *n.* **1** a belief, answer, act, etc. that is untrue, incorrect, or wrong; mistake [an *error* in multiplication]. **2** a play by a baseball fielder which is poorly made, but which would have resulted in an out if it had been properly made.

es·say (es′ā) *n.* a short piece of writing on some subject, giving the writer's personal ideas.

Eu·rope (yoor′əp) the continent between Asia and the Atlantic Ocean.

ev·er·y·bod·y (ev′rē bäd′ē *or* ev′rē bud′ē) *pron.* every person; everyone [*Everybody* loves a good story.]

ex·change (eks chānj′) *v.* to give in return for something else; trade [She *exchanged* the bicycle for a larger one.] —**ex·changed′, ex·chang′ing**

ex·cuse (ek skyoōz′) *v.* **1** to be a proper reason or explanation for [That was a selfish act that nothing will *excuse*.] **2** to think of a fault or wrongdoing as not important; overlook; forgive; pardon [Please *excuse* this interruption.] **3** to allow to leave or go [You may be *excused* from the table.] —**ex·cused′, ex·cus′ing** ◆*n.* (ek skyoōs′) a reason given to explain some action or behavior; apology [Ignorance of the law is no *excuse* for wrongdoing.]

ex·er·cise (ek′sər sīz) *n.* **1** active use of the body in order to make it stronger or healthier [Long walks are good outdoor *exercise*.] **2** *usually* **exercises**, *pl.* a series of movements done regularly to make some part of the body stronger or to develop some skill [These *exercises* will strengthen your legs.] **3** a problem to be studied and worked on by a student in order to get more skill [piano *exercises*]. ◆*v.* to put into use or do certain regular movements, in order to develop or train [*Exercise* your weak ankle. I *exercise* every morning.] —**ex′er·cised, ex′er·cis·ing**

ex·pen·sive (ek spen′siv) *adj.* costing much; having a high price [She wears *expensive* clothes.] —**ex·pen′sive·ly** *adv.*

ex·plore (ek splôr′) *v.* **1** to travel in a region that is unknown or not well known, in order to find out more about it [to *explore* a wild jungle]. **2** to look into or examine carefully [to *explore* a problem]. —**ex·plored′, ex·plor′ing** —**ex′plo·ra′tion** *n.* —**ex·plor′er** *n.*

ex·press (ek spres′) *v.* **1** to put into words; state [It is hard to *express* my feelings.] **2** to give or be a sign of; show [a frown that *expressed* doubt]. ☆**3** to send goods by a fast way. ◆*adj.* taking the shortest and fastest route; not making many stops [an *express* train or bus].

ex·tend (ek stend′) *v.* to make longer; stretch out [Careful cleaning *extends* the life of a rug.]

ex·tinct (ek stiŋkt′) *adj.* **1** no longer living; having died out [Dinosaurs are *extinct*.] **2** no longer burning or active [an *extinct* volcano].

ex·tin·guish·er (ek stiŋ′gwish ər) *n.* a person or thing that extinguishes; especially, a device for putting out a fire by spraying a liquid or gas on it.

eye·lash (ī′lash) *n.* **1** any of the hairs that grow along the edge of the eyelid. **2** a fringe of these hairs. —*pl.* **eye′lash·es**

equator

a	ask, fat
ā	ape, date
ä	car, lot
e	elf, ten
ē	even, meet
i	is, hit
ī	ice, fire
ō	open, go
ô	law, horn
oi	oil, point
oo	look, pull
o͞o	ooze, tool
ou	out, crowd
u	up, cut
u	fur, fern
ə	a in ago
	e in agent
	e in father
	i in unity
	o in collect
	u in focus
ch	chin, arch
ŋ	ring, singer
sh	she, dash
th	thin, truth
th	then, father
zh	s in pleasure

fa·ble (fā′bəl) *n.* **1** a very short story that teaches a lesson. It is usually about animals who act and talk like people [Aesop's *fable* "The Grasshopper and the Ant" teaches the need to work hard and be thrifty.]

fac·to·ry (fak′tər ē *or* fak′trē) *n.* a building or group of buildings where products are made by machinery. —*pl.*fac′to·ries

fair (fer) *adj.* **1** beautiful [your *fair* city]. **2** light in color; blond [*fair* hair; *fair* skin]. **3** clear and sunny [*fair* weather]. **4** just and honest; according to what is right [a *fair* price; *fair* play]. —**fair′ness** *n.*

fame (fām) *n.* the condition of being well known or much talked about; great reputation [Marie Curie's scientific research brought her much *fame.*]

fa·mil·iar (fə mil′yər) *adj.* friendly; intimate; well-acquainted [a *familiar* face in the crowd].

fam·i·ly (fam′ə lē) *n.* **1** a group made up of two parents and all of their children. **2** the children alone [a widow who raised a large *family*]. **3** a group of people who are related by marriage or a common ancestor; relatives; clan. —*pl.* **fam′i·lies**

fan·cy (fan′sē) *n.* the power of picturing in the mind things that are not real, especially in a light and playful way; imagination ["Alice's Adventures in Wonderland" is the product of Lewis Carroll's *fancy.*] —*pl.* **fan′cies** ◆*adj.* **1** having much design and decoration; not plain; elaborate [a *fancy* tie]. **2** of better quality than the usual; special [a *fancy* grade of canned pears]. —**fan′ci·er, fan′ci·est** ◆*v.* to have a liking for [He *fancies* Swiss chocolate.] —**fan′cied, fan′cy·ing**

far·ther (fär′thər) *the comparative of* **far.** ◆*adj.* more distant [My home is *farther* from school than yours.] ◆*adv.* at or to a greater distance [I can swim *farther* than you can.]

fault (fôlt) *n.* **1** a thing that keeps something from being perfect; defect; flaw [His main *fault* is that he's lazy.] **2** an error; mistake. **3** blame; responsibility [It isn't my *fault* that we're late.]

fawn (fôn *or* fän) *n.* a young deer, less than one year old.

fear·less (fir′ləs) *adj.* having no fear; not afraid; brave. —**fear′less·ly** *adv.*

feath·er (feth′ər) *n.* any of the parts that grow out of the skin of birds, covering the body and filling out the wings and tail. Feathers are soft and light. —**feath′er·y** *adj.*

flamingo

fend·er (fen′dər) *n.* ☆**1** a metal piece over the wheel of a car to keep off splashing mud. **2** a metal piece at the front of a locomotive to throw off things that are hit.

field (fēld) *n.* **1** a wide piece of open land without many trees; especially, a piece of land for growing crops, grazing animals, etc. **2** a piece of land having a special use or producing a certain thing [a landing *field*; an oil *field*]. **3** an area where games or athletic events are held; also, the part of such an area where such events as high jump, long jump, pole vault, shot put, etc. are held. ◆*v.* to stop or catch and return a batted ball.

fight (fīt) *v.* to use fists, weapons, or other force in trying to beat or overcome someone or something [to *fight* a war]. —**fought, fight′ing**

film (film) *n.* **1** a thin skin or coating [a *film* of ice on the pond]. **2** a sheet or roll of material covered with a chemical substance that is changed by light, used for taking photographs or making movies. **3** a movie.

fin·ish (fin′ish) *v.* **1** to bring or come to an end; complete or become completed [Did you *finish* your work? The game *finished* early.] **2** to give final touches to; perfect [We *finished* the room by putting up molding.] **3** to use up; consume completely [*Finish* your milk.] ◆*n.* the kind of surface a thing has [an oil *finish* on wood].

fish (fish) *n.* an animal that lives in water and has a backbone, fins, and gills for breathing [The aquarium exhibits many *fishes.*] —*pl.* **fish′es**

fla·min·go (flə miŋ′gō) *n.* a wading bird that has a very long neck and legs, and pink or red feathers. It lives in tropical regions. —*pl.* **fla·min′gos** *or* **fla·min′goes**

flash (flash) *v.* **1** to send out a short and bright burst of light [Electric signs *flashed* all along the street.] **2** to sparkle or gleam [Her eyes *flashed* with anger.] **3** to come, move, or send swiftly or suddenly [The train *flashed* by. The news was *flashed* to Paris by radio.] ◆*n.* a short burst of light or of something bright [a *flash* of lightning; a *flash* of wit, hope, etc.] —*pl.* **flash′es**

fleet¹ (flēt) *n.* **1** a group of warships under one command [our Pacific *fleet*]. **2** any group of ships, trucks, buses, etc. moving together or under one control.

fleet² (flēt) *adj.* moving swiftly; swift.

flew (flo͞o) *past tense of* **fly¹.**

flies (flīz) **1** *the form of the verb* **fly¹**, *used in the present with* he, she, *or* it. **2** *the plural of* **fly¹** *and* **fly².**

flight (flīt) *n.* **1** the act or way of flying or moving through space. **2** a trip through the air, as by an airplane, bird, etc. [a 500-mile *flight*]. **3** a group of things flying together [a *flight* of wild swans].

Flor·i·da (flôr′i də) a State in the southeastern part of the U.S.: abbreviated **Fla., FL**

flu (flo͞o) *n.* a disease caused by a virus, like a bad cold only more serious.

flue (flo͞o) *n.* a tube, pipe, or shaft through which smoke, steam, or hot air can escape [the *flue* in a chimney].

fly[1] (flī) *v.* **1** to move through the air by using wings, as a bird. **2** to travel or carry through the air, as in an aircraft. **3** to pilot an aircraft. **4** to wave or float in the air, or cause to float in the air, as a flag or kite. **5** to move swiftly [The door *flew* open. Time *flies*.] —**flew, flown, fly′ing** ◆*n.* a baseball batted high in the air inside the foul lines. —*pl.* **flies**

fly[2] (flī) *n.* **1** a flying insect having one pair of wings, as the housefly and gnat. Some insects with two pairs of wings are called flies, as the mayfly. **2** an object used in fishing, made of bright feathers, silk, etc. tied to a fishhook to look like a fly. —*pl.* **flies**

folk (fōk) *n.* **folk** or **folks**, *pl.* people or persons [The farmer disliked city *folk. Folks* differ in customs.] —*pl.* **folk** or **folks** ◆*adj.* of the common people [a *folk* saying].

folk tale a story made and handed down by word of mouth among the common people: *also* **folk story.**

fol·low·ing (fä′lō iŋ) *adj.* going or coming after; next after [the *following* week]. ◆*n.* people who follow; followers. ◆*prep.* after [*Following* dinner we played cards.]

fond (fänd) *v.* loving and tender; affectionate [*fond* parents].

fool·ish (fo͞ol′ish) *adj.* without good sense; silly. —**fool′ish·ly** *adv.* —**fool′ish·ness** *n.*

force (fôrs) *n.* **1** power or energy that can do or make something [Electricity is a powerful natural *force*. The *force* of the high winds broke the windows.] **2** power or strength used against a person or thing [The police used *force* to scatter the crowd.] **3** the power to cause motion or to stop or change motion [the *force* of gravity]. ◆*v.* **1** to make do something by using strength or power of some kind [You shouldn't *force* a child to eat. The blizzard *forced* us to stay home.] **2** to break open or through by using strength [He *forced* the lock with a pick.] —**forced, forc′ing**

fore·head (fôr′hed *or* fär′hed) *n.* the part of the face above the eyebrows.

forth (fôr*th*) *adv.* **1** forward or onward [She never left the house from that day *forth*.] **2** out; into view [The bears came *forth* from their den.]

fought (fôt *or* fät) *past tense and past participle of* **fight.**

fox (fäks) *n.* **1** a wild animal of the dog family, with pointed ears, a bushy tail, and, usually, reddish-brown fur. —*pl.* **foxes**

France (frans) a country in western Europe.

fraud (frôd *or* fräd) *n.* **1** a cheating, tricking, or lying; dishonesty. **2** a person who cheats or is not what he or she pretends to be.

fray (frā) *v.* to wear down so as to become ragged and have loose threads showing [a coat *frayed* at the elbows].

free·dom (frē′dəm) *n.* **1** the condition of being free; liberty; independence. **2** a being able to use or move about in as one wishes [Has your dog been given *freedom* of the house?]

freight·er (frāt′ər) *n.* a ship for freight.

front (frunt) *n.* **1** the part that faces forward; most important side [The *front* of a house usually faces the street.] **2** the part ahead of the rest; first part; beginning [That chapter is toward the *front* of the book.] **3** outward look or behavior [I put on a bold *front* in spite of my fear.] **4** the land alongside a lake, ocean, street, etc. [docks on the water*front*].

fron·tier (frun tir′) *n.* **1** the line or border between two countries. ☆**2** the part of a settled country that lies next to a region that is still a wilderness. **3** any new field of learning or any part of it still to be explored [the *frontiers* of medicine].

fry (frī) *v.* to cook in hot fat over direct heat. —**fried, fry′ing** ◆*n.* ☆**1** a kind of picnic at which food is fried and eaten [a fish *fry*]. **2** **fries**, *pl.* things fried, as potatoes. —*pl.* **fries**

fun·ny (fun′ē) *adj.* **1** causing smiles or laughter; amusing; comical. **2** odd or unusual: *used only in everyday talk* [It's *funny* that he's late.] —**fun′ni·er, fun′ni·est** ◆☆*n.* *usually* **funnies**, *pl.* comic strips: *used only in everyday talk.* —*pl.* **fun′nies** —**fun′ni·ness** *n.*

Florida

gal·ax·y (gal′ək sē) *often* **Galaxy**, *another name for* **Milky Way**. ◆*n.* **1** any vast group of stars. **2** a group of very famous people. —*pl.* **gal′ax·ies**

gal·ley (gal′ē) *n.* **1** a large, low ship of long ago, having both sails and many oars. The oars were usually rowed by slaves or prisoners in chains. **2** the kitchen of a ship. —*pl.* **gal′leys**

gal·lon (gal′ən) *n.* a measure of liquids, equal to four quarts or eight pints. One gallon equals 3.785 liters.

gar·bage (gär′bij) *n.* spoiled or waste food that is thrown away.

gasp (gasp) *v.* to breathe in suddenly [She *gasped* in sudden surprise.]

a	ask, fat
ā	ape, date
ä	car, lot
e	elf, ten
ē	even, meet
i	is, hit
ī	ice, fire
ō	open, go
ô	law, horn
oi	oil, point
o͝o	look, pull
o͞o	ooze, tool
ou	out, crowd
u	up, cut
u	fur, fern
ə	a in ago
	e in agent
	e in father
	i in unity
	o in collect
	u in focus
ch	chin, arch
ŋ	ring, singer
sh	she, dash
th	thin, truth
th	then, father
zh	s in pleasure

giraffe

gath·er (gath'ər) **v. 1** to bring or come together in one place or group [The child *gathered* her toys together. The families *gathered* for a reunion.] **2** to get or collect gradually; accumulate [to *gather* wealth; to *gather* one's strength; to *gather* news for a paper]. **3** to pick or glean [to *gather* crops]. —**gath'er·er n.**

gaunt (gônt *or* gänt) **adj. 1** so thin that the bones show; worn and lean, as from hunger or illness. **2** looking gloomy and deserted [the *gaunt*, rocky coast of the island]. —**gaunt'ly adv.** —**gaunt'ness n.**

geese (gēs) **n.** *plural of* **goose.**

gen·tle (jent'l) **adj. 1** mild, soft, or easy; not rough [a *gentle* touch; a *gentle* scolding]. **2** tame; easy to handle [a *gentle* horse]. **3** gradual; not sudden [a *gentle* slope]. —**gen'tler, gen'tlest** —**gen'tle·ness n.**

ge·og·ra·phy (jē ôg'rə fē *or* jē ä'grə fē) **n. 1** the study of the surface of the earth and how it is divided into continents, countries, seas, etc. Geography also deals with the climates, plants, animals, minerals, etc. of the earth. **2** the natural features of a certain part of the earth [the *geography* of Ohio]. —**ge·og'ra·pher n.**

ger·bil or **ger·bille** (jur'bəl) **n.** an animal like a mouse but with very long hind legs. It is found in Africa and Asia.

ghost (gōst) **n. 1** a pale, shadowy form that some people think they can see and that is supposed to be the spirit of a dead person. **2** a mere shadow or slight trace [not a *ghost* of a chance].

gift (gift) **n. 1** something given to show friendship, thanks, support, etc.; a present [Christmas *gifts*; a *gift* of $5,000 to a museum]. **2** a natural ability; talent [a *gift* for writing catchy tunes].

gi·raffe (ji raf') **n.** a large animal of Africa that chews its cud. It has a very long neck and legs and a spotted coat, and is the tallest animal alive.

give (giv) **v. 1** to pass or hand over to another [*Give* me your coat and I'll hang it up.] **2** to hand over to another to keep; make a gift of [My uncle *gave* a book to me for my birthday.] **3** to cause to have [Music *gives* me pleasure.] **4** to be the source of; supply [Cows *give* milk.] —**gave, giv'en, giv'ing**

gla·cier (glā'shər) **n.** a large mass of ice and snow that moves very slowly down a mountain or across land until it melts. Icebergs are pieces of a glacier that have broken away into the sea.

glove

glove (gluv) **n. 1** a covering to protect the hand, with a separate part for each finger and the thumb [Surgeons wear rubber *gloves*. Padded *gloves* are worn in playing baseball.] **2** a padded mitt worn in boxing: also **boxing glove.** ◆**v.** to put gloves on. —**gloved, glov'ing**

glow (glō) **v. 1** to give off light because of great heat; be red-hot or white-hot [embers *glowing* in a fire]. **2** to give out light without flame or heat [Fireflies *glow* in the dark.]

glue (glōō) **n. 1** a thick, sticky substance made by boiling animal hoofs and bones, used for sticking things together. **2** any sticky substance like this. ◆**v. 1** to stick together with glue. **2** to keep or hold without moving [The exciting movie kept us *glued* to our seats.] —**glued, glu'ing** —**glue'y adj.**

gnaw (nô *or* nä) **v.** to bite and wear away bit by bit with the teeth [The rat *gnawed* the rope in two. The dog *gnawed* on the bone.]

gob·ble (gäb'əl) **v.** to eat quickly and greedily [She *gobbled* half the pizza before I finished a single piece.] —**gob'bled, gob'bling**

goose (gōōs) **n.** a swimming bird that is like a duck but has a larger body and a longer neck; especially, the female of this bird. The male is called a *gander*. —*pl.* **geese**

gov·ern·ment (guv'ərn mənt) **n. 1** control or rule, as over a country, city, etc. **2** a system of ruling or controlling [a centralized *government*; democratic *governments*]. **3** all the people who control the affairs of a country, city, etc. [The French *government* moved to Vichy during World War II.] —☆**gov'ern·men'tal adj.**

grab (grab) **v. 1** to seize or snatch suddenly. **2** to take by force or in a selfish way. —**grabbed, grab'bing** ◆**n. 1** the act of grabbing [He made a *grab* for the handle.] **2** something grabbed.

grace·ful (grās'fəl) **adj.** having grace, or beauty of form or movement. —**grace'ful·ly adv.** —**grace'ful·ness n.**

gram (gram) **n.** the basic unit of weight in the metric system. It is the weight of one cubic centimeter of distilled water at 4°C; one gram equals about 1/28 of an ounce.

graph (graf) **n.** a chart or diagram that shows the changes taking place in something, by the use of connected lines, a curve, etc. [a *graph* showing how sales figures vary during the year].

Greece (grēs) a country in southeastern Europe, on the Mediterranean.

greed·y (grēd'ē) **adj.** wanting or taking all that one can get with no thought of what others need [The *greedy* girl ate all the cookies.] —**greed'i·er, greed'i·est** —**greed'i·ly adv.** —**greed'i·ness n.**

grid·dle (grid'əl) **n.** a heavy, flat, metal plate or pan for cooking pancakes, etc.

griz·zly (griz'lē) **n.** a large, ferocious bear found in western North America. —*pl.* **griz'zlies**

groan (grōn) **v.** to make a deep sound showing sorrow, pain, annoyance, or disapproval [We *groaned* when our team lost.]

gro·cer·y (grō′sər ē) **n.** ☆**1** a store selling food and household supplies. **2 groceries**, *pl.* the goods sold by a grocer. —*pl.* **gro′cer·ies**

guess (ges) **v. 1** to judge or decide about something without having enough facts to know for certain [Can you *guess* how old he is?] **2** to judge correctly by doing this [She *guessed* the exact number of beans in the jar.] **3** to think or suppose [I *guess* you're right.] ◆*n.* a judgment formed by guessing; surmise [Your *guess* is as good as mine.] —**guess′er n.**

gulp (gulp) **v.** to swallow in a hurried or greedy way [She *gulped* her breakfast and ran to school.] —**gulped, gulp′ing**

hair (her) **n. 1** any of the thin growths, like threads, that come from the skin of animals and human beings. **2** the whole number of these growths that cover a person's head, the skin of an animal, etc. [I must comb my *hair*.]

half (haf) **n. 1** either of the two equal parts of something [Five is *half* of ten.] **2** either of two almost equal parts: *thought by some people to be not a proper use* [Take the smaller *half* of the pie.] **3** a half hour [It is *half* past two.]—*pl.* **halves** ◆*adv.*

half·way (haf′wā′) **adj. 1** at the middle between two points or limits [to reach the *halfway* mark]. **2** not complete; partial [to take *halfway* measures]. ◆*adv.* **1** to the midway point; half the distance [They had gone *halfway* home.] **2** partially [The house is *halfway* built.]

halt (hôlt) **n., v.** stop [I worked all morning without a *halt*. Rain *halted* the game.]

halves (havz) **n.** *plural of* **half**.

ham·mer (ham′ər) **n. 1** a tool for driving in nails, breaking stones, shaping metal, etc. It usually has a metal head and a handle. **2** a thing like this in shape or use, as the part that strikes against the firing pin of a gun or any of the parts that strike the strings of a piano. ◆*v.* to hit with many blows [They *hammered* on the door with their fists.]

hand (hand) **n. 1** the end of the arm beyond the wrist, including the palm, fingers, and thumb. **2** any of the pointers on a clock or watch. **3** a person hired to work with the hands [a farm *hand*; dock *hand*]. **4** help [Give me a *hand* with this job.] **5** a clapping of hands; applause [Give the dancer a big *hand*.] ◆*v.* to give with the hand; pass [*Hand* me the book, please.]

hand·ker·chief (haŋ′kər chif) **n.** a small piece of cloth for wiping the nose, eyes, or face, or worn as a decoration. —*pl.* **hand′ker·chiefs**

hap·py (hap′ē) **adj. 1** feeling or showing pleasure or joy; glad; contented [a *happy* child; a *happy* song]. **2** lucky; fortunate [The story has a *happy* ending.] —**hap′pi·er, hap′pi·est** —**hap′pi·ly adv.** —**hap′pi·ness n.**

har·bor (här′bər) **n. 1** a place where ships may anchor and be safe from storms; port; haven. **2** any place where one is safe; shelter. ◆*v.* to shelter or hide [to *harbor* an outlaw].

hare (her) **n.** a swift animal with long ears, a split upper lip, large front teeth used for gnawing, and long, powerful hind legs. Hares are related to rabbits but are usually larger.

har·vest (här′vəst) **n.** the act or process of gathering a crop of grain, fruit, or vegetables when it becomes ripe.

has·n't (haz′ənt) has not.

haunt (hônt *or* hänt) **v. 1** to spend much time at; visit often [We like to *haunt* bookstores. A *haunted* house is one that is supposed to be visited by a ghost.] **2** to keep coming back to the mind [Memories *haunt* her.] ◆*n.* a place often visited [They made the library their *haunt*.]

heal (hēl) **v.** to get or bring back to good health or a sound condition; cure or mend [The wound *healed* slowly. Time *heals* grief.]

heart (härt) **n. 1** the hollow muscle that gets blood from the veins and sends it through the arteries by squeezing together and expanding. **2** the part at the center [*hearts* of celery; the *heart* of the jungle]. **3** the main or most important part [Get to the *heart* of the matter.] **4** the human heart thought of as the part that feels love, kindness, pity, sadness, etc. [a tender *heart*; a heavy *heart*].

hearth (härth) **n.** the stone or brick floor of a fireplace.

heav·y (hev′ē) **adj. 1** hard to lift or move because of its weight; weighing very much [a *heavy* load]. **2** weighing more than is usual for its kind [Lead is a *heavy* metal.] **3** larger, deeper, greater, etc. than usual [a *heavy* vote; a *heavy* sleep; a *heavy* blow]. —**heav′i·er, heav′i·est** ◆*adv.* in a heavy manner [*heavy*-laden].

heel (hēl) **n. 1** the back part of the foot, below the ankle and behind the arch. **2** that part of a stocking or sock which covers the heel. **3** the part of a shoe that is built up to support the heel.

a	ask, fat
ā	ape, date
ä	car, lot
e	elf, ten
ē	even, meet
i	is, hit
ī	ice, fire
ō	open, go
ô	law, horn
oi	oil, point
oo	look, pull
o͞o	ooze, tool
ou	out, crowd
u	up, cut
ᵊ	fur, fern
ə	a in ago
	e in agent
	e in father
	i in unity
	o in collect
	u in focus
ch	chin, arch
ŋ	ring, singer
sh	she, dash
th	thin, truth
th	then, father
zh	s in pleasure

heron

horseshoe

herd (hʉrd) *n.* a number of cattle or other large animals feeding or living together [a *herd* of cows; a *herd* of elephants]. ✦*v.* **1** to form into a herd, group, or crowd. **2** to take care of a herd of animals.

her·on (her′ən) *n.* a wading bird with long legs, a long neck, and a long, pointed bill. Herons live in marshes or along river banks.

hes·i·tate (hez′i tāt′) *v.* **1** to stop or hold back, as because of feeling unsure [Never *hesitate* to speak the truth. He *hesitated* at the door before entering.] **2** to feel unwilling [I *hesitate* to ask you for money.] —**hes′i·tat·ed, hes′i·tat·ing**

high·way (hī′wā) *n.* a main road.

hob·by (häb′ē) *n.* something that one likes to do, study, etc. for pleasure in one's spare time [Her *hobby* is collecting coins.] —*pl.* **hob′bies**

hoe (hō) *n.* a garden tool with a thin, flat blade on a long handle. It is used for removing weeds, loosening the soil, etc. ✦*v.* to dig, loosen soil, etc. with a hoe. —**hoed, hoe′ing**

hol·i·day (häl′ə dā) *n.* **1** a day on which most people do not have to work, often one set aside by law [Thanksgiving is a *holiday* in all States.] **2** a religious festival; holy day [Easter is a Christian *holiday*.]

hol·low (häl′ō) *adj.* **1** having an empty space on the inside; not solid [a *hollow* log]. **2** shaped like a bowl; concave. **3** sunken in [*hollow* cheeks]. —**hol′low·ness** *n.*

home·work (hōm′wʉrk) *n.* **1** lessons to be studied or schoolwork to be done outside the classroom. **2** any work to be done at home.

hom·o·nym (häm′ə nim) *n.* a word that is pronounced like another word but that has a different meaning and is usually spelled differently ["Bore" and "boar" are *homonyms*.]

hon·est (än′əst) *adj.* **1** that does not steal, cheat, or lie; upright or trustworthy [an *honest* person]. **2** got in a fair way, not by stealing, cheating, or lying [to earn an *honest* living]. **3** sincere or genuine [He made an *honest* effort.]

hoof (hoof *or* hʊf) *n.* **1** the horny covering on the feet of cows, horses, deer, pigs, etc. **2** the whole foot of such an animal. —*pl.* **hoofs** or **hooves**

hor·ri·fy (hôr′ə fī) *v.* to fill with horror [He was *horrified* at the sight of the victims.] —**hor′ri·fied, hor′ri·fy·ing**

horse·shoe (hôrs′shoo) *n.* **1** a flat metal plate shaped like a U, nailed to a horse's hoof to protect it. **2** anything shaped like this. **3** **horseshoes**, *pl.* a game in which the players toss horseshoes at a stake in the ground.

host·ess (hōs′təs) *n.* **1** a woman who has guests in her own home, or who pays for their entertainment away from home. **2** a

woman hired by a restaurant to welcome people and show them to their tables. —*pl.* **host′ess·es**

hour (our) *n.* **1** any of the 24 equal parts of a day; 60 minutes. **2** a particular time [At what *hour* shall we meet?] **3** *often* **hours**, *pl.* a particular period of time [the dinner *hour*; the doctor's office *hours*].

how (hou) *adv.* **1** in what way [*How* do you start the motor? She taught him *how* to dance.] **2** in what condition [*How* is your mother today?] **3** for what reason; why [*How* is it that you don't know?]

how's (houz) **1** how is. **2** how has. **3** how does.

hum (hum) *v.* **1** to make a low, steady, buzzing sound like that of a bee or a motor. **2** to sing with the lips closed, not saying the words. —**hummed, hum′ming**

☆**hum·ming·bird** (hum′iŋ bʉrd′) *n.* a tiny bird with a long, thin bill, that it uses to suck nectar from flowers. Its wings move very fast, with a humming sound, and it can hover in the air.

hun·dred (hun′drəd) *n., adj.* ten times ten; the number 100.

hur·ri·cane (hʉr′ə kān) *n.* a very strong windstorm, often with heavy rain, in which the wind blows in a circle at 73 or more miles per hour. Hurricanes usually start in the West Indies and move northward.

hur·ry (hʉr′ē) *v.* **1** to move, send, or carry quickly or too quickly [You fell because you *hurried*. A taxi *hurried* us home.] **2** to make happen or be done more quickly [Please try to *hurry* those letters.] **3** to try to make move or act faster [Don't *hurry* me when I'm eating.] —**hur′ried, hur′ry·ing**

hy·giene (hī′jēn) *n.* the practice of keeping clean [good personal *hygiene*].

i·de·a (ī dē′ə) *n.* **1** something one thinks, knows, imagines, feels, etc.; belief or thought. **2** a plan or purpose [an *idea* for making money].

im·mov·a·ble (im moov′ə bəl) *adj.* **1** that cannot be moved; firmly fixed [The ancients thought the earth *immovable*.] **2** not changing; steadfast [an *immovable* purpose].

im·pa·tient (im pā′shənt) *adj.* not patient; not willing to put up with delay or annoyance [*impatient* customers standing in line].

im·per·fect (im pʉr′fikt) *adj.* **1** not perfect; having some fault or flaw. **2** lacking in something; not complete; unfinished [an *imperfect* knowledge of Russian]. —**im·per′fect·ly** *adv.*

im·per·son·al (im pur′sən əl) *adj.* not referring to any particular person [The teacher's remarks about cheating were *impersonal* and meant for all the students.] —**im·per′son·al·ly** *adv.*

im·prac·ti·cal (im prak′ti kəl) *adj.* not practical; not useful, efficient, etc.

im·pure (im pyoor′) *adj.* 1 not clean; dirty [Smoke made the air *impure*.] 2 mixed with things that do not belong [*impure* gold]. 3 not decent or proper [*impure* thoughts].

in·de·pend·ent (in′dē pen′dənt) *adj.* 1 not ruled or controlled by another; self-governing [Many colonies became *independent* countries after World War II.] 2 not connected with others; separate [an *independent* grocer]. 3 not influenced by others; thinking for oneself [an *independent* voter]. —**in′de·pend′ent·ly** *adv.*

In·di·a (in′dē ə) 1 a large peninsula of southern Asia. 2 a country in the central and southern part of this peninsula.

in·ju·ry (in′jər ē) *n.* harm or damage done to a person or thing [*injuries* received in a fall; *injury* to one's good name]. —*pl.* **in′ju·ries**

in·stant (in′stənt) *n.* a very short time; moment [Wait just an *instant*.]

in·stead (in sted′) *adv.* in place of the other; as a substitute [If you have no cream, use milk *instead*.]

in·tel·li·gent (in tel′ə jənt) *adj.* having or showing intelligence, especially high intelligence.

is·land (ī′lənd) *n.* 1 a piece of land smaller than a continent and surrounded by water. 2 any place set apart from what surrounds it [The oasis was an *island* of green in the desert.]

It·a·ly (it′l ē) a country in southern Europe, including the islands of Sicily and Sardinia.

Jj

jag·uar (jag′wär) *n.* a large wildcat that looks like a large leopard. It is yellowish with black spots and is found from the southwestern U.S. to Argentina.

Jan·u·ar·y (jan′yoo er′ē) *n.* the first month of the year, which has 31 days: abbreviated **Jan.**

Ja·pan (jə pan′) a country east of Korea, made up of many islands.

jaw (jô *or* jä) *n.* 1 either of the two bony parts that form the frame of the mouth and that hold the teeth. 2 either of two parts that close to grip or crush something [A vise and a pair of pliers have *jaws*.] 3 **jaws**, *pl.* the mouth; also, the entrance of a canyon, valley, etc.

jog (jäg) *v.* 1 to give a little shake to; jostle or nudge [*Jog* him to see if he's awake.] 2 to shake up or rouse, as the memory or the mind. —**jogged, jog′ging** ✦*n.* 1 a little shake or nudge. 2 a jogging pace; trot. —**jog′ger** *n.*

jour·nal (jur′nəl) *n.* 1 a daily record of what happens, such as a diary [She kept a *journal* of her trip.] 2 a written record of what happens at the meetings of a legislature, club, etc. 3 a newspaper or magazine.

jour·ney (jur′nē) *n.* a traveling from one place to another; trip. —*pl.* **jour′neys** ✦*v.* to go on a trip; travel. —**jour′neyed, jour′ney·ing**

judge (juj) *n.* 1 a public official with power to hear cases in a law court and decide what laws apply to them. 2 a person chosen to decide the winner in a contest or to settle an argument. ✦*v.* 1 to decide the winner of a contest or settle an argument [to *judge* a beauty contest]. 2 to form an opinion on something [Don't *judge* by first impressions.] —**judged, judg′ing** —**judge′ship′** *n.*

juic·y (jōō′sē) *adj.* full of juice [a *juicy* plum]. —**juic′i·er, juic′i·est**

Ju·ly (jōō lī′) *n.* the seventh month of the year, which has 31 days: abbreviated **Jul.**

June (jōōn) *n.* the sixth month of the year, which has 30 days: abbreviated **Jun.**

Kk

kay·ak (kī′ak) *n.* an Eskimo canoe made of a wooden frame covered with skins all around, except for an opening for the paddler.

kelp (kelp) *n.* a brown seaweed that is large and coarse.

kil·o·gram (kil′ə gram) *n.* a unit of weight, equal to 1,000 grams.

kil·o·li·ter (kil′ə lēt′ər) *n.* a unit of volume, equal to 1,000 liters or one cubic meter.

kiss (kis) *v.* 1 to touch with the lips as a way of showing love, respect, etc. or as a greeting. 2 to touch lightly [Her bowling ball just *kissed* the last pin.] ✦*n.* a touch or caress with the lips. —*pl.* **kiss′es**

knap·sack (nap′sak) *n.* a leather or canvas bag worn on the back, as by hikers, for carrying supplies.

knead (nēd) *v.* to keep pressing and squeezing dough or clay to make it ready for use [to *knead* bread dough].

knife (nīf) *n.* 1 a tool having a flat, sharp blade set in a handle, used for cutting. 2 a cutting blade that is part of a machine. —*pl.* **knives** ✦*v.* to cut or stab with a knife. —**knifed, knif′ing**

kayak

a	ask, fat
ā	ape, date
ä	car, lot
e	elf, ten
ē	even, meet
i	is, hit
ī	ice, fire
ō	open, go
ô	law, horn
oi	oil, point
oo	look, pull
ōō	ooze, tool
ou	out, crowd
u	up, cut
ʉ	fur, fern
ə	a in ago
	e in agent
	e in father
	i in unity
	o in collect
	u in focus
ch	chin, arch
ŋ	ring, singer
sh	she, dash
th	thin, truth
th	then, father
zh	s in pleasure

knives (nīvz) *n. plural of* **knife**.

know (nō) *v.* **1** to be sure of or have the facts about [Do you *know* why grass is green? She *knows* the law.] **2** to be aware of; realize [He suddenly *knew* he would be late.] **3** to have in one's mind or memory [The actress *knows* her lines.] **4** to be acquainted with [I *know* your brother well.] —**knew, known, know′ing**

knowl·edge (nä′lij) *n.* the fact or condition of knowing [*Knowledge* of the crime spread through the town.]

known (nōn) *past participle of* **know**.

knuck·le (nuk′əl) *n.* **1** a joint of the finger; especially, a joint connecting a finger to the rest of the hand. **2** the knee or hock joint of a pig, calf, etc., used as food. —☆**knuckle down,** to work hard. —**knuckle under,** to give in.

kook·a·bur·ra (kꝏk′ə bur ə) *n.* an Australian bird related to the kingfisher. Its cry sounds like someone laughing loudly.

kookaburra

la·dy (lā′dē) *n.* **1** a woman, especially one who is polite and refined and has a sense of honor. **2** a woman belonging to a family of high social standing, as the wife of a lord. —*pl.* **la′dies**

land·ing (lan′diŋ) *n.* **1** a coming to shore or a putting on shore [the *landing* of troops]. **2** a place where a ship can land; pier or dock. **3** a platform at the end of a flight of stairs. **4** a coming down after flying, jumping, or falling.

late (lāt) *adj., n.* **1** happening or coming after the usual or expected time; tardy [*late* for school; a *late* train]. **2** happening or appearing just before now; recent [a *late* news broadcast]. —**lat′er** or **lat′ter, lat′est** or **last** ◆*adv.* **1** after the usual or expected time [Roses bloomed *late* last year.] **2** toward the end of some period [They came *late* in the day.] —**lat′er, lat′est** —**late′ness** *n.*

lat·i·tude (lat′ə tꝏd *or* lat′ə tyꝏd) *n.* **1** freedom from strict rules; freedom to do as one wishes [Our school allows some *latitude* in choosing courses.] **2** distance north or south of the equator, measured in degrees [Minneapolis is at 45 degrees north *latitude*.]

laugh (laf) *v.* **1** to make a series of quick sounds with the voice that show one is amused or happy or, sometimes, that show scorn. One usually smiles or grins when laughing. ◆*n.* the act or sound of laughing.

launch (lônch *or* länch) *v.* **1** to throw, hurl, or send off into space [to *launch* a rocket]. **2** to cause to slide into the water; set afloat [to *launch* a new ship]. **3** to start or begin [to *launch* an attack].

law·yer (lô′yər *or* lä′yər) *n.* a person whose profession is giving advice on law or acting for others in lawsuits.

lead (lēd) *v.* **1** to show the way for; guide [*Lead* us along the path. The lights *led* me to the house.] **2** to go or make go in some direction [This path *leads* to the lake. Drainpipes *lead* the water away.] **3** to be at the head of or be first [He *leads* the band. Their team was *leading* at the half.] —**led, lead′ing** ◆*n.* **1** the first place or position [The bay horse is in the *lead*.] **2** a clue [The police followed up every *lead*.]

lead·ing (lē′diŋ) *adj.* **1** that leads; guiding [A *leading* question guides one toward a certain answer.] **2** most important; playing a chief role [She played a *leading* part in our campaign.]

leaf (lēf) *n.* **1** any of the flat, green parts growing from the stem of a plant or tree. **2** a petal [a rose *leaf*]. **3** a sheet of paper in a book [Each side of a *leaf* is a page.] —*pl.* **leaves**

learn (lurn) *v.* **1** to get some knowledge or skill, as by studying or being taught [I have *learned* to knit. Some people never *learn* from experience.] **2** to find out about something; come to know [When did you *learn* of his illness?] **3** to fix in the mind; memorize [*Learn* this poem by tomorrow.] —**learned** (lurnd) **or learnt** (lurnt), **learn′ing** —**learn′er** *n.*

leash (lēsh) *n.* a strap or chain by which a dog, etc. is led or held. —*pl.* **leash′es** ◆*v.* to put a leash on.

leaves (lēvz) *n. plural of* **leaf**.

leg·end (lej′ənd) *n.* **1** a story handed down through the years and connected with some real events, but probably not true in itself [The story of King Arthur is a British *legend*.] **2** all such stories as a group [famous in Irish *legend*].

☆**length·y** (leŋkth′ē) *adj.* long or too long [a *lengthy* speech]. —**length′i·er, length′i·est** —**length′i·ly** *adv.*

leop·ard (lep′ərd) *n.* **1** a large, fierce animal of the cat family, having a tan coat with black spots. It is found in Africa and Asia. **2** *another name for* **jaguar**.

let's (lets) let us.

let·ter (let′ər) *n.* **1** any of the marks used in writing or printing to stand for a sound of speech; character of an alphabet. **2** a written message, usually sent by mail. ◆*v.* to print letters by hand [Will you *letter* this poster?]

li·brar·y (lī′brer ē) *n.* **1** a place where a collection of books is kept for reading or borrowing. **2** a collection of books. —*pl.* **li′brar′ies**

life (līf) *n.* **1** the quality of plants and animals that makes it possible for them to take in food, grow, produce others of their kind, etc. and that makes them different from rocks, water, etc. [Death is the loss of *life*.] **2** a living thing; especially, a human being [The crash took six *lives*.] —*pl.* **lives**

life·boat (līf′bōt) *n.* **1** any of the small boats carried by a ship for use if the ship must be abandoned. **2** a sturdy boat kept on a shore, for use in rescuing people in danger of drowning.

lift (lift) *v.* **1** to bring up to a higher place; raise [Please *lift* that box onto the truck.] **2** to rise or go up [Our spirits *lifted* when spring came.] ◆*n.* **1** a ride in the direction one is going. **2** a device for carrying people up or down a slope [a ski *lift*].

lis·ten (lis′ən) *v.* to pay attention in order to hear; try to hear [*Listen* to the rain. *Listen* when the counselor speaks.] —**lis′ten·er** *n.*

li·ter (lēt′ər) *n.* the basic unit of capacity in the metric system, equal to 1 cubic decimeter. A liter is equal to a little more than a quart in liquid measure and to a little less than a quart in dry measure.

lives (līvz) *n.* *plural of* **life.**

loaf (lōf) *n.* **1** a portion of bread baked in one piece, usually oblong in shape. **2** any food baked in this shape [a meat *loaf*]. —*pl.* **loaves**

loan (lōn) *n.* **1** the act of lending [Thanks for the *loan* of your pen.] **2** something lent, especially a sum of money. ◆*v.* to lend, especially a sum of money or something to be returned.

loaves (lōvz) *n.* *plural of* **loaf.**

lo·cate (lō′kāt *or* lō kāt′) *v.* **1** to set up or place; situate [Their shop is *located* in the new mall.] **2** to find out where something is [Have you *located* the gloves that you lost?] —**lo′cat·ed, lo′cat·ing**

lock (läk) *n.* **1** a device for fastening a door, safe, etc. by means of a bolt. A lock can usually be opened only by a special key, etc. **2** an enclosed part of a canal, river, etc. with gates at each end. Water can be let in or out of it to raise or lower ships from one level to another. ◆*v.* to fasten or become fastened with a lock [I *locked* the door.] —**locked, lock′ing**

lo·co·mo·tive (lō′kə mō′tiv) *n.* a steam, electric, or diesel engine on wheels, that pulls or pushes railroad trains. ◆*adj.* moving or able to move from one place to another.

lodge (läj) *n.* **1** a place to live in; especially, a small house for some special purpose [a hunting *lodge*]. **2** the hut or tent of an American Indian. ◆*v.* **1** to provide with a place to live or sleep in for a time [She agreed to *lodge* the strangers overnight.] **2** to come to rest and stick firmly [A fish bone *lodged* in her throat.] —**lodged, lodg′ing**

lone·ly (lōn′lē) *adj.* **1** unhappy because one is alone or away from friends or family [Billy was *lonely* his first day at camp.] **2** without others nearby; alone [a *lonely* cottage]. **3** with few or no people [a *lonely* island]. —**lone′li·er, lone′li·est** —**lone′li·ness** *n.*

love (luv) *n.* **1** a deep and tender feeling of fondness and devotion [parents' *love* for their children; the *love* of Romeo and Juliet] . **2** a strong liking [a *love* of books]. **3** a person that one loves [my own true *love*]. ◆*v.* to feel love for [to *love* one's parents; to *love* all people]. —**loved, lov′ing**

love·ly (luv′lē) *adj.* very pleasing in looks or character; beautiful [a *lovely* person]. —**love′li·er, love′li·est**

loy·al (loi′əl) *adj.* **1** faithful to one's country [a *loyal* citizen]. **2** faithful to one's family, duty, or beliefs [a *loyal* friend].

luck·y (luk′ē) *adj.* having good luck [She is *lucky* to go to Rome.] —**luck′i·er, luck′i·est**

lug·gage (lug′ij) *n.* the suitcases, trunks, etc. of a traveler; baggage.

manatee

Mm

mag·ni·fy (mag′nə fī) *v.* to make look or seem larger than is really so [to *magnify* an object with a lens]. —**mag′ni·fied, mag′ni·fy·ing**

mam·mal (mam′əl) *n.* any animal with glands in the female that produce milk for feeding its young. —**mam·ma·li·an** (mə mā′lē ən) *adj., n.*

mam·moth (mam′əth) *n.* a type of large elephant that lived long ago. Mammoths had a hairy skin and long tusks that curved upward. ◆*adj.* very big; huge.

man (man) *n.* an adult male human being. **2** any human being; person ["that all *men* are created equal"]. —*pl.* **men**

man·ag·er (man′ij ər) *n.* a person who manages a business, baseball team, etc.

man·a·tee (man′ ə tē) *n.* a large animal that lives in shallow tropical waters and feeds on plants. It has flippers and a broad, flat tail; sea cow.

March (märch) *n.* the third month of the year, which has 31 days: abbreviated **Mar.**

marsh·mal·low (märsh′mel′ō *or* märsh′mal′ō) *n.* a soft, white, spongy candy coated with powdered sugar.

mas·cot (mas′kät) *n.* a person, animal, or thing thought to bring good luck by being present [Our team's *mascot* is the lion.]

match[1] (mach) *n.* **1** a slender piece of wood or cardboard having a tip coated with a chemical that catches fire when rubbed on a certain surface. **2** a slowly burning cord or wick once used for firing a gun or cannon. —*pl.* **match′es**

a	ask, fat
ā	ape, date
ä	car, lot
e	elf, ten
ē	even, meet
i	is, hit
ī	ice, fire
ō	open, go
ô	law, horn
oi	oil, point
ᴏᴏ	look, pull
ᴏ̄ᴏ̄	ooze, tool
ou	out, crowd
u	up, cut
u	fur, fern
ə	a in ago
	e in agent
	e in father
	i in unity
	o in collect
	u in focus
ch	chin, arch
ŋ	ring, singer
sh	she, dash
th	thin, truth
th	then, father
zh	s in pleasure

match² (mach) *n.* **1** two or more people or things that go well together [That suit and tie are a good *match*.] **2** a game or contest between two persons or teams [a tennis *match*].

mead·ow (med′ō) *n.* **1** a piece of land where grass is grown for hay. **2** low, level grassland near a stream or lake.

mean·ing (mēn′iŋ) *n.* what is meant; what is supposed to be understood; significance [She repeated her words to make her *meaning* clear. What is the *meaning* of this poem?] ◆*adj.* that has some meaning [a *meaning* smile].

meas·ure (mezh′ər) *v.* **1** to find out the size, amount, or extent of, as by comparing with something else [*Measure* the child's height with a yardstick. How do you *measure* a person's worth?] **2** to set apart or mark off a certain amount or length of [*Measure* out three pounds of sugar.] **3** to be of a certain size, amount, or extent [The table *measures* five feet on each side.] —**meas′ured, meas′ur·ing** ◆*n.* the size, amount, or extent of something, found out by measuring [The *measure* of the bucket is 15 liters.] **2** the notes or rests between two bars on a staff of music. **3** rhythm or meter, as of a poem or song.

meat (mēt) *n.* **1** the flesh of animals used as food. Meat usually does not include fish and often does not include poultry. **2** the part that can be eaten [the *meat* of a nut].

med·i·cine (med′ə sən) *n.* **1** any substance used in or on the body to treat disease, lessen pain, heal, etc. **2** the science of treating and preventing disease. **3** the branch of this science that makes use of drugs, diet, etc., especially as separate from surgery.

mel·o·dy (mel′ə dē) *n.* **1** an arrangement of musical tones in a series so as to form a tune; often, the main tune in the harmony of a musical piece [The *melody* is played by the oboes.] **2** any pleasing series of sounds [a *melody* sung by birds]. —*pl.* **mel′o·dies**

mem·ber (mem′bər) *n.* **1** any of the persons who make up a church, club, political party, or other group. **2** a leg, arm, or other part of the body.

mem·o·ry (mem′ər ē) *n.* **1** the act or power of remembering [to have a good *memory*]. **2** all that one remembers. **3** something remembered [The music brought back many *memories*.] **4** the part of a computer that stores information. —*pl.* **mem′o·ries**

men (men) *n.* plural of man.

mend (mend) *v.* to put back in good condition; repair; fix [to *mend* a torn shirt]. —**mend′ed, mend′ing**

men·u (men′yo͞o) *n.* a list of the foods served at a meal [a restaurant's dinner *menu*].

me·ter (mēt′ər) *n.* **1** a measure of length that is the basic unit in the metric system. One meter is equal to 39.37 inches. **2** rhythm in poetry; regular arrangement of accented and unaccented syllables in each line. **3** rhythm in music; arrangement of beats in each measure [Marches are often in 4/4 *meter*, with four equal beats in each measure.]

Mi·am·i (mī am′ē) a city on the southeastern coast of Florida.

mice (mīs) *n. plural of* **mouse**.

mi·cro·wave (mī′krō wāv′) *n.* any radio wave within a certain range, usually between 300,000 and 300 megahertz. Those of a certain wavelength create great heat when they pass through substances such as food. A **microwave oven** uses these waves for fast cooking. Others are used to transmit signals to and from communications satellites.

mi·grate (mī′grāt) *v.* **1** to move from one place or country to another, especially in order to make a new home. **2** to move from one region to another when the season changes, as some birds do in the spring and fall. —**mi′grat·ed, mi′grat·ing** —**mi·gra′tion** *n.*

milk (milk) *n.* a white liquid formed in special glands of female mammals for suckling their young. The milk that is a common food comes from cows. ◆*v.* to squeeze milk out from a cow, goat, etc. —**milk′er** *n.* —**milk′ing** *n.*

mil·li·gram (mil′i gram) *n.* a unit of weight, equal to one thousandth of a gram.

mil·li·li·ter (mil′i lēt′ər) *n.* a unit of volume, equal to one thousandth of a liter.

mil·li·me·ter (mil′i mēt′ər) *n.* a unit of measure, equal to one thousandth of a meter (.03937 inch).

min·er·al (min′ər əl) *n.* **1** a substance formed in the earth by nature; especially, a solid substance that was never animal or vegetable [Iron, granite, and salt are *minerals*. Coal is sometimes called a *mineral*, too.] **2** any of certain elements, as iron or phosphorus, needed by plants and animals.

miss (mis) *v.* **1** to fail to hit, meet, reach, get, catch, see, hear, etc. [The arrow *missed* the target. We *missed* our plane. I *missed* you at the play last night.] **2** to let go by; fail to take [You *missed* your turn.] **3** to escape; avoid [He just *missed* being hit.]

mol·lusk or **mol·lusc** (mäl′əsk) *n.* an animal with a soft body that is usually protected by a shell, as the oyster, clam, snail, etc.

☆**moose** (mo͞os) *n.* a large animal related to the deer, of the northern U.S. and Canada. The male has broad antlers with many points. —*pl.* **moose**

mollusk

moun·tain (mount′n) *n.* **1** a part of the earth's surface that rises high into the air; very high hill. **2 mountains**, *pl.* a chain or group of such high hills.

mouse (mous) *n.* **1** a small, gnawing animal found in houses and fields throughout the world. **2** a small device moved by the hand, as on a flat surface, so as to make the cursor move on a computer terminal. —*pl.* **mice** (mīs)

mov·er (mo͞ov′ər) *n.* a person or thing that moves; especially, ☆one whose work is moving people's furniture from one home to another.

mug·ger (mug′ər) *n.* a person who assaults others, usually in order to rob them.

mul·ti·ply (mul′tə plī) *v.* **1** to become more, greater, etc.; increase [Our troubles *multiplied*.] **2** to repeat a certain figure a certain number of times [If you *multiply* 10 by 4, or repeat 10 four times, you get the product 40.] —**mul′ti·plied, mul′ti·ply·ing**

mus·cle (mus′l) *n.* **1** the tissue in an animal's body that makes up the fleshy parts. Muscle can be stretched or tightened to move the parts of the body. **2** any single part or band of this tissue [The biceps is a *muscle* in the upper arm.] **3** strength that comes from muscles that are developed; brawn.

mu·si·cal (myo͞o′zi kəl) *adj.* **1** of music or for making music [a *musical* score; a *musical* instrument]. **2** like music; full of melody, harmony, etc. [Wind has a *musical* sound.] **3** fond of music or skilled in music. —**mu′si·cal·ly** *adv.*

☆**musk·rat** (musk′rat) *n.* **1** a North American animal that is like a large rat. It lives in water and has glossy brown fur.

mys·ter·y (mis′tər ē *or* mis′trə) *n.* **1** any event or thing that remains unexplained or is so secret that it makes people curious [That murder is still a *mystery*.] **2** a story or play about such an event [She read a murder *mystery*.] —*pl.* **mys′ter·ies**

Nn

need (nēd) *v.* to require; want [She *needs* a car.]

neigh·bor (nā′bər) *n.* **1** a person who lives near another. **2** a person or thing that is near another [France and Spain are *neighbors*.] **3** another human being; fellow person ["Love thy *neighbor*."]

neph·ew (nef′yo͞o) *n.*] **1** the son of one's brother or sister. **2** the son of one's brother-in-law or sister-in-law.

nerv·ous (nʉr′vəs) *adj.* feeling fear or expecting trouble [He is *nervous* about seeing the dentist.]

night·in·gale (nīt′n gāl) *n.* a small European thrush. The male is known for its sweet singing.

noise (noiz) *n.* sound, especially a loud, harsh, or confused sound [the *noise* of fireworks; *noises* of a city street]. —*pl.* **nois·es** ◆*v.* to make public by telling; spread [to *noise* a rumor about]. —**noised, nois′ing**

nom·i·nate (näm′ə nāt) *v.* **1** to name as a candidate for an election [Each political party *nominates* a person to run for president.] **2** to appoint to a position [The President *nominates* the members of the Cabinet.] —**nom′i·nat·ed, nom′i·nat·ing**

non·fic·tion (nän fik′shən) *n.* a piece of writing about the real world, real people, or true events, as a biography or history.

non·prof·it (nän präf′it) *adj.* not intending to make a profit [a *nonprofit* hospital].

non·sense (nän′sens) *n.* **1** speech or writing that is foolish or has no meaning [I read the letter but it just sounded like *nonsense* to me.] **2** silly or annoying behavior [She is a teacher who will put up with no *nonsense* in the classroom.] ◆*interj.* how silly! how foolish! indeed not!

non·stop (nän′stäp′) *adj., adv.* without making a stop [to fly *nonstop* from New York to Seattle].

North America the northern continent in the Western Hemisphere. Canada, the United States, Mexico, and the countries of Central America are in North America.

north·west (nôrth west′ *or* nôr west′) *n.* **1** the direction halfway between north and west. **2** a place or region in or toward this direction. ◆*adj.* **1** in, of, or toward the northwest [the *northwest* part of the county]. **2** from the northwest [a *northwest* wind]. ◆*adv.* in or toward the northwest [to sail *northwest*].

numb (num) *adj.* not able to feel, or feeling very little; deadened [My toes were *numb* with cold. He sat *numb* with grief.] ◆*v.* to make numb. —**numb′ly** *adv.* **numb′ness** *n.*

nurse (nʉrs) *n.* a person who has been trained to take care of sick people and help doctors.

nu·tri·ent (no͞o′trē ənt *or* nyo͞o′trē ənt) *adj.* nourishing. ◆*n.* any of the substances in food that are needed for health, such as proteins, minerals, vitamins, etc.

Oo

o·cean·og·ra·phy (ō′shən äg′rə fē) *n.* the science that studies the oceans and the animals and plants that live in them. —**o′cean·og′ra·pher** *n.*

muskrat

a	ask, fat
ā	ape, date
ä	car, lot
e	elf, ten
ē	even, meet
i	is, hit
ī	ice, fire
ō	open, go
ô	law, horn
oi	oil, point
o͝o	look, pull
o͞o	ooze, tool
ou	out, crowd
u	up, cut
ʉ	fur, fern
ə	a in ago
	e in agent
	e in father
	i in unity
	o in collect
	u in focus
ch	chin, arch
ŋ	ring, singer
sh	she, dash
th	thin, truth
th	then, father
zh	s in pleasure

organ

penguin

of·ten (ôf′ən *or* ôf′tən) *adv.* many times; frequently.

o·pen (ō′pən) *adj.* not closed, shut, covered, or stopped up [*open* eyes; *open* doors; an *open* jar; an *open* drain]. ◆*v.* **1** to make or become open, or no longer closed [Please *open* that trunk.   The door suddenly *opened.*] **2** to begin or start [We *opened* the program with a song.] **3** to start operating [She *opened* a new store.   School will *open* in September.] —**o′pen·ly** *adv.* —**o′pen·ness** *n.*

op·er·a·t or (äp′ər ātər) *n.* ☆**1** a person who operates a machine or device [a telephone *operator*]. **2** an owner or manager of a factory, mine, etc.

or·gan (ôr′gən) *n.* **1** a musical instrument having sets of pipes that make sounds when keys or pedals are pressed to send air through the pipes. *Also called* **pipe organ**. **2** a part of an animal or plant that has some special purpose [The heart, lungs, and eyes are *organs* of the body.]

or·gan·i·za·tion (ôr′gə ni zā′shən) *n.* **1** the act of organizing or arranging. **2** a group of persons organized for some purpose.

or·gan·ize (ôr′gə nīz) *v.* to arrange or place according to a system [The library books are *organized* according to their subjects.] —**or′gan·ized, or′gan·iz·ing** —**or′gan·iz′er** *n.*

or·phan (ôr′fən) *n.* a child whose parents are dead or, sometimes, one of whose parents is dead. ◆*adj.* **1** being an orphan [an *orphan* child]. **2** of or for orphans [an *orphan* home]. ◆*v.* to cause to become an orphan [children *orphaned* by war].

os·trich (äs′trich) *n.* a very large bird of Africa and southwestern Asia, with a long neck and long legs.   It cannot fly, but runs swiftly.

ot·ter (ät′ər) *n.* **1** a furry animal related to the weasel.   It has webbed feet used in swimming and a long tail, and it eats small animals and fish.

☆**out·doors** (out′dôrz′) *adv.* in or into the open; outside [We went *outdoors* to play.] ◆*n.* (out dôrz′) the world outside of buildings; the open air.

out·fit (out′fit) *n.* the clothing or equipment used in some work, activity, etc. [a hiking *outfit*]. ◆*v.* to supply with what is needed [Their store *outfits* campers.] —**out′fit·ted, out′fit·ting**

out·stand·ing (out′ stan′diŋ) *adj.* that stands out as very good or important [an *outstanding* lawyer].

☆**o·ver·coat** (ō′vər kōt) *n.* a heavy coat worn outdoors in cold weather.

ox (äks) *n.* **1** a castrated male of the cattle family, used for pulling heavy loads. **2** any animal of a group that chew their cud and have cloven hoofs, including the buffalo, bison, etc. —*pl.* **ox·en** (äk′s′n)

pace (pās) *n.* **1** a step in walking or running. **2** the length of a step or stride, thought of as about 30 to 40 inches. **3** the rate of speed at which something moves or develops [The scoutmaster set the *pace* in the hike.   Science goes forward at a rapid *pace.*] ◆*v.* **1** to walk back and forth across [While waiting for the verdict, I *paced* the floor nervously.] **2** to measure by paces [*Pace* off 30 yards.] —**paced, pac′ing** —**pac′er** *n.*

pad (pad) *n.* **1** anything made of or stuffed with soft material, and used to protect against blows, to give comfort, etc.; cushion [a shoulder *pad*; seat *pad*]. **2** the under part of the foot of some animals, as the wolf, lion, etc. ◆*v.* to stuff or cover with soft material [a *padded* chair]. —**pad′ded, pad′ding**

par·don (pärd′n) *n.* the act of forgiving or excusing. —*pl.* **par′dons**

par·ty (pär′tē) *n.* **1** a gathering of people to have a good time [a birthday *party*]. **2** a group of people who share the same political opinions and work together to elect certain people, to promote certain policies, etc. [the Republican *Party*]. **3** a group of people working or acting together [a hunting *party*]. —*pl.* **par′ties**

pas·sen·ger (pas′ən jər) *n.* a person traveling in a car, bus, plane, ship, etc., but not driving or helping to operate it.

pa·ti·o (pat′ē ō *or* pät′ē ō) *n.* ☆**1** in Spain and Spanish America, a courtyard around which a house is built.   ☆**2** a paved area near a house, with chairs, tables, etc. for outdoor lounging, dining, etc. —*pl.* **pa′ti·os**

pa·trol (pə trōl′) *v.* to make regular trips around a place in order to guard it [The watchman *patrolled* the area all night.] —**pa·trolled′, pa·trol′ling**

peace (pēs) *n.* **1** freedom from war or fighting [a nation that lives in *peace* with all other nations]. **2** law and order [The rioters were disturbing the *peace.*] **3** calm or quiet [to find *peace* of mind].

pen·cil (pen′səl) *n.* a long, thin piece of wood, metal, etc. with a center stick of graphite or crayon that is sharpened to a point for writing or drawing. ◆*v.* to mark, write, or draw with a pencil. —**pen′ciled** or **pen′cilled, pen′cil·ing** or **pen′cil·ling**

pen·guin (peŋ′gwin) *n.* a sea bird mainly of the antarctic region, with webbed feet and flippers for swimming and diving.   Penguins cannot fly.

pen·in·su·la (pə nin′sə lə) *n.* a long piece of land almost completely surrounded by water [Italy is a *peninsula*.] —**pen·in′su·lar** *adj.*

per·ceive (pər sēv′) *v.* **1** to become aware of through one of the senses, especially through seeing [to *perceive* the difference between two shades of red]. **2** to take in through the mind [I quickly *perceived* the joke.] —**per·ceived′, per·ceiv′ing**

perch (purch) *n.* **1** a small fish living in lakes and streams. It is used for food. **2** a similar saltwater fish. —*pl.* **perch** or **perch′es**

per·fect (pur′fəkt) *adj.* complete in every way and having no faults or errors [a *perfect* test paper].

per·form·er (pər fôrm′ər) *n.* one who does something to entertain an audience [The *performer* sang and danced.]

per·fume (pur′fyo͞om *or* pər fyo͞om′) *n.* **1** a sweet smell; pleasing odor; fragrance [the *perfume* of roses]. **2** a liquid with a pleasing smell, for use on the body, clothing, etc. ◆*v.* (pər fyo͞om′) to give a pleasing smell to, as with perfume. —**per·fumed′, per·fum′ing**

per·son (pur′sən) *n.* a human being; man, woman, or child [every *person* in this room].

pet·ri·fy (pe′tri fī) *v.* **1** to change into a substance like stone by replacing the normal cells with minerals [Trees buried under lava for a great many years can become *petrified*.] **2** to make unable to move or act, as because of fear or surprise. —**pet′ri·fied, pet′ri·fy·ing**

phase (fāz) *n.* **1** any of the sides or views of a subject by which it may be looked at, thought about, or shown [We discussed the many *phases* of the problem.] **2** any stage in a series of changes [Adolescence is a *phase* we all go through.] ◆*v.* —**phased, phas′ing**

☆**pho·ny** or **pho·ney** (fō′nē) *adj.* not real or genuine; fake; false. —**pho′ni·er, pho′ni·est** ◆*n.* a person or thing that is not really what it is supposed to be. —*pl.* **pho′nies** *This is a slang word.*

pho·to (fōt′ō) *n.* *a shorter name for* **photograph:** *used only in everyday talk.* —*pl.* **pho′tos**

pho·to·graph (fōt′ə graf) *n.* a picture made with a camera. ◆*v.* **1** to take a photograph of. **2** to look a certain way in photographs [She *photographs* taller than she is.]

pho·tog·ra·pher (fə täg′rə fər) *n.* a person who takes photographs, especially for a living.

phrase (frāz) *n.* a group of words that is not a complete sentence, but that gives a single idea, usually as a separate part of a sentence.

pi·an·o (pē ä′nō) *n.* a large musical instrument with many wire strings in a case and a keyboard. When a key is struck, it makes a small hammer hit a string so that it gives out a tone. **grand piano** *and* **upright.** —*pl.* **pi·an′os**

pic·ture (pik′chər) *n.* a likeness of a person, thing, scene, etc. made by drawing, painting, or photography; also, a printed copy of this. ◆*v.* **1** to make a picture of. **2** to show; make clear [Joy was *pictured* in her face.] **3** to describe or explain [Dickens *pictured* life in England.] **4** to form an idea or picture in the mind; imagine [You can *picture* how pleased I was!] —**pic′tured, pic·tur·ing**

pie (pī) *n.* a dish with a filling made of fruit, meat, etc., baked in a pastry crust.

piece (pēs) *n.* **1** a part broken or separated from a whole thing [The glass shattered and I swept up the *pieces*.] **2** a part or section of a whole, thought of as complete by itself [a *piece* of meat; a *piece* of land]. **3** any one of a set or group of things [a dinner set of 52 *pieces*; a chess *piece*]. ◆*v.* to join the pieces of, as in mending [to *piece* together a broken jug].

pine·ap·ple (pīn′ap əl) *n.* **1** a juicy tropical fruit that looks a little like a large pine cone. **2** the plant it grows on, having a short stem and curved leaves with prickly edges.

pi·o·neer (pī ə nir′) *n.* ☆ a person who goes before, opening up the way for others to follow, as an early settler or a scientist doing original work [Daniel Boone was a *pioneer* in Kentucky. Marie Curie was a *pioneer* in the study of radium.] ◆*v.* to act as a pioneer; open up the way for others [The Wright brothers *pioneered* in air travel.]

Pitts·burgh (pits′burg) a city in southwestern Pennsylvania.

pit·y (pit′ē) *v.* to feel sorrow for another's suffering or trouble [to *pity* someone's misfortune]. —**pit′ied, pit′y·ing**

plain (plān) *adj.* **1** open; clear; not blocked [in *plain* view]. **2** easy to understand; clear to the mind [The meaning is *plain*.] **3** simple; easy [I can do a little *plain* cooking.] —**plain′ly** *adv.* —**plain′ness** *n.*

plane[1] (plān) *adj.* **1** flat; level; even. ◆*n.* **2** *a shorter form of* **airplane.**

plane[2] (plān) *n.* a tool used by carpenters for shaving wood in order to make it smooth or level. ◆*v.* to make smooth or level with a plane. —**planed, plan′ing**

plat·form (plat′fôrm) *n.* a flat surface or stage higher than the ground or floor around it [a *platform* at a railroad station; a speaker's *platform*].

po·et·ry (pō′ə trē) *n.* **1** the art of writing poems. **2** poems [the *poetry* of Keats].

po·lit·i·cal (pə lit′i kəl) *adj.* **1** having to do with government, politics, etc. [*political* parties]. **2** of or like political parties or politicians [a *political* speech]. —**po·lit′i·cal·ly** *adv.*

perch

a	ask, fat
ā	ape, date
ä	car, lot
e	elf, ten
ē	even, meet
i	is, hit
ī	ice, fire
ō	open, go
ô	law, horn
oi	oil, point
o͝o	look, pull
o͞o	ooze, tool
ou	out, crowd
u	up, cut
u	fur, fern
ə	a in ago
	e in agent
	e in father
	i in unity
	o in collect
	u in focus
ch	chin, arch
ŋ	ring, singer
sh	she, dash
th	thin, truth
th	then, father
zh	s in pleasure

poll (pōl) *n.* **1** a voting or listing of opinions by persons; also, the counting of these votes or opinions [A *poll* of our class shows that most of us want a party.] **2** the number of votes cast. **3** a list of voters. ☆**4 polls**, *pl.* a place where people go to vote.

porch (pôrch) *n.* **1** a covered entrance to a building, usually with a roof that is held up by posts. **2** a room on the outside of a building, either open or enclosed by screens, etc.

porpoise

por·poise (pôr′pəs) *n.* **1** a water animal that is like a small whale. It is dark above and white below and has a blunt snout. **2** *another name for* **dolphin**.

port·hole (pôrt′hōl) *n.* a small opening in a ship's side, as for letting in light and air.

pow·er·ful (pou′ər fəl) *adj.* having much power; strong or influential [a *powerful* hand; a *powerful* leader]. —**pow′er·ful·ly** *adv.*

prac·tice (prak′tis) *v.* **1** to do or carry out regularly; make a habit of [to *practice* what one preaches; to *practice* charity]. **2** to do something over and over again in order to become skilled at it [She *practices* two hours a day on the piano.] **3** to work at as a profession or occupation [to *practice* medicine]. —**prac′ticed, prac′tic·ing**

☆**prai·rie** (prer′ē) *n.* a large area of level or rolling grassy land without many trees.

praise (prāz) *v.* **1** to say good things about; give a good opinion of [to *praise* someone's work]. **2** to worship, as in song [to *praise* God]. —**praised, prais′ing**

pre·cau·tion (prē kô′shən *or* prē kä′shən) *n.* care taken ahead of time, as against danger, failure, etc. [She took the *precaution* of locking the door before she left.] —**pre·cau′tion·ar′y** *adj.*

pre·cip·i·ta·tion (prē sip′ə tā′shən) *n.* **1** a sudden bringing about of something [the *precipitation* of a cold by getting chilled]. **2** sudden or reckless haste. **3** rain, snow, etc. or the amount of this.

pre·dict (prē dikt′) *v.* to tell what one thinks will happen in the future [I *predict* that you will win.] —**pre·dict′a·ble** *adj.*

pre·fix (prē′fiks) *n.* a syllable or group of syllables joined to the beginning of a word to change its meaning. Some common prefixes are *un-, non-, re-, anti-,* and *in-*.

pre·paid (prē pād′) *past tense and past participle of* **prepay**.

pre·pay (prē pā′) *v.* to pay for ahead of time [Postage is normally *prepaid*.] —**pre·paid′, pre·pay′ing**

pre·set (prē set′) *v.* to set or adjust ahead of time [He *presets* the oven so it will be ready for the cake.] —**pre·set′, pre·set′ting**

pret·ty (prit′ē) *adj.* **1** pleasant to look at or hear, especially in a delicate, dainty, or graceful way [a *pretty* girl; a *pretty* voice; a *pretty* garden]. **2** fine; good; nice: —**pret′ti·er, pret′ti·est**

pre·view (prē′vyo͞o) *n.* ☆a view or showing ahead of time; especially, a private showing of a movie before showing it to the public. ◆*v.* to give a preview of.

price (prīs) *n.* **1** the amount of money asked or paid for something; cost [What is the *price* of that coat?] **2** value or worth [a painting of great *price*]. ◆*v.* to set the price of [The rug was *priced* at $40.] —**priced, pric′ing**

pride (prīd) *n.* **1** an opinion of oneself that is too high; vanity [Her *pride* blinded her to her own faults.] **2** proper respect for oneself; dignity; self-respect [He has too much *pride* to go begging.] **3** pleasure or satisfaction in something done, owned, etc. [We take *pride* in our garden.] **4** a person or thing that makes one proud [She is her father's *pride* and joy.] —**prid′ed, prid′ing**

prince (prins) *n.* a son or grandson of a king or queen.

prin·ci·pal (prin′sə pəl) *n.* the head of a school.

print·ing (print′iŋ) *n.* **1** the act of one that prints. **2** the making of printed material, as books, newspapers, etc. **3** printed words. —**print′er** *n.*

pro·ceed (prō sēd′) *v.* **1** to go on, especially after stopping for a while [After eating, we *proceeded* to the next town.] **2** to begin and go on doing something [I *proceeded* to build a fire.]

prod·uct (präd′əkt) *n.* **1** something produced by nature or by human beings [Wood is a natural *product*. A desk is a manufactured *product*.] **2** result [The story is a *product* of her imagination.] **3** a number that is the result of multiplying [28 is the *product* of 7 multiplied by 4.]

pro·gram (prō′gram) *n.* **1** the acts, speeches, or musical pieces that make up a ceremony or entertainment [a commencement *program*]. **2** a scheduled broadcast on radio or TV.

prom·ise (präm′is) *n.* **1** an agreement to do or not to do something; vow [to make and keep a *promise*]. **2** a sign that gives reason for expecting success; cause for hope [She shows *promise* as a singer.] ◆*v.* to make a promise to [I *promised* them I'd arrive at ten.] —**prom′ised, prom′is·ing**

prompt (prämpt) *adj.* **1** quick in doing what should be done; on time [He is *prompt* in paying his bills.] **2** done, spoken, etc. without waiting [We would like a *prompt* reply.] ◆*v.* to urge or stir into action [Tyranny *prompted* them to revolt.] —**prompt′ly** *adv.* —**prompt′ness** *n.*

prop·er (präp′ər) *adj.* **1** right, correct, or suitable [the *proper* tool for this job; the *proper* clothes for a party]. **2** not to be ashamed of; decent; respectable [*proper* manners]. —**prop′er·ly** *adv.*

pro·tect (prō tekt′) *v.* to guard or defend against harm or danger; shield [armor to *protect* the knight's body]. —**pro·tec′tor** *n.*

pro·te·in (prō′tēn) *n.* a substance containing nitrogen and other elements, found in all living things and in such foods as cheese, meat, eggs, beans, etc. It is a necessary part of an animal's diet.

pro·test (prō test′ *or* prō′test) *v.* **1** to speak out against; object [They joined the march to *protest* against injustice.] **2** to say in a positive way; insist [Bill *protested* that he would be glad to help.] ◆*n.* (prō′test) the act of protesting; objection [They ignored my *protest* and continued hammering.] —**pro·test′er** or **pro·tes′tor** *n.*

prove (prōōv) *v.* **1** to show that something is true or correct [She showed us the method of *proving* our arithmetic problems.] **2** to put to a test or trial; find out about through experiments [A *proving* ground is a place for testing new equipment, as aircraft.] **3** to turn out to be [Your guess *proved* right.] —**proved, proved** or **prov′en, prov′ing**

pub·lic (pub′lik) *adj.* of or having to do with the people as a whole [*public* opinion]. ◆*n.* the people as a whole [what the *public* wants].

punc·tu·a·tion (puŋk′choo ā′shən) *n.* **1** the use of commas, periods, etc. in writing [rules of *punctuation*]. **2** punctuation marks [What *punctuation* is used to end sentences?]

purse (purs) *n.* a bag of leather or cloth used for carrying money, cosmetics, keys, and so on. —*pl.* **purs′es**

quit·ter (kwit′ər) *n.* ☆a person who quits or gives up too easily.

rail·road (rāl′rōd) *n.* **1** a road on which there is a track made up of parallel steel rails along which trains run. **2** a series of such roads managed as a unit, together with the cars, engines, stations, etc. that belong to it.

rai·sin (rā′zən) *n.* a sweet grape dried for eating.

rake (rāk) *n.* a tool with a long handle having a set of teeth or prongs at one end. It is used for gathering loose grass, leaves, etc. or for smoothing broken ground. ◆*v.* to gather together or smooth as with a rake [to *rake* leaves; to *rake* a gravel path]. —**raked, rak′ing**

☆**ranch** (ranch) *n.* a large farm, especially in the Western part of the U.S., where cattle, horses, or sheep are raised. —*pl.* **ranch′es** ◆*v.* to work on or manage a ranch. —**ranch′er** *n.*

rap·id (rap′id) *adj.* very swift or quick [a *rapid* journey]. ◆☆*n.* usually **rapids**, *pl.* a part of a river where the water moves swiftly. —**rap′id·ly** *adv.*

reach (rēch) *v.* **1** to stretch out one's hand, arm, etc. [He *reached* up and shook the branch.] **2** to touch, as by stretching out [Can you *reach* the top shelf?] **3** to stretch out in time, space, amount, etc. [Her fame *reaches* into all parts of the world.]

re·ac·tion (rē ak′shən) *n.* an action, happening, etc. in return or in response to some other action, happening, force, etc. [What was their *reaction* to your suggestion? A rubber ball bounces as a *reaction* to hitting the ground.]

rea·son (rē′zən) *n.* **1** something said to explain or try to explain an act, idea, etc. [Write the *reasons* for your answer.] **2** a cause for some action, feeling, etc.; motive [Noisy neighbors were our *reason* for moving.] **3** the power to think, get ideas, decide things, etc. [Human beings are the only creatures that truly have *reason*.]

re·ceipt (rē sēt′) *n.* **1** a receiving or being received [Upon *receipt* of the gift, she thanked him.] **2** a written statement that something has been received [My landloard gave me a *receipt* when I paid my rent.] **3** **receipts**, *pl.* the amount of money taken in, as in a business

re·ceive (rē sēv′) *v.* **1** to take or get what has been given or sent to one [to *receive* a letter]. **2** to meet with,; be given; undergo [to *receive* punishment; to *receive* applause]. **3** to find out about; learn [He *received* the news calmly.] **4** to greet guests and let them come in [Our hostess *received* us at the door.] —**re·ceived′, re·ceiv′ing**

re·count (rē kount′) *v.* to count again [You had better *recount* your change just to make sure.]

re·duce (rē dōōs′ *or* rē dyōōs′) *v* **1** to make smaller, less, fewer, etc.; decrease [to *reduce* speed; to *reduce* taxes]. **2** to loose weight, as by dieting. **3** to make lower, as in rank or condition; bring down [to *reduce* a major to rank of captain; a family *reduced* to poverty.] —**re·duced′, re·duc′ing** —**re·duc′er** *n.* —**re·duc′i·ble** *adj*

reel (rēl) *n.* **1** a frame or spool on which film, fishing line, wire, etc. is wound. **2** the amount of movie film, wire, etc. usually wound on one reel. ◆*v.* to wind on a reel

reel

a	ask, fat
ā	ape, date
ä	car, lot
e	elf, ten
ē	even, meet
i	is, hit
ī	ice, fire
ō	open, go
ô	law, horn
oi	oil, point
͝oo	look, pull
͞oo	ooze, tool
ou	out, crowd
u	up, cut
ʉ	fur, fern
ə	a in ago
	e in agent
	e in father
	i in unity
	o in collect
	u in focus
ch	chin, arch
ŋ	ring, singer
sh	she, dash
th	thin, truth
th	then, father
zh	s in pleasure

177

reindeer

re·fill (rē fil′) *v.* to fill again. ◆*n.* (rē′fil)**1** something to refill a special container [a *refill* for a ball point pen]. **2** any extra filling of a prescription for medicine. —**re·fill′a·ble** *adj.*

re·frig·er·a·tor (ri frij′ər āt′ər) *n.* a box or room in which the air is kept cool to keep food, etc. from spoiling.

re·fund (rē fund′) *v.* to give back money, etc.; repay [We will *refund* the full price if you are not satisfied.] ◆*n.* (rē′fund) the act of refunding or the amount refunded. —**re·fund′a·ble** *adj.*

reg·is·ter (rej′is tər) *n.* **1** a record or list of names, events, or things; also, a book in which such a record is kept [a hotel *register*; *register* of accounts]. **2** a device for counting and keeping a record of [a cash *register*]. ◆*v.* ☆**1** to keep a record of in a register [to *register* a birth]. **2** to put one's name in a register, as of voters.

reg·u·lar (reg′yə lər) *adj.* formed or arranged in an orderly way; balanced [a face with *regular* features].

rein·deer (rān′dir) *n.* a large deer found in northern regions, where it is tamed and used for work or as food. Both the male and female have antlers. —*pl.* **rein′deer**

re·lief (rē lēf′) *n.* **1** a lessening of pain, discomfort, worry, etc. [This salve will give *relief* from itching.] **2** anything that lessens pain, worry, etc. or gives a pleasing change [It's a *relief* to get out of that stuffy hall.] **3** help given to poor people, to victims of a flood, etc.

re·ly (rē lī′) *v.* to trust or depend [You can *rely* on me to be on time.] —**re·lied′, re·ly′ing**

re·mem·ber (rē mem′bər) *v.* **1** to think of again [I suddenly *remembered* I was supposed to mow the lawn.] **2** to bring back to mind by trying; recall [I just can't *remember* your name.] **3** to be careful not to forget [*Remember* to look both ways before crossing.]

re·move (rē mo͞ov′) *v.* to move to another place; take away or take off [They *removed* their coats.]

re·pair (rē per′) *v.* **1** to put into good condition again; fix; mend [to *repair* a broken toy]. **2** to set right; correct [to *repair* a mistake; to *repair* an injustice]. ◆*n.* **1** the act of repairing. **2** *usually* **repairs**, *pl.* work done in repairing [to make *repairs* on a house]. —**re·pair′a·ble** *adj.*

re·ply (rē plī′) *v.* to answer by saying or doing something [to *reply* to a question; to *reply* to the enemy's fire with a counterattack]. —**re·plied′, re·ply′ing** ◆*n.* an answer. —*pl.* **re·plies′**

re·port (rē pôrt′) *v.* **1** to tell about; give an account of [I *reported* on my trip to the Falls.] **2** to tell as news [The papers *reported* little damage as a result of the storm.] ◆*n.* an account of something, often one in written or printed form [a financial *report*].

☆**res·tau·rant** (res′tər änt *or* res′tränt) *n.* a place where meals can be bought and eaten.

re·turn (rē turn′) *v.* **1** to go or come back [When did you *return* from your trip?] **2** to bring, send, carry, or put back [Our neighbor *returned* the ladder.] **3** to pay back by doing the same [to *return* a visit; to *return* a favor]. **4** to report back [The jury *returned* a verdict of "not guilty."]

rid·er (rīd′ər) *n.* a person who rides.

rise (rīz) *v.* **1** to stand up or get up from a lying or sitting position [*rise* to greet the guests.] **2** to get up after sleeping [She *rises* early.] —**rose** (rōz), **ris′en** (riz′en), **ris′ing**

risk (risk) *n.* the chance of getting hurt, or of losing, failing, etc.; danger [He ran into the burning house at the *risk* of his life.] ◆*v.* to take the chance of [Are you willing to *risk* a fight for your beliefs?]

roast (rōst) *v.* **1** to cook with little or no liquid, as in an oven or over an open fire [to *roast* a chicken or a whole ox]. **2** to dry or brown with great heat [to *roast* coffee]. ◆*n.* a piece of roasted meat.

ro·dent (rōd′nt) *n.* an animal having sharp front teeth for gnawing. Rats, mice, rabbits, squirrels, woodchucks, and beavers are rodents.

rough·ly (ruf′lē) *adv.* **1** in a rough manner. **2** more or less; about [*Roughly* 50 people came to the party.]

roy·al·ty (roi′əl tē) *n.* **1** a royal person, or royal persons as a group [a member of British *royalty*]. **2** the rank or power of a king or queen. **3** royal quality or nature; nobility, splendor, etc. —*pl.* **roy′al·ties**

rude (ro͞od) *adj.* without respect for others; impolite [It was *rude* of them not to thank you.] —**rud′er, rud′est**

rule (ro͞ol) *n.* **1** a statement or law that is meant to guide or control the way one acts or does something [the *rules* of grammar; baseball *rules*]. **2** a usual way of doing something, behaving, etc. [to make it a *rule* never to rush]. **3** government or reign [the *rule* of Elizabeth I].

☆**run·way** (run′wā) *n.* a track or path on which something moves, as a paved strip on an airfield used by airplanes in taking off and landing.

Ss

safe (sāf) *adj.* **1** free from harm or danger; secure [a *safe* hiding place; *safe* in bed]. **2** not hurt or harmed [We emerged *safe* from the wreck.] **3** that can be trusted [a *safe* investment]. —**saf′er, saf′est** —**safe′ly** *adv.*

sal·ad (sal′əd) *n.* any mixture of vegetables, fruits, fish, eggs, etc., with a dressing of oil, vinegar, spices, etc.   It is usually served cold, often on lettuce leaves.

sand·wich (san′dwich *or* san′wich) *n.* slices of bread with a filling of meat, cheese, etc. between them. —*pl.* **sand′wich·es** ✦*v.* to squeeze in [a shed *sandwiched* between two houses].

San Fran·cis·co (san′ fran sis′kō) a city on the coast of central California.

sar·dine (sär dēn′) *n.* a small fish, as a young herring, preserved in oil and packed in cans.

sash (sash) *n.* a band, ribbon, or scarf worn over the shoulder or around the waist. —*pl.* **sash′es**

sat·el·lite (sat′l īt) *n.* **1** a heavenly body that revolves around another, larger one [The moon is a *satellite* of the earth.] **2** an artificial object put into orbit around the earth, the moon, or some other heavenly body.

sat·is·fy (sat′is fī) *v.* **1** to meet the needs or wishes of; content; please [Only first prize will *satisfy* him.] **2** to make feel sure; convince [The jury was *satisfied* that he was innocent.] —**sat·is·fied, sat·is·fy·ing**

sauce (sôs *or* säs) *n.* **1** a liquid or soft dressing served with food to make it tastier [spaghetti with tomato *sauce*]. ☆**2** fruit that has been stewed [apple*sauce*].

sauce·pan (sôs′pan *or* s′äs′pan) *n.* a small metal pot with a long handle, used for cooking.

sau·cer (sô′sər *or* sä′sər) *n.* a small, shallow dish, especially one for a cup to rest on.

save (sāv) *v.* **1** to rescue or keep from harm or danger [He was *saved* from drowning.] **2** to keep or store up for future use [She *saved* her money for a vacation.] **3** to keep from being lost or wasted [Traveling by plane *saved* many hours.] —**saved, sav′ing** —**sav′er** *n.*

scale[1] (skāl) *n.* **1** a series of marks along a line, with regular spaces in between, used for measuring [A Celsius thermometer has a basic *scale* of 100 degrees.] **2** the way that the size of a map, model, or drawing compares with the size of the thing that it stands for [One inch on a map of this *scale* equals 100 miles of real distance.] **3** a series of steps or degrees based on size, amount, rank, etc. [A passing grade on this *scale* is 70.]

scale[2] (skāl) *n.* **1** any of the thin, flat, hard plates that cover and protect certain fish and reptiles. **2** a thin piece or layer; flake [*scales* of rust in a water pipe]. ✦*v.* to scrape scales from [to *scale* a fish]. —**scaled, scal′ing**

scale[3] (skāl) *n.* **1** either of the shallow pans of a balance. **2** often **scales**, *pl.* the balance itself; also, any device or machine for weighing. ✦*v.* to weigh. —**scaled, scal′ing**

scare (sker) *v.* to make or become afraid; frighten. —**scared, scar′ing** ✦*n.* a sudden fear; fright [The loud noise gave me quite a *scare*.]

scarf (skärf) *n.* **1** a long or broad piece of cloth worn about the head, neck, or shoulders for warmth or decoration. **2** a long, narrow piece of cloth used as a covering on top of a table, bureau, etc. —*pl.* **scarfs** or **scarves** (skärvz)

scent (sent) *n.* **1** a smell; odor [the *scent* of apple blossoms]. **2** the sense of smell [Lions hunt partly by *scent*.] **3** a smell left by an animal [The dogs lost the fox's *scent* at the river.]

school·house (skōōl′hous) *n.* a building used as a school.

scout (skout) *n.* a soldier, ship, or plane sent to spy out the strength or movements of the enemy.

scram·ble (skram′bəl) *v.* to climb or crawl in a quick, rough way [The children *scrambled* up the steep hill.] —**scram′bled, scram′bling**

scratch (skrach) *n.* **1** a mark or cut made in a surface by something sharp. **2** a slight wound. —*pl.* **scratch′es**

scrawl (skrôl) *v.* to write or draw in a hasty, careless way. ✦*n.* careless or poor handwriting that is hard to read.

screech (skrēch) *v.* to give a harsh, high shriek. ✦*n.* a harsh, high shriek.

screen (skrēn) *n.* **1** a mesh woven loosely of wires so as to leave small openings between them.   Screens are used in windows, doors, etc. to keep insects out. **2** a covered frame or curtain used to hide, separate, or protect. **3** anything that hides, separates, or protects [a smoke *screen*; a *screen* of trees].

scrub (skrub) *v.* to clean or wash by rubbing hard [to *scrub* floors]. —**scrubbed, scrub′bing** ✦*n.* the act of scrubbing.

scur·ry (skur′ē) *v.* to run quickly; scamper. —**scur′ried, scur′ry·ing** ✦*n.* the act or sound of scurrying.

sea·son (sē′zən) *n.* **1** any of the four parts into which the year is divided: spring, summer, fall, or winter. **2** a special time of the year [the Easter *season*; the hunting *season*]. **3** a period of time [the busy *season* at a factory]. ✦*v.* to add to or change the flavor of [to *season* meat with herbs].

Se·at·tle (sē at′l) a city in Washington.

satellite

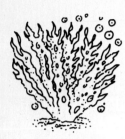

seaweed

sea·weed (sē'wēd) *n.* any plant or plants growing in the sea, especially algae. There are some plants like these that grow in fresh water and are also called seaweed.

seek (sēk) *v.* 1 to try to find; search for [to *seek* gold]. 2 to try to get; aim at [to *seek* a prize]. —**sought, seek'ing**

seize (sēz) *v.* 1 to take hold of in a sudden, strong, or eager way; grasp [to *seize* a weapon and fight; to *seize* an opportunity] . 2 to capture or arrest, as a criminal. 3 to take over as by force [The troops *seized* the fort. The city *seized* the property for nonpayment of taxes.] —**seized, seiz'ing**

sense (sens) *n.* 1 any of the special powers of the body and mind that let one see, hear, feel, taste, smell, etc. 2 a feeling or sensation [a *sense* of warmth; a *sense* of guilt]. 3 an understanding or appreciation; special awareness [a *sense* of honor; a *sense* of beauty; a *sense* of rhythm; a *sense* of humor]. 4 judgment or intelligence; reasoning [He showed good *sense* in his decision. There's no *sense* in going there late.]

serve (surv) *v.* 1 to work for someone as a servant [I *served* in their household for ten years.] 2 to do services for; aid; help [She *served* her country well.] 3 to hold a certain office [She *served* as mayor for two terms.] 4 to offer or pass food, drink, etc. to [May I *serve* you some chicken?] —**served, serv'ing**

sev·en (sev'ən) *n., adj.* one more than six; the number 7.

shake (shāk) *v.* to move quickly up and down, back and forth, or from side to side [She *shook* her head in disapproval.] —**shook, shak'en, shak'ing**

share (sher) *n.* a part that each one of a group gets or has [your *share* of the cake; my *share* of the blame]. ◆*v.* 1 to divide and give out in shares [The owners *shared* the profits with their employees.] 2 to have a share of with others; have or use together [The three of you will *share* the back seat.] —**shared, shar'ing**

shawl

sharp (shärp) *adj.* 1 having a thin edge for cutting, or a fine point for piercing [a *sharp* knife; a *sharp* needle]. 2 not gradual; abrupt [a *sharp* turn]. 3 severe or harsh [a *sharp* reply]. ◆*adv.* in a sharp manner; keenly, alertly, briskly, etc. [Look *sharp* when crossing streets.] —**sharp'ly** *adv.* —**sharp'ness** *n.*

shawl (shôl) *n.* a large piece of cloth worn, especially by women, over the shoulders or head.

sheep (shēp) *n.* an animal that chews its cud and is related to the goat. Its body is covered with heavy wool and its flesh is used as food, called mutton. —*pl.* **sheep**

shelf (shelf) *n.* a thin, flat length of wood, metal, etc. fastened against a wall or built into a frame so as to hold things [the top *shelf* of a bookcase. —*pl.* **shelves**

she'll (shēl) 1 she will. 2 she shall.

shel·ter (shel'tər) *n.* a place or thing that covers or protects from the weather or danger [The *shelter* protected us from the rain.]

sher·bet (shur'bət) *n.* a frozen dessert of fruit juice, sugar, and water, milk, etc.

ship·ment (ship'mənt) *n.* 1 the shipping of goods by any means. 2 the goods shipped.

shoe (shoo) *n.* an outer covering for the foot, usually of leather. ◆*v.* to furnish with shoes; put shoes on [to *shoe* a horse].

shore (shôr) *n.* 1 land at the edge of a sea or lake. 2 land, not water [The retired sailor lives on *shore.*]

short·en (shôrt'n) *v.* to make or become short or shorter [to *shorten* a skirt.]

should·n't (shood'nt) should not.

shov·el (shuv'əl) *n.* 1 a tool with a broad scoop and a handle, for lifting and moving loose material. 2 a machine with a part like a shovel, used for digging or moving large amounts of loose material [a steam *shovel*]. ◆*v.* to lift and move with a shovel [to *shovel* coal]. —**shov'eled** or **shov'elled, shov'el·ing** or **shov'el·ling**

show·er (shou'ər) *n.* 1 a short fall of rain or hail. 2 a sudden, very full fall or flow, as of sparks, praise, etc. ☆3 a bath in which the body is sprayed with fine streams of water. *The full name is* **shower bath.**

shriek (shrēk) *n.* a loud, sharp, shrill cry; screech; scream. ◆*v.* to cry out with a shriek [to *shriek* in terror.]

shrimp (shrimp) *n.* a small shellfish with a long tail, used as food.

shut·tle (shut'əl) *n.* 1 a device in weaving that carries a thread back and forth between the threads that go up and down. ☆2 a bus, train, or airplane that makes frequent trips back and forth over a short route. ◆*v.* to move rapidly to and fro. —**shut'tled, shut'tling**

☆**side·walk** (sīd'wôk) *n.* a path for walking, usually paved, along the side of a street.

si·lent (sī'lənt) *adj.* 1 not speaking or not talking much. 2 with no sound or noise; noiseless [Find a *silent* place to study. We went to a *silent* movie.] 3 not spoken or told [*silent* grief; the *silent* "b" in "debt".] —**si'lent·ly** *adv.*

sing·er (siŋ'ər) *n.* 1 a person that sings. 2 a bird that sings.

sink (siŋk) *v.* to go or put down below the surface [The boat is *sinking.*] —**sank** or **sunk, sink'ing**

sink·er (siŋk'ər) *n.* something that sinks, as a lead weight put on the end of a fishing line.

sis·ter (sis'tər) *n.* 1 a girl or woman as she is related to the other children of her parents. 2 a girl or woman who is close to one in some way; especially, a fellow member of the same race, religion, club, etc. 3 a nun.

sit (sit) **v.** **1** to rest the weight of the body upon the buttocks or haunches [She is *sitting* on a bench. The dog *sat* still.] **2** to perch, rest, lie, etc. [A bird *sat* on the fence. Cares *sit* lightly on him.] —**sat, sit′ting**

sit·ting (sit′iŋ) **n.** **1** the act or position of one that sits, as for a picture. **2** a meeting, as of a court or a council. **3** a period of being seated [I read the book in one *sitting.*]

skat·er (skāt′ər) **n.** one who moves along on skates [The *skater* twirled on the ice.]

skill (skil) **n.** **1** ability that comes from training, practice, etc. [He plays the violin with *skill.*] **2** an art, craft, or science, especially one that calls for use of the hands or body [Weaving is a *skill* often taught to the blind.]

skim (skim) **v.** **1** to take off floating matter from the top of a liquid [to *skim* cream from milk; to *skim* molten lead]. **2** to look through a book, magazine, etc. quickly without reading carefully. **3** to glide lightly, as over a surface [bugs *skimming* over the water]. —**skimmed, skim′ming**

☆**skunk** (skuŋk) **n.** **1** an animal having a bushy tail and black fur with white stripes down its back. It sprays out a very bad-smelling liquid when frightened or attacked.

☆**sleigh** (slā) **n.** a carriage with runners instead of wheels, for travel over snow or ice. ◆**v.** to ride in or drive a sleigh.

slen·der (slen′dər) **adj.** small in width as compared with the length or height; long and thin [a *slender* woman].

slice (slīs) **n.** a thin, broad piece cut from something [a *slice* of cheese; a *slice* of bread] . ◆**v.** **1** to cut into slices [to *slice* a cake]. **2** to cut as with a knife [The plow *sliced* through the soft earth.] —**sliced, slic′ing** —**slic′er n.**

slip (slip) **v.** **1** to go or pass quietly or without being noticed; escape [We *slipped* out the door. It *slipped* my mind. Time *slipped* by.] **2** to pass slowly into a certain condition [to *slip* into bad habits]. **3** to move, shift, or drop, as by accident [The plate *slipped* from my hand.] **4** to slide by accident [He *slipped* on the ice.] —**slipped, slip′ping**

slip·per (slip′ər) **n.** a light, low shoe that is usually worn while a person is relaxing at home.

smooth (smo͞oth) **adj.** having an even or level surface, with no bumps or rough spots [*smooth* water on the lake].

snap (snap) **v.** to bite, grasp, or snatch suddenly [The frog *snapped* at the fly.] —**snapped, snap′ping**

sneeze (snēz) **v.** to blow out breath from the mouth and nose in a sudden way that cannot be controlled [My cold made me *sneeze.*] —**sneezed, sneez′ing**

soar (sôr) **v.** to rise or fly high into the air [The plane *soared* out of sight.]

sof·ten (sôf′ən *or* säf′ən) **v.** to make or become soft or softer. —**sof′ten·er n.**

soft·ware (sôft′wer′ *or* sft′wer) **v.** the special instructions, information, etc. that make a computer operate.

sol·id (säl′id) **adj.** **1** keeping its shape instead of flowing or spreading out like a liquid or gas; quite firm or hard [Ice is water in a *solid* form.] **2** filled with matter throughout; not hollow [a *solid* block of wood]. **3** that has length, width, and thickness [A prism is a *solid* figure.] **4** strong, firm, sound, dependable, etc. [*solid* thinking; a *solid* building]. —**sol′id·ly adv.**

sor·row (sär′ō) **n.** **1** a sad or troubled feeling; sadness; grief. **2** a loss, death, or trouble causing such a feeling [Our grandmother's illness is a great *sorrow* to us.] ◆**v.** to feel or show sorrow [We are *sorrowing* over his loss.]

sort (sôrt) **n.** **1** a group of things that are alike in some way; kind; class [various *sorts* of toys]. **2** quality or type [phrases of a noble *sort*]. ◆**v.** to separate or arrange according to class or kind [*Sort* out the clothes that need mending.]

sought (sôt *or* sät) **v.** *past tense and past participle of* **seek.**

sound (sound) **n.** **1** the form of energy that acts on the ears so that one can hear. Sound consists of waves of vibrations carried in the air, water, etc. [In air, *sound* travels at a speed of about 332 meters per second, or 1,088 feet per second.] **2** anything that can be heard; noise, tone, etc. [the *sound* of bells]. **3** any of the noises made in speaking [a vowel *sound*]. ◆**v.** to make a sound [Your voice *sounds* hoarse.]

soup (so͞op) **n.** a liquid food made by cooking meat, vegetables, etc. as in water or milk.

South America the southern continent in the Western Hemisphere. —**South American**

south·east (south ēst′ *or* sou ēst′) **n.** **1** the direction halfway between south and east. **2** a place or region in or toward this direction. ◆**adj.** **1** in, of, or toward the southeast [the *southeast* part of the county]. **2** from the southeast [a *southeast* wind]. ◆**adv.** in or toward the southeast [to sail *southeast*].

south·ern (suth′ərn) **adj.** **1** in, of, or toward the south [the *southern* sky]. **2** from the south [a *southern* wind]. **3** **Southern,** of the South.

soy·bean (soi′bēn) **n.** **1** the seed, or bean, of a plant of Asia, now grown throughout the world. The beans are ground into flour, pressed for oil, etc. **2** the plant itself.

sleigh

a	ask, fat
ā	ape, date
ä	car, lot
e	elf, ten
ē	even, meet
i	is, hit
ī	ice, fire
ō	open, go
ô	law, horn
oi	oil, point
o͝o	look, pull
o͞o	ooze, tool
ou	out, crowd
u	up, cut
ʉ	fur, fern
ə	a in ago
	e in agent
	e in father
	i in unity
	o in collect
	u in focus
ch	chin, arch
ŋ	ring, singer
sh	she, dash
th	thin, truth
th	then, father
zh	s in pleasure

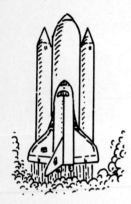

spacecraft

space (spās) *n.* **1** the area that stretches in all directions, has no limits, and contains all things in the universe [The earth, the sun, and all the stars exist in *space*.] **2** the distance or area between things or inside of something, especially as used for some purpose [a closet with much *space*; parking *space*]. **3** *a shorter name for* **outer space.** ◆*v.* to arrange with spaces in between [The trees are evenly *spaced*.] —**spaced, spac′ing**

space·craft (spās′kraft) *n.* any spaceship or satellite designed for use in outer space. —*pl.* **space′craft**

spare (sper) *v.* **1** to save or free from something [*Spare* us the trouble of listening to that story again.] **2** to get along without; give up [We can't *spare* the money or the time for a vacation trip.] —**spared, spar′ing** ◆*adj.* **1** kept for use when needed [a *spare* room; a *spare* tire]. **2** not taken up by regular work or duties; free [*spare* time]. —**spar′er, spar′est** ◆*n.* **1** an extra part or thing. ☆**2** in bowling, the act of knocking down all ten pins with two rolls of the ball. —**spare′ly** *adv.*

spark (spärk) *n.* **1** a small bit of burning matter, as one thrown off by a fire. **2** any flash of light like this [the *spark* of a firefly] . **3** the small flash of light that takes place when an electric current jumps across an open space, as in a spark plug.

spar·row (sper′ō) *n.* a small gray and brown songbird with a short beak. The common sparrow seen on city streets is the **English sparrow.**

spe·cies (spē′shēz *or* spē′sēz) *n.* a group of plants or animals that are alike in certain ways [The lion and tiger are two different *species* of cat.] —*pl.* **spe′cies**

speed (spēd) *n.* **1** fast motion; swiftness. **2** rate of motion; velocity [a *speed* of 10 miles per hour]. **3** swiftness of any action [reading *speed*]. ◆*v.* **1** to go or move fast or too fast [The arrow *sped* to its mark.] **2** to make go or move fast [He *sped* the letter on its way.] —**sped** *or* **speed′ed, speed′ing**

spend (spend) *v.* **1** to pay out or give up, as money, time, or effort [He *spent* $50 for food. Try to *spend* some time with me.] **2** to pass [She *spent* the summer at camp.] —**spent, spend′ing** —**spend′er** *n.*

spent (spent) *past tense and past participle of* **spend.** ◆*adj.* tired out; used up.

spice (spīs) *n.* any one of several vegetable substances used to give a special flavor or smell to food [Cinnamon, nutmeg, and pepper are kinds of *spices*.]

splash (splash) *v.* **1** to make a liquid scatter and fall in drops [to *splash* water or mud about]. **2** to dash a liquid on, so as to wet or soil [The car *splashed* my coat.] ◆*n.* the act or sound of splashing. —*pl.* **splash′es** —**splash′y** *adj.*

splen·did (splen′did) *adj.* very bright, brilliant, showy, or magnificent [a *splendid* gown].

splin·ter (splin′tər) *v.* to break or split into thin, sharp pieces [Soft pine *splinters* easily.] ◆*n.* a thin, sharp piece of wood, bone, etc. broken off.

spoil (spoil) *v.* **1** to make or become useless, worthless, rotten, etc.; damage; ruin [Ink stains *spoiled* the paper. Illness *spoiled* my attendance record. Meat *spoils* fast in warm weather.] **2** to cause a person to ask for or expect too much by giving in to all of that person's wishes [to *spoil* a child]. —**spoiled** *or* **spoilt, spoil′ing**

sponge (spunj) *n.* **1** a sea animal that is like a plant and grows fixed to surfaces under water. **2** the light, elastic skeleton of such an animal, that is full of holes and can soak up much water. Sponges are used for washing, bathing, etc. **3** any artificial substance like this, as of plastic or rubber, used in the same way. ◆*v.* to wipe, clean, make wet, or soak up as with a sponge [to *sponge* up gravy with a crust of bread]. —**sponged, spong′ing**

sport (spôrt) *n.* **1** active play, a game, etc. taken up for exercise or pleasure and, sometimes, as a profession [Football, golf, bowling, swimming, etc. are *sports*.] **2** fun or play [They thought it was great *sport* to fool others on the telephone.]

sprain (sprān) *v.* to twist a muscle or ligament in a joint without putting the bones out of place [to *sprain* one's wrist]. ◆*n.* an injury caused by this.

sprin·kle (sprin′kəl) *v.* **1** to scatter in drops or bits [to *sprinkle* salt on an egg]. **2** to scatter drops or bits on [to *sprinkle* a lawn with water]. **3** to rain lightly. —**sprin′kled, sprin′kling** ◆*n.* **1** the act of sprinkling. **2** a light rain. —**sprin′kler** *n.*

spy (spī) *n.* a person who watches others secretly and carefully. —*pl.* **spies**

squall (skwôl) *n.* a short, violent windstorm, usually with rain or snow. ◆*v.* to storm for a short time. —**squall′y** *adj.*

stage (stāj) *n.* **1** a raised platform or other area on which plays, speeches, etc. are given. **2** the profession of acting; the theater [He left the *stage* to write.] **3** *a shorter name for* **stagecoach.** **4** a period or step in growth or development [She has reached a new *stage* in her career.] ◆*v.* to present on a stage, as a play. —**staged, stag′ing**

stamp (stamp) *v.* **1** to bring one's foot down with force ["No!" she cried, *stamping* on the floor.] **2** to beat, press, or crush as with the foot [to *stamp* out a fire; to *stamp* out a revolt]. **3** to press or print marks, letters, a design, etc. on something [He *stamped* his initials on all his books.] ◆*n.* **1** a machine, tool, or die used for stamping. **2** a small piece of paper printed and sold by a government for sticking on letters, packages, etc. as proof that postage or taxes were paid.

stand (stand) *v.* **1** to be or get in an upright position on one's feet [*Stand* by your desk.] **2** to be or place in an upright position on its base, bottom, etc. [Our trophy *stands* on the shelf. *Stand* the broom in the corner.] **3** to put up with; endure; bear [The boss can't *stand* noise.] —**stood, stand′ing** ◆*n.* **1** an opinion, belief, or attitude [What is the Senator's *stand* on higher taxes?] **2** *often* **stands,** *pl.* seats in rising rows, as in a stadium, from which to watch games, races, etc. **3** a booth or counter where goods are sold [a popcorn *stand*]. **4** a rack, framework, etc. for holding something [a music *stand*].

stare (ster) *v.* to look steadily with the eyes wide open [to *stare* in curiosity]. —**stared, star′ing**

starve (stärv) *v.* to die or suffer from lack of food [Many pioneers *starved* during the long winter.] —**starved, starv′ing**

sta·tion (stā′shən) *n.* **1** the place where a person or thing stands or is located, as one's post when on duty, a building for a special purpose, etc. [a sentry's *station*; a police *station*]. **2** a regular stopping place, as for a bus or train; also, a building at such a place.

☆**steam·boat** (stēm′bōt) *n.* a steamship, especially a small one.

step (step) *v.* to move by taking a step or steps [We *stepped* into the car.] —**stepped, step′ping**

stern[1] (sturn) *adj.* strict or harsh; not gentle, tender, easy, etc. [*stern* parents; *stern* treatment]. —**stern′ly** *adv.* —**stern′ness** *n.*

stern[2] (sturn) *n.* the rear end of a ship or boat.

stick (stik) *n.* **1** a twig or branch broken or cut off. **2** any long, thin piece of wood, with a special shape for use as a cane, club, etc. [a walking *stick*; a hockey *stick*]. **3** a long, thin piece [a *stick* of celery; a *stick* of chewing gum]. ◆*v.* **1** to press a sharp point into; pierce; stab [He *stuck* his finger with a needle.] **2** to fasten or be fastened as by pinning or gluing [I *stuck* my name tag on my coat. The stamp *sticks* to the paper.] —**stuck, stick′ing**

stiff (stif) *adj.* **1** that does not bend easily; firm [*stiff* cardboard]. **2** not able to move easily [*stiff* muscles]. **3** not relaxed; tense or formal [a *stiff* smile]. —**stiff′ly** *adv.* —**stiff′ness** *n.*

stitch (stich) *n.* **1** one complete movement of a needle and thread into and out of the material in sewing. **2** one complete movement done in various ways in knitting, crocheting, etc. **3** a loop made by stitching [Tight *stitches* pucker the cloth.] —**stitches**

sto·ry[1] (stôr′ē) *n.* **1** a telling of some happening, whether true or made-up [the *story* of the first Thanksgiving]. **2** a made-up tale, written down, that is shorter than a novel [the *stories* of Poe]. —*pl.* **sto′ries**

sto·ry[2] (stôr′ē) *n.* the space or rooms making up one level of a building, from a floor to the ceiling above it [a building with ten *stories*]. —*pl.* **sto′ries**

stove (stōv) *n.* a device for cooking or heating by the use of gas, oil, electricity, etc.

straight (strāt) *adj.* **1** having the same direction all the way; not crooked, curved, wavy, etc. [a *straight* line; *straight* hair]. **2** upright or erect [*straight* posture]. **3** level or even [a *straight* hemline]. **4** direct; staying right to the point, direction, etc. [a *straight* course; a *straight* answer].

strange (strānj) *adj.* **1** not known, seen, or heard before; not familiar [I saw a *strange* person at the door.] **2** different from what is usual; peculiar; odd [wearing a *strange* costume]. **3** not familiar; without experience [She is *strange* to this job.] —**strang′er, strang′est** —**strange′ly** *adv.*

straw (strô *or* strä) *n.* **1** hollow stalks, as of wheat or rye, after the grain has been threshed out. Straw is used as stuffing or is woven into hats, etc. **2** a tube, as of plastic, used for sucking a drink.

strength (streŋkth *or* strenth) *n.* the quality of being strong; force; power [the *strength* of a blow].

stretch (strech) *v.* **1** to reach out or hold out, as a hand, object, etc. **2** to draw out to full length, to a greater size, to a certain distance, etc.; extend [She *stretched* out on the sofa. Will this material *stretch*? *Stretch* the rope between two trees. The road *stretches* for miles through the hills.] **3** to pull or draw tight; strain [to *stretch* a muscle].

strict (strikt) *adj.* **1** keeping to rules in a careful, exact way [a *strict* supervisor]. **2** never changing; rigid [a *strict* rule]. —**strict′ly** *adv.* —**strict′ness** *n.*

stuff (stuf) *n.* **1** what anything is made of; material; substance. **2** a collection of objects, belongings, etc. [I emptied the *stuff* from my bag.] ◆*v.* **1** to fill or pack [pockets *stuffed* with candy]. **2** to fill with seasoning, bread crumbs, etc. before roasting [to *stuff* a turkey]. **3** to force or push [I *stuffed* the money in my wallet.]

stum·ble (stum′bəl) *v.* to trip or almost fall while walking or running [to *stumble* over a curb]. —**stum′bled, stum′bling**

stur·dy (stur′dē) *adj.* strong and hardy [a *sturdy* oak]. —**stur′di·er, stur′di·est** —**stur′di·ly** *adv.* —**stur′di·ness** *n.*

sub·trac·tion (səb trak′shən) *n.* the act of subtracting one part, number, etc. from another.

☆**su·per·mar·ket** (sōō′pər mär′kət) *n.* a large food store in which shoppers serve themselves from open shelves and pay at the exit.

steamboat

a	ask, fat
ā	ape, date
ä	car, lot
e	elf, ten
ē	even, meet
i	is, hit
ī	ice, fire
ō	open, go
ô	law, horn
oi	oil, point
͞oo	look, pull
o͞o	ooze, tool
ou	out, crowd
u	up, cut
u	fur, fern
ə	a in ago
	e in agent
	e in father
	i in unity
	o in collect
	u in focus
ch	chin, arch
ŋ	ring, singer
sh	she, dash
th	thin, truth
th	then, father
zh	s in pleasure

183

sword

sup·ply (sə plī′) **v. 1** to give what is needed; furnish [The camp *supplies* sheets and towels. The book *supplied* us with the facts.] **2** to take care of the needs of [to *supply* workers with tools]. —**sup·plied′, sup·ply′ing** ◆**n. 1** the amount at hand; store; stock [I have a small *supply* of money but a large *supply* of books.] **2 supplies**, *pl.* things needed; materials; provisions [school *supplies*]. —*pl.* **sup·plies′**

sur·prise (sər prīz′) **v.** to cause to feel wonder by being unexpected [Her sudden anger *surprised* us.] —**sur·prised′, sur·pris′ing**

sur·pris·ing (sər prīz′iŋ) *adj.* causing surprise; strange. —**sur·pris′ing·ly adv.**

sur·vey (sər vā′) **v. 1** to look over in a careful way; examine; inspect [The lookout *surveyed* the horizon.] **2** to measure the size, shape, boundaries, etc. of a piece of land by the use of special instruments [to *survey* a farm]. ◆**n.** (sʉr′vā) a general study covering the main facts or points [The *survey* shows that we need more schools. This book is a *survey* of American poetry.] —*pl.* **sur′veys**

sur·viv·al (sər vī′vəl) **n.** the act or fact of surviving, or continuing to exist [Nuclear war threatens the *survival* of all nations.]

swal·low (swä′lō) **v. 1** to let food, drink, etc. go through the throat into the stomach. **2** to move the muscles of the throat as in swallowing something [I *swallowed* hard to keep from crying.] **3** to take in; engulf [The waters of the lake *swallowed* him up.]

swamp (swämp) **n.** a piece of wet, spongy land; marsh; bog: *also called* ☆**swamp′land. —swamp′y adj.**

sway (swā) **v. 1** to swing or bend back and forth or from side to side [The flowers *swayed* in the breeze.] **2** to lean or go to one side; veer [The car *swayed* to the right on the curve.] **3** to change the thinking or actions of; influence [We will not be *swayed* by their promises.]

sweat (swet) **v. 1** to give out a salty liquid through the pores of the skin; perspire [Running fast made me *sweat*.] —**sweat** or **sweat′ed, sweat′ing** ◆**n. 1** the salty liquid given out through the pores of the skin.

sweat shirt (swet shʉrt) **n.** a heavy, loose cotton shirt with long or short sleeves.

swift (swift) *adj.* **1** moving or able to move very fast [a *swift* runner]. **2** coming, happening, or done quickly [a *swift* reply]. **3** acting quickly; prompt [They were *swift* to help us.] —**swift′ly adv.** —**swift′ness n.**

sword (sôrd) **n.** a weapon having a long, sharp blade, with a handle, or hilt, at one end.

syl·la·ble (sil′ə bəl) **n. 1** a word or part of a word spoken with a single sounding of the voice ["Moon" is a word of one *syllable*. "Moonlight" is a word of two *syllables*.] **2** any of the parts into which a written word is divided to show where it may be broken at the end of a line [The *syllables* of the entry words in this dictionary are divided by tiny dots.]

syn·o·nym (sin′ə nim) **n.** a word having the same or almost the same meaning as another ["Big" and "large" are *synonyms*.]

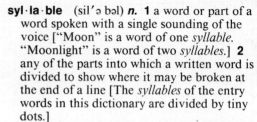

tail (tāl) **n. 1** the part at the rear of an animal's body that sticks out beyond the backbone. **2** any thing or part like this [the *tail* of a shirt; a pig*tail*]. **3** the hind or last part [the *tail* of a parade]. **tails**, *pl.* —**tail′less adj.**

tai·lor (tā′lər) **n.** a person who makes or repairs suits, coats, etc. ◆**v. 1** to work as a tailor or make as a tailor does [suits *tailored* for stout people]. **2** to make or change so as to fit a certain need [That movie was *tailored* to please children.]

tale (tāl) **n.** a story, especially about things that are imagined or made up [The sitter read the child both folk *tales* and fairy *tales*.]

tar·dy (tär′dē) *adj.* not on time; late; delayed [to be *tardy* for class]. —**tar′di·er, tar′di·est** —**tar′di·ly adv.** —**tar′di·ness n.**

tast·y (tās′tē) *adj.* tasting good; full of flavor [a *tasty* meal] —**tast′i·er, tast′i·est**

tax (taks) **n.** money that citizens and businesses must pay to help support a government. —*pl.* **tax′es**

tax·pay·er (taks′pā ər) **n.** a person who pays a tax or taxes.

teach·er (tēch′ər) **n.** a person who teaches, especially in a school or college.

tea·spoon (tē′spoon) **n. 1** a spoon for stirring tea, coffee, etc. and eating some soft foods. **2** *a shorter form of* **teaspoonful.**

teeth (tēth) **n.** *plural of* **tooth.**

tel·e·scope (tel′ə skōp) **n.** a device for making far-off things seem closer and larger, used especially in astronomy. It consists of one or more tubes containing lenses and, often, mirrors.

tel·e·vi·sion (tel′ə vizhən) **n. 1** a way of sending pictures through space by changing the light rays into electric waves which are picked up by a receiver that changes them back to light rays shown on a screen. The sound that goes with the picture is sent by radio at the same time. **2** such a receiver, usually in a cabinet.

telescope

tem·per·ate (tem′pər ət *or* tem′prət) *adj.* **1** using or showing temperance in one's actions, appetites, etc.; moderate [Although she was angry, she made a *temperate* reply.] **2** neither very hot nor very cold [a *temperate* climate]. —**tem′per·ate·ly** *adv.*

ten·der (ten′dər) *adj.* **1** soft or delicate and easily chewed, cut, etc. [*tender* meat; *tender* blades of grass]. **2** that is hurt or feels pain easily; sensitive [My sprained ankle still feels *tender*.] —**ten′der·ly** *adv.* —**ten′der·ness** *n.*

tense[1] (tens) *adj.* **1** stretched tight; taut [a *tense* rope; *tense* muscles]. **2** feeling or showing nervous strain, anxious [a *tense* silence]. **3** causing a nervous feeling [a *tense* situation]. —**tens′er, tens′est** ◆*v.* to make or become tense; tighten, as muscles. —**tensed, tens′ing** —**tense′ly** *adv.*

tense[2] (tens) *n.* any of the forms of a verb that show the time of the action or condition [Present, past, and future *tenses* of "sail" are "sail" or "sails," "sailed," and "will sail."]

☆**te·pee** (tē′pē) *n.* a tent made of animal skins and shaped like a cone, used by some Native Americans.

ter·ri·to·ry (ter′ə tôr′ē) *n.* **1** the land ruled by a nation or state. **2 Territory,** a large division of a country or empire, that does not have the full rights of a province or state, as in Canada or Australia [the Northwest *Territories*]. **3** any large stretch of land; region. **4** the particular area chosen as its own by an animal or group of animals. —*pl.* **ter′ri·to′ries**

thank·ful (thaŋk′fəl) *adj.* feeling or showing thanks; grateful.

their (*th*er) *adj.* of them or done by them. *This possessive form of* **they** *is used before a noun and thought of as an adjective* [*their* house; *their* work].

there (*th*er) *adv.* **1** at or in that place [Who lives *there*?] **2** to, toward, or into that place [Go *there*.]

there·fore (*th*er′fôr) *adv.* for this or that reason; as a result of this or that; hence. *This word is often used as a conjunction* [We missed the bus; *therefore*, we were late.]

there's (*th*erz) there is.

these (*th*ēz) *pron., adj. plural of* **this.**

they'll (*th*āl) **1** they will. **2** they shall.

thief (thēf) *n.* a person who steals, especially secretly. —*pl.* **thieves** (thēvz)

think (thiŋk) *v.* to use the mind; reason [*Think* before you act.] —**thought, think′ing**

this (*th*is) *pron.* **1** the person or thing mentioned or understood [*This* is Juan. *This* tastes good.] **2** the thing that is present or nearer [*This* is prettier than that.] **3** the fact, idea, etc. about to be told [Now hear *this*!] —*pl.* **these** (*th*ēz) ◆*adj.* **1** being the one that is mentioned or understood [Copy down *this* rule.] **2** being the one that is present or nearer [*This* house is newer than that one.] ◆*adv.* to such a degree; so [It was *this* big.]

thought[1] (thôt *or* or thät) *n.* **1** the act or process of thinking [When deep in *thought*, he doesn't hear.] **2** what one thinks; idea, opinion, plan, etc. [a penny for your *thoughts*].

thought[2] (thôt *or* thät) *past tense and past participle of* **think**.

thou·sand (thou′zənd) *n., adj.* ten times one hundred; the number 1,000.

thumb (thum) *n.* the short, thick finger nearest the wrist.

thun·der (thun′dər) *n.* **1** the loud noise that comes after a flash of lightning. It is caused when the discharge of electricity disturbs the air. **2** any loud, rumbling noise like this [We heard the *thunder* of stampeding cattle.]

Thurs·day (thurz′dē) *n.* the fifth day of the week.

tight (tīt) *adj.* **1** put together firmly or closely [a *tight* knot]. **2** fitting too closely [a *tight* shirt]. **3** stretched and strained; taut [a *tight* wire; *tight* nerves]. —**tight′ly** *adv.* —**tight′ness** *n.*

tim·id (tim′id) *adj.* feeling or showing fear or shyness.

tip·toe (tip′tō) *n.* the tip of a toe. ◆*v.* to walk on one's tiptoes in a quiet or careful way. —**tip′toed, tip′toe·ing**

to·ma·to (tə māt′ō *or* tə mät′ō) *n.* a red or yellow, round fruit with a juicy pulp. —*pl.* **to·ma′toes**

tooth (tōōth) *n.* **1** any of the white, bony parts growing from the jaws and used for biting and chewing. **2** any part more or less like a tooth, as on a saw, comb, gearwheel, etc. —*pl.* **teeth** (tēth) —**tooth′less** *adj.*

tooth·ache (tōōth′āk) *n.* pain in or near a tooth.

tooth·brush (tōōth′brush) *n.* a small brush for cleaning the teeth. —*pl.* **tooth′brush·es**

tor·na·do (tôr nā′dō) *n.* a high, narrow column of air that is whirling very fast. It is often seen as a slender cloud shaped like a funnel, that usually destroys everything in its narrow path. —*pl.* **tor·na′does** or **tor·na′dos**

toss (tôs *or* täs) *v.* **1** to throw from the hand in a light, easy way [to *toss* a ball]. **2** to throw about; fling here and there [The waves *tossed* the boat.]

tough (tuf) *adj.* **1** able to bend or twist without tearing or breaking [*tough* rubber]. **2** not able to be cut or chewed easily [*tough* meat]. **3** very difficult or hard [a *tough* job].

town (toun) *n.* **1** a place where there are a large number of houses and other buildings, larger than a village but smaller than a city. **2** *another name for* **city.** **3** the business center of a city or town.

tepee

a	ask, fat
ā	ape, date
ä	car, lot
e	elf, ten
ē	even, meet
i	is, hit
ī	ice, fire
ō	open, go
ô	law, horn
oi	oil, point
͞oo	look, pull
͞oo	ooze, tool
ou	out, crowd
u	up, cut
u	fur, fern
ə	a in ago
	e in agent
	e in father
	i in unity
	o in collect
	u in focus
ch	chin, arch
ŋ	ring, singer
sh	she, dash
th	thin, truth
th	then, father
zh	s in pleasure

tuba

trace (trās) *n.* **1** a mark, track, sign, etc. left by someone or something [no human *trace* on the island]. **2** a very small amount [a *trace* of garlic in the dressing]. ◆*v.* **1** to follow the trail of; track [The hunter *traced* the lions to their den.] **2** to follow or study the course of [We *traced* the history of Rome back to Caesar.] **3** to copy a picture, drawing, etc. by following its lines on a thin piece of paper placed over it. —**traced, trac′ing**

trade (trād) *n.* **1** any work done with the hands that needs special skill got by training [the plumber's *trade*]. **2** all those in a certain business or kind of work [the book *trade*]. **3** the act of giving one thing for another; exchange [an even *trade* of my comic books for your football]. ◆*v.* **1** to carry on a business; buy and sell [This company *trades* in tea. Our country *trades* with other countries.] **2** to exchange [I *traded* my stamp collection for a camera.] —**trad′ed, trad′ing**

traf·fic (traf′ik) *n.* the movement or number of automobiles, persons, ships, etc. along a road or route of travel [to direct *traffic* on city streets; the heavy *traffic* on weekends]. —**traf′ficked, traf′fick·ing**

trail·er (trā′lər) *n.* a wagon, van, cart, etc. made to be pulled by an automobile, truck, or tractor. Some trailers are outfitted as homes.

treat (trēt) *v.* **1** to deal with or act toward in a certain way [We were *treated* with respect. Don't *treat* this matter lightly.] **2** to try to cure or heal, as with medicine [The doctor *treated* my cuts.] **3** to act upon, as by adding something [The water is *treated* with chlorine.]

tribe (trīb) *n.* a group of people or families living together under a leader or chief [a North American Indian *tribe*; the *tribes* of ancient Israel]. —**trib′al** *adj.*

trim (trim) *v.* **1** to make neat or tidy, especially by clipping, smoothing, etc. [She had her hair *trimmed*.] **2** to cut, clip, etc. [He *trimmed* dead branches off the tree.] —**trimmed, trim′ming** ◆*n.* good condition or order [An athlete must keep in *trim*.] —**trim′mer, trim′mest** —**trim′ly** *adv.* —**trim′ness** *n.*

trip (trip) *v.* to stumble or make stumble [She *tripped* over the rug. Bill put out his foot and *tripped* me.] —**tripped, trip′ping**

tro·phy (trō′fē) *n.* anything kept as a token of victory or success, as a deer's head from a hunting trip, a silver cup from a sports contest, or a sword from a battle. —*pl.* **tro′phies**

trop·i·cal (träp′i kəl) *adj.* of, in, or like the tropics [heavy *tropical* rains; *tropical* heat].

trou·ble (trub′əl) *n.* **1** worry, care, annoyance, suffering, etc. [My mind is free of *trouble*.] **2** a difficult or unhappy situation; disturbance [We've had no *trouble* with our neighbors.] —**trou′bled, trou′bling**

trust (trust) *n.* a strong belief that some person or thing is honest or can be depended on; faith [You can put your *trust* in that bank.] ◆*v.* **1** to have or put trust in; rely; depend [I *trust* him to be on time. Don't *trust* that rickety ladder.] **2** to put something in the care of [Her mother *trusted* her with the car.] **3** to believe [I *trust* her story.]

try (trī) *v.* **1** to make an effort; attempt [We must *try* to help them.] **2** to seek to find out about, as by experimenting; test [Please *try* my recipe. *Try* the other window, which may not be locked.] **3** to put to a severe test or strain [Such exercise *tried* my strength.] —**tried, try′ing** ◆*n.* an effort; attempt; trial [He made a successful jump on his third *try*.] —*pl.* **tries**

tu·ba (tōō′bə *or* tyōō′bə) *n.* a large brass-wind instrument with a full, deep tone.

tun·dra (tun′drə *or* tōōn′drə) *n.* a large, flat plain without trees in the arctic regions.

turn (turn) *v.* **1** to move around a center point or axis; revolve; rotate [The wheels *turn*. *Turn* the key.] **2** to do by moving in a circle [*Turn* a somersault.] **3** to change in position or direction [*Turn* your chair around. *Turn* to the left. The tide has *turned*.]

twelve (twelv) *n., adj.* two more than ten; the number 12.

twist·er (twis′tər) *n.* **1** a person or thing that twists. ☆**2** a tornado or cyclone.

type·writ·er (tīp′rīt ər) *n.* a machine with a keyboard for making printed letters or figures on paper.

um·pire (um′pīr) *n.* **1** a person who rules on the plays of a game, as in baseball. **2** a person chosen to settle an argument. ◆*v.* to be an umpire in a game or dispute. —**um′pired, um′pir·ing**

un·cle (uŋ′kəl) *n.* **1** the brother of one's father or mother. **2** the husband of one's aunt.

un·clear (un klir′) *adj.* not clear; hard to see or understand.

un·fold (un fōld′) *v.* **1** to open and spread out something that has been folded [to *unfold* a map]. **2** to make or become known [to *unfold* one's plans].

u·ni·verse (yōōn′ə vʉrs) **n.** all space and everything in it; earth, the sun, stars, and all things that exist.

u·ni·ver·si·ty (yōōn′ə vʉr′sə tē) **n.** a school of higher education, made up of a college or colleges. —*pl.* **u′ni·—ver′si·ties**

un·known (un nōn′) **adj. 1** not known, seen, or heard before [a song *unknown* to me]. **2** not discovered, identified, etc. [an *unknown* writer]. ◆*n.* an unknown person or thing.

un·pleas·ant (un plez′ənt) **adj.** not pleasant or agreeable; offensive; disagreeable [an *unpleasant* taste]. —**un·pleas′ant·ly adv.** —**un·pleas′ant·ness n.**

un·pre·pared (un′prē perd′) **adj.** not prepared or ready [We are still *unprepared* for the visitors.]

un·re·al (un rēl′) **adj.** not real; imaginary or made up. —**un·re·al·i·ty** (un′rē al′ə tē) **n.**

un·re·lat·ed (un rē lāt′əd) **adj.** not of the same family or kind.

un·til (un til′) **prep. 1** up to the time of; till [Wait *until* noon.] **2** before [Don't leave *until* tomorrow.] ◆*conj.* **1** up to the time when [He was lonely *until* he met her.] **2** to the point, degree, or place that [She ate *until* she was full.] **3** before [Don't stop *until* he does.]

un·wise (un wīz′) **adj.** not wise; not showing good sense; foolish. —**un·wise′ly adv.**

ur·gent (ʉr′jənt) **adj. 1** needing quick action [an *urgent* situation]. **2** demanding in a strong and serious way; insistent [an *urgent* call for help]. —**ur′gent·ly adv.**

Vv

vague (vāg) **adj.** not clear, definite, or distinct, as in form, meaning, or purpose [*vague* figures in the fog; a *vague* answer]. —**va′guer, va′guest** —**vague′ly adv.** —**vague′ness n.**

val·ley (val′ē) **n. 1** low land lying between hills or mountains. **2** the land that is drained or watered by a large river and its branches [the Mississippi *valley*]. —*pl.* **val′leys**

veil (vāl) **n.** a piece of thin cloth, such as net or gauze, worn especially by women over the face or head [a bride's *veil*].

ves·sel (ves′əl) **n.** a ship or large boat.

Vi·et·nam (vē′ət näm′) a country in southeastern Asia. —**Vi·et·nam·ese** (vē′et nə mēz′ or vē′et nə mēs′) **adj., n.**

vi·ta·min (vīt′ə min) **n.** any of certain substances needed by the body to keep healthy. Vitamin A is found in fish-liver oil, yellow vegetables, egg yolk, etc. One kind of vitamin B, called vitamin B_1, is found in cereals, green peas, beans, liver, etc. Vitamin C is found in citrus fruits, tomatoes, etc. Vitamin D is found in fish-liver oil, milk, eggs, etc. Lack of these vitamins or others can cause certain diseases.

voice (vois) **n. 1** sound made through the mouth, especially by human beings in talking, singing, etc. **2** anything thought of as like speech or the human voice [the *voice* of the sea; the *voice* of one's conscience]. **3** the right to say what one wants, thinks, or feels [Each voter has a *voice* in the government.] ◆*v.* to put into words, as an idea, feeling, etc.; utter. —**voiced, voic′ing** —**voice′less adj.**

vote (vōt) **n.** one's decision on some plan or idea, or one's choice between persons running for office, shown on a ballot, by raising one's hand, etc. ◆*v.* **1** to give or cast a vote [For whom did you *vote*?] **2** to decide, elect, or bring about by vote [Congress *voted* new taxes.] —**vot′ed, vot′ing**

walrus

Ww

waist (wāst) **n. 1** the part of the body between the ribs and the hips. **2** the part of a garment that covers the body from the shoulders to the waistline.

wait·er (wāt′ər) **n. 1** a man who waits on table, as in a restaurant. **2** one who waits.

wait·ress (wā′trəs) **n.** a woman who waits on table, as in a restaurant.

walk·er (wôk′ər) **n. 1** a person or animal that walks. ☆**2** a frame with or without wheels for use by babies in learning to walk or by people who have trouble walking because of injuries or disease.

wal·rus (wôl′rəs) **n.** a large sea animal like the seal, found in northern oceans. It has two tusks and a thick layer of blubber.

Wash·ing·ton (wôsh′iŋ tən or wäsh′iŋ tən) the capital of the U.S., in the District of Columbia.

watch (wäch or wôch) **v. 1** to keep one's sight on; look at [We *watched* the parade.] **2** to pay attention to; observe [I've *watched* her career with interest.] **3** to take care of; look after; guard [The shepherd *watched* his flock.]

a	ask, fat
ā	ape, date
ä	car, lot
e	elf, ten
ē	even, meet
i	is, hit
ī	ice, fire
ō	open, go
ô	law, horn
oi	oil, point
͞oo	look, pull
͞o͞o	ooze, tool
ou	out, crowd
u	up, cut
ʉ	fur, fern
ə	a in ago
	e in agent
	e in father
	i in unity
	o in collect
	u in focus
ch	chin, arch
ŋ	ring, singer
sh	she, dash
th	thin, truth
th	then, father
zh	s in pleasure

wheat

wa·ter·fall (wôt′ər fôl *or* wät′ər fôl) **n.** a steep fall of water, as from a high cliff.

wax (waks) **n.** **1** a yellow substance that bees make and use for building honeycombs; beeswax. **2** any substance like this, as paraffin. Wax is used to make candles, polishes, etc. ◆**v.** to put wax or polish on.

wea·ry (wir′ē) **adj.** **1** tired; worn out [*weary* after a day's work]. **2** having little or no patience or interest left; bored [I grew *weary* of listening to them.] —**wea′ri·er, wea′ri·est** —**wea′ried, wea′ry·ing** —**wea′ri·ly adv.** —**wea′ri·ness n.**

Wednes·day (wenz′dē) **n.** the fourth day of the week.

weigh (wā) **v.** **1** to use a scales, balance, etc. to find out how heavy a thing is [to *weigh* oneself]. **2** to have a certain weight [The suitcase *weights* six pounds.]

we're (wir) we are.

west·ward (west′wərd) **adv., adj.** in the direction of the west.

wheat (hwēt *or* wēt) **n.** **1** the cereal grass whose grain is used in making the most common type of flour. **2** this grain.

where (hwer *or* wer) **adv.** **1** in or at what place? [*Where* is the car?] **2** in what way? how? [*Where* is she at fault?]

where's (hwerz *or* werz) **1** where is. **2** where has.

wheth·er (hweth′ər *or* weth′ər) **conj.** **1** if it is true or likely that [I don't know *whether* I can go.] **2** in either case that [It makes no difference *whether* he comes or not.]

which (hwich *or* wich) **pron.** **1** what one or what ones of those being talked about or suggested [*which* will you choose?] **2** the one or the ones that [I know *which* I like best.] **3** that [the story *which* we all know]. ◆**adj.** what one or ones [*Which* apples are the best for baking?]

whisk·er (hwis′kər *or* wis′kər) **n.** **1** **whiskers,** *pl.* the hair growing on a man's face, especially the beard on the cheeks. **2** a single hair of a man's beard **3** any of the long, stiff hairs on the upper lip of a cat, rat, etc. —**whisk′ered adj.**

whis·tle (hwis′əl *or* wis′əl) **n.** a device for making high, shrill sounds.

who's (hōōz) **1** who is. **2** who has.

whose (hōōz) **pron.** the one or the ones belonging to whom [*Whose* are these books?]

wife (wīf) **n.** the woman to whom a man is married. —*pl.* **wives**

wild (wīld) **adj.** **1** living or growing in nature; not tamed or cultivated by human beings [*wild* animals; *wild*flowers]. **2** not civilized; savage [*wild* tribes]. **3** not controlled; unruly, rough, noisy, etc. [*wild* children]. —**wild′ly adv.** —**wild′ness n.**

win·ner (win′ər) **n.** **1** one that wins. **2** a person who seems very likely to win or be successful: *used only in everyday talk.*

wish (wish) **v.** **1** to have a longing for; want; desire [You may have whatever you *wish*.] **2** to have or express a desire about [I *wish* you were here. We *wished* her good luck.] ◆**n.** something wanted or hoped for [He got his *wish*.] —*pl.* **wish′·es**

witch (wich) **n.** **1** a person, now especially a woman, who is imagined to have magic power with the help of the devil. **2** an ugly and mean old woman.

with·out (with out′ *or* with out′) **prep.** free from; not having [a person *without* a worry; a cup *without* a saucer].

wit·ness (wit′nəs) **n.** a person who saw or heard something that happened [A *witness* saw the fire start.] —*pl.* **wit′nes·ses**

wives (wīvz) **n.** *plural of* **wife.**

wom·an (woom′ən) **n.** an adult, female human being. —*pl.* **wom′en**

wom·en (wim′ən) **n.** *plural of* **woman.**

wor·ry (wur′ē) **v.** **1** to be or make troubled in mind; feel or make uneasy or anxious [Don't *worry*. Her absence *worried* us.] **2** to annoy, bother, etc. [Stop *worrying* me with such unimportant matters.] —**wor′ried, wor′ry·ing** ◆**n.** **1** a troubled feeling; anxiety; care [sick with *worry*]. **2** a cause of this [He has many *worries*.] —*pl.* **wor′ries**

would·n't (wood′nt) would not.

wrap (rap) **v.** **1** to wind or fold around something [She *wrapped* a scarf around her head.] **2** to cover in this way [They *wrapped* the baby in a blanket.] **3** to cover with paper, etc. [to *wrap* a present]. —**wrapped** *or* **wrapt** (rapt), **wrap′ping**

wreck (rek) **n.** **1** the loss of a ship, or of a building, car, etc. through storm, accident, etc. **2** the remains of something that has been destroyed or badly damaged [an old *wreck* stranded on the reef]. ◆**v.** **1** to destroy or damage badly; ruin [to *wreck* a car in an accident; to *wreck* one's plans for a picnic]. **2** to tear down; raze [to *wreck* an old house].

wrench (rench) **n.** **1** a sudden, sharp twist or pull [With one *wrench*, he loosened the lid.] **2** an injury, as to the back or an arm, caused by a twist. **3** a sudden feeling of sadness, as at parting with someone. **4** a tool for holding and turning nuts, bolts, pipes, etc.

wrin·kle (riŋ′kəl) **n.** a small or uneven crease or fold [*wrinkles* in a blouse].

wrist (rist) **n.** the joint or part of the arm between the hand and forearm.

writ·ing (rīt′iŋ) **n.** **1** the act of one who writes. **2** something written, as a letter, article, poem, book, etc. [the *writings* of Thomas Jefferson]. **3** written form [to put a request in *writing*]. **4** handwriting [Can you read her *writing*?]

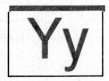

yacht (yät) *n.* a large boat or small ship for racing, taking pleasure cruises, etc. ◆*v.* to sail in a yacht. —**yacht′ing** *n.*

yak (yak) *n.* an ox with long hair, found wild or raised in Tibet and central Asia.

yawn (yôn *or* yän) *v.* to open the mouth wide and breathe in deeply in a way that is not controlled, as when one is sleepy or tired.

your·self (yʊr self′) *pron.* **1** your own self. *This form of* **you is used when the object is** *the same as the subject of the verb* [Did you cut *yourself?*] **2** your usual or true self [You are not *yourself* today.] *Yourself* is also used to give force to the subject [You *yourself* told me so.] —*pl.* **your·selves** (yʊr selvz′)

a	ask, fat
ā	ape, date
ä	car, lot
e	elf, ten
ē	even, meet
i	is, hit
ī	ice, fire
ō	open, go
ô	law, horn
oi	oil, point
ʊ	look, pull
ōō	ooze, tool
ou	out, crowd
u	up, cut
ʉ	fur, fern
ə	a in ago
	e in agent
	e in father
	i in unity
	o in collect
	u in focus
ch	chin, arch
ŋ	ring, singer
sh	she, dash
th	thin, truth
th	then, father
zh	s in pleasure